D1596704

Killing Pat Garrett

The Wild West's Most Famous Lawman – Murder or Self-Defense?

First Edition

David G. Thomas

Mesilla Valley History Series, Vol 5

Doc45 Publishing, P. O. Box 5044, Las Cruces, N. M. 88003
books@doc45.com

To obtain books, visit:
doc45.com

Cover artwork by Dusan Arsenic.

ISBN 978-0-9828709-5-2

000

DOC45 PUBLISHING

Dedicated To

Friends of Pat Garrett

friendsofpatgarrett.com

Mesilla Valley History Series

La Posta – From the Founding of Mesilla, to Corn Exchange Hotel, to Billy the Kid Museum, to Famous Landmark – by David G. Thomas

Giovanni Maria de Agostini, Wonder of The Century – The Astonishing World Traveler Who Was A Hermit – by David G. Thomas

Screen with a Voice – A History of Moving Pictures in Las Cruces, New Mexico – by David G. Thomas

Billy the Kid's Grave – A History of the Wild West's Most Famous Death Marker – by David G. Thomas

Killing Garrett, The Wild West's Most Famous Lawman – Murder or Self-Defense? – by David G. Thomas

Doc 45

Buenas noches boys,
A social call no doubt –
Do we talk it over,
Or do we shoot it out?

I'm Doc 45,
Toughest man alive.
Hand over those golden bills
Or I'll dose you up with dirty leaden pills.

Contents

Acknowledgments

I thank Sally Kading and Karla Steen for permission to use the tintype image of Pat Garrett on the cover and in the text. I thank Pauline Garrett Tillinghast, Sally Kading, and Karla Steen for access to and permission to use the letters of Pat Garrett to his wife and children.

I thank Robert J. Stahl for extensive suggestions during the manuscript stage of the book, which improved it greatly. I thank Dan Aranda, Dan Crow, and Lucinda Allshouse for proofing the manuscript and making corrections and suggestions.

Special thanks to the many who sought out source materials and provided invaluable help in my research efforts: Dennis Daily, Elizabeth Villa, and Teddie Moreno, Library Archives & Special Collections, NMSU; Evan Davies, Institute of Historical Survey Foundation; Angelica Valenzuela, Dona County Clerks Office; Karl Laumbach, Human Systems Research; Claudia Rivers, Abbie H. Weiser, and Anne M. Allis, C. L. Sonnichsen Special Collections, UTEP; Gail Packard, Lynne Newton, and Marcus Flores, State Archives of New Mexico; Daniel Kosharek, Palace of the Governors Photo Archives, New Mexico History Museum; Amanda Morales, El Paso Public Library; Center for Southwest Research and Special Collections, UNM; Collections, Geronimo Springs Museum; Cathy Smith, Nita Stewart Haley Memorial Library and J. Evetts Haley History Center; Whitney Hamm, Special Collections, MSSU; Loretta Deaver, Library of Congress; Stephanie Joyner and Chris Reid, Pinal County Historical Society Museum; and L. Tom Perry Special Collections, BYU.

For photographs and permission to use them, I thank Albert J. Fountain, IV; Karl Laumbach; Kenneth L. Beal; Kathy Easterling; Bob Gamboa; Dan Crow; and Gordon Steele.

Unattributed photos are from the author's collection.

List of Images

Patrick Floyd Jarvis Garrett, tintype, circa 1878. Never before published photo.
Courtesy Sally Kading and Karla Steen.

Introduction

Who killed Patrick Floyd Jarvis Garrett?
Was it murder?
Was it self-defense?

When I began the research for this book – twelve years ago – I was not focused on these questions. Instead, I was obsessed with learning absolutely everything I could about the life of the man who killed Billy the Kid, who suffered a similar fate himself, violent death by gunshot. A fate numerous commentators have implied was karmic justice.

I quickly realized no biographer of Garrett has been able to answer the questions posed above. All have expressed opinions. None have presented evidence that would stand up in a court of law.

To understand who killed Garrett, and why he was killed, you have to begin with the first event in the chain of events that led to his death. For Garrett, that first event was his decision to re-locate to Las Cruces, New Mexico, from Uvalde, Texas. That is where this book begins.

Garrett's sojourn in Las Cruces, between the killing that began it, and the killing that ended it, contain the most eventful and fascinating years of his life.

In approaching this book, I wanted to write a book that was different from the other books about Garrett. I wanted as much as possible to tell Garrett's story in his own words, and in the words of the people with whom he interacted. So you will find an enormous number of quotes in this book – probably more than in any other history book you have read.

You will also find 102 images, including never before published photos of Garrett, his wife, and their children; his Dona Ana County ranch sites; Wildy Well, the location of Garrett's famous shootout with Oliver Lee; Wayne Brazel, the man who confessed to killing Garrett; the spot on the lonely desert road where Garrett was shot; the tiny adobe house in Las Cruces where Garrett's widow and seven children moved following Garrett's killing; and Garrett's original burial location.

Garrett's life has been extensively researched. Yet, I was able to uncover an enormous amount of new information. I had access to over 80 letters that Garrett wrote to his wife. I discovered a multitude of new documents and details concerning Garrett's killing, the events surrounding it, and the personal life of the man who was placed on trial for killing Garrett.

A few examples:

- The true actions of "Deacon Jim" Miller, a professional killer, who was in Las Cruces the day Garrett was killed.
- The place on the now abandoned old road to Las Cruces where Garrett was killed.
- The coroner's jury report on Garrett's death, lost for over 100 years.
- Garrett's original burial location and tombstone.
- The sworn courtroom testimony of the only witness to Garrett's killing.
- The New Mexico Territorial Policeman who provided the decisive evidence in the trial of the man accused of murdering Garrett.
- The location of Garrett's Rock House and Home Ranches.
- The marriage of Wayne Brazel to Olive Elizabeth Boyd and the birth of their son.
- New family details: Garrett had a four-month-old daughter the day he killed Billy the Kid. She died tragically at 15. Another daughter was blinded by a well-intended eye treatment; a son was paralyzed by childhood polio; and Pat Garrett, Jr., named after his father, lost his right leg to amputation at age 12.
- The images of Garrett in this book are the first new images of Garrett that have been published in more than 50 years. No images of Garrett's family, of which there are four in this book, have ever been published before!

Garrett's life was a remarkable adventure, with enormous highs. He met two United States presidents: President William McKinley Jr. and President Theodore Roosevelt. President Roosevelt he met five times, three times in the White House. He brought the law to hardened gunmen. He oversaw hangings. His national fame was so extensive the day he died that newspapers from the East to the West Coast only had to write "Pat Garrett" for readers to know to whom they were referring.

He also had devastating lows. He experienced heartbreaking family tragedy. He was blocked for re-appointment as El Paso Customs Collector by unjustified personal animus. He was pursued ruthlessly for a loan that he had co-signed as a favor for a friend. He had his ranches and livestock confiscated and sold on the Las Cruces public square. In spite of his reputation as a gunman, when faced with public humiliation, he responded with commendable dignity. Queried after losing the Custom Collector job, he replied:

"I simply take my medicine." (See page 108.)

I have tried to write this book so you experience his life as he did, as it happened, event by event. I hope you enjoy it!

Note: All places not otherwise identified are in New Mexico.

See the publisher's website doc45.com for a bibliography.

Chapter 1 | A Fresh Start

Proffer and Acceptance

Pat Garrett was brought to Las Cruces, New Mexico, by murder.

On February 21, 1896, New Mexico Governor William T. Thornton, Las Cruces attorneys Albert B. Fall and William H. H. Llewellyn, and several other prominent citizens of New Mexico met in El Paso, Texas, to decide what to do about the unexplained disappearance and apparent killing three weeks earlier of Colonel Albert J. Fountain and his 8-year-old son Henry.[1]

The meeting was not pre-planned. Most of the men were in El Paso to see the Fitzsimmons-Maher prizefight. Governor Thornton was there with the sheriff of Dona Ana County to prevent it from taking place in New Mexico territory. When the fight was also blocked by the governors of Texas and Chihuahua, Mexico, the two fighters and about 115 spectators boarded a special train for Langtry, Texas, where the fight was held on a sandbar island in the Rio Grande River between Texas and Mexico. To ensure the fight was not held secretly in El Paso or Juarez, Texas posted 12 Texas Rangers to El Paso, Mexico sent five companies of national infantry to Juarez.[2]

The result of the impromptu El Paso meeting, which, according to one newspaper, took place in a *"fistic carnival"* atmosphere, was a resolution to hire Patrick Floyd Jarvis Garrett as a private detective to determine who had killed Colonel Fountain and his son. Governor Thornton told the press afterward, he was:

> *"...confident that Mr. Garrett's familiarity with every foot of the country in which the [alleged] crime was committed, wide acquaintance among the inhabitants thereof, and recognized courage and discretion [would] prove of great value...."* [3]

Governor Thornton did not add to this statement – for he knew it unnecessary – that Pat Garrett was the West's most famous lawman, even 15 years after the singular event for which he was famous – the killing of William Henry McCarty, alias Billy the Kid, in Pete Maxwell's darkened bedroom, at about midnight, on July 14, 1881, in Fort Sumner, New Mexico.[4] The terms offered Garrett were exceedingly generous. Here is his personal description in a letter he wrote to his wife after his acceptance:

> *"I made a trade yesterday to go to work for the committee that has been selected by the most prominent men of New Mexico to hunt and bring to justice the murderers of Col. Fountain and his little eight year old boy. They pay my expenses and $150.00 per month, and $8,000 in case I succeed in arresting and convicting the murderers."* [5]

Garrett had moved to Uvalde, Texas, from Roswell, New Mexico in 1891. His move was motivated by a rapidly deteriorating financial situation. In Uvalde, he acquired a small ranch, but he quickly found it necessary to supplement his ranch income by racing horses at county fairs. He would compete for the race purse, which was often only $50, and bet on the race outcomes.[6]

Colonel Albert J. Fountain and his 8-year-old son Henry. They disappeared February 1, 1896. The evidence found by the posses sent to look for them strongly indicated that they had been murdered. Their bodies were never found. *El Paso Daily Herald,* June 3, 1899.

Oliver Milton Lee and James R. "Jim" Gililland. Both men were tried for the murder of Colonel Fountain and his son and were acquitted. *El Paso Daily Herald,* May 3, 1899.

The offer by Governor Thornton and the others was so attractive to and so desperately needed by Garrett that he immediately left Uvalde – even though his wife was nine-months pregnant. Just hours before he arrived in Las Cruces on February 23 to meet with Governor Thornton, his wife had a baby son, Patrick Floyd Garrett, Jr. In a letter to his daughter Ida in Uvalde – before he knew the baby had been born safely – Garrett wrote that he dreamed his wife had *"had a blue-eyed baby boy."* [7]

Knowing he had a new child to support, Garrett was especially grateful for the job offer. He notified his wife of his acceptance by letter:

"You know if it were not that we are so poor, I would not be away for a minute, so, if I am successful we will get located in this country, and I will never be away from you and the children again." [8]

Besides the private detective proffer, Governor Thornton told Garrett that he would also be able to make him sheriff of Dona Ana County. The right of the current sheriff to serve was being legally disputed due to voter fraud, and it was virtually certain that the county court would remove him.[9] Garrett told his wife:

"[There is] a chance for me to get the Sheriff's Office of Dona Ana County, which is worth $6,000 a year." [10]

But Governor Thornton was not going to rely solely on Garrett. As a backup plan, he hired a Pinkerton Detective Agency operative (*"the eye that never sleeps"*) to come to Las Cruces *"in disguise,"* to pursue an undercover investigation of the Fountain case.[11]

The Fountain Murders

On January 28, 1896, Colonel Albert J. Fountain stepped out of the county courthouse in Lincoln, New Mexico. A man he did not recognize came up to him and handed him a folded sheet of paper. When Colonel Fountain unfolded the paper, he read:

"If you drop this [to the ground] we will be your friends. If you go on with it you will never reach home alive." [12]

Colonel Fountain had just helped convince a Lincoln County grand jury to indict 23 men for cattle stealing and brand defacing.[13]

Tracking down and convicting cattle rustlers was his job. Two years earlier he had been hired as the staff attorney and lead investigator for the Southeastern New Mexico Stock Growers' Association, whose members were experiencing costly, wide-spread cattle rustling.[14]

Colonel Fountain was well aware that he had a risky job, that the men he was pursuing were capable of extreme violence. He had received many examples of this since taking the Stock Growers' job:

"I was anonymously notified that if I attempted to prosecute these parties I would be killed. Of course I paid no attention to these threats." [15]

It was this self-evident danger, in fact, that had induced Colonel Fountain's wife Mariana to convince Colonel Fountain to take eight-year-old Henry with him on his trip to Lincoln. She believed that the presence of her youngest son would prevent any violence directed at Colonel Fountain.[16]

Sutherland house in La Luz where Colonel Fountain and Henry spent their last night (January 31, 1896) before disappearing. 2007 photo.

Oliver Milton Lee's Dog Canyon Ranch house, circa 1936. Courtesy Archives and Special Collections, NMSU.

Travelling by horse-drawn buggy, the trip to Lincoln had taken Colonel Fountain and Henry three days. The return trip would take the same.

Ignoring the "coffin notice" he had been handed, Colonel Fountain started immediately for his home in Las Cruces. That day he made about 50 miles, spending the night at Blazer's Mill, a site famous for the killing of "Buckshot" Roberts during the infamous Lincoln County Wars. He discussed his grand jury appearance with the mill's owner, Doctor Joseph F. Blazer. Blazer later testified in court that:

> *"[Fountain said] he had secured indictments against a gang of cattle thieves, and he had enough evidence to convict and send them to the penitentiary, if they did not succeed in making away either with him or his witnesses."* [17]

Colonel Fountain also told Doctor Blazer that he had been followed all day by two men on horseback. They had stayed far enough away to be unrecognizable.[18]

The second night Colonel Fountain and Henry stayed with a friend in the small village of La Luz, about 30 miles from Blazer's Mill.[19]

On leaving La Luz the next morning, several people observed that Colonel Fountain and his son were being shadowed, this time by three men on horses, one riding a striking white horse. One of these witnesses, Saturnino Barela, a mail carrier, felt compelled to stop Colonel Fountain and warn him:

> *"...I told him about the men whom I had seen.... Col. Fountain asked me if I knew the horsemen. I told him I did not."* [20]

The next day, just past the spot where he had last observed Colonel Fountain, Barela noticed that Fountain's buggy tracks left the road, heading south. Worried, because of what he had seen the day before, he followed the buggy tracks far enough to determine that foul play was likely.[21]

Barela raced to Las Cruces and reported what he had found.[22] Fountain's family was already upset because he had been expected home the previous evening.[23]

Fountain's two oldest sons, father-in-law, and several friends immediately rode out to look for Colonel Fountain and Henry. A little later, a more official posse, which included the county sheriff, left to join the search.[24]

Both posses found evidence that Colonel Fountain had been murdered, and that Henry had been taken alive, and killed later.

The Crime Scenes

A short distance beyond where postman Barela had ventured the previous day, the searchers found where Colonel Fountain's buggy had been ambushed, as testified to by Major Eugene Van Patton:

> *"I found several human tracks and prints of knees behind a bush and several empty shells."* [25]

Also found at the site was *"a pool of blood:"*

> *"It was 7 or 8 inches deep and twice or three times as large as a spittoon."* [26]

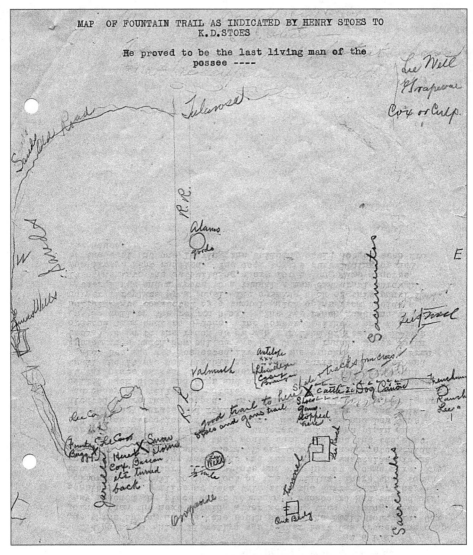

Map of the routes taken by the Fountain posses as described by posse member Henry Stoes to his wife Katherine D. Stoes. The map shows:

(a) The road from Tularosa that Fountain was travelling when he disappeared;
(b) The spot where Fountain's buggy was found;
(c) The trail of horse tracks from the buggy toward Oliver Lee's Dog Canyon Ranch;
(d) The spot – marked by an "X" – where Lee's cattle were driven over the tracks;
(e) Lee's Dog Canyon Ranch house, showing the tunnel dug from the residence to an outbuilding (see page 66);
(f) Wildy Well – marked as "Lee Well;"
(g) The towns of Alamogordo, Valmont (Camp City), and Orogrande;

Courtesy Archives and Special Collections, NMSU.

William McNew, *El Paso Daily Herald,* May 3, 1899.

Attorney Albert B. Fall. 1905 photo. Courtesy Library of Congress.

John Conklin Fraser, Pinkerton National Detective Agency operative, sent to
Las Cruces March 5, 1896, to investigate the disappearance of Colonel Albert J.
Fountain and his son Henry. Undated photo. Courtesy Library of Congress.

From the apparent ambush site, tracks trailed about a mile south to where the buggy was found (see map page 8). [27] The buggy had been searched by the ambushers:

"The valise and boxes had been opened and their contents were either missing or scattered around. The little hat of Henry's had been left behind inside the valise. A bottle of liquor had been broken. The tracks of three men were plainly visible in the sand at and around the [buggy]...." [28]

The visible evidence suggested that after abandoning the ransacked buggy, the ambushers took Colonel Fountain's horses and rode southwest.[29] About five miles distant, the searchers found the *"charred remnants of a campfire."* [30]

Marks on the ground at the campfire suggested that Colonel Fountain's body had been carried there wrapped in a blanket, and that Henry was still alive: [31]

"There were 3 or 4 child's tracks, all made by the right shoe." [32]

One of the searchers thought the tracks had been faked by someone who *"had taken the child's shoe in his hand or on a stick and made impressions with it." [33]*

From the campfire site, the searchers followed the tracks to a point where they split. One set of horse tracks led to Wildy Well, the site of a future shootout between Garrett and Oliver Milton Lee and James R. "Jim" Gililland, two men Garrett would eventually indict for the Fountain murders. The other sets led toward Lee's Dog Canyon Ranch.[34]

A few miles distant from Lee's ranch, the searchers encountered a problem:

"A herd of cattle, driven by a man, crossed the trail and obliterated it." [35]

The man was one of Lee's ranch hands. His action appeared to be intentional.

The old road from Tularosa trailing down the west side of Chalk Hill. Colonel Albert J. Fountain and Henry were ambushed at this location, as they descended the hill in their buggy. The abandoned road is badly eroded today. Located on the White Sands Missile Range. 2019 photo.

John "Jack" W. Maxwell. Garrett and C. C. Perry signed a contract with Maxwell which promised him $2,000 if his testimony led to the conviction of the persons who killed the Fountains. Undated painting. Courtesy Karl Laumbach.

Operative Fraser Arrives

"I arrived at Las Cruces at 10:05 a.m. and took the bus from the depot to the Rio Grande hotel (the only one in town)." [36]

The "I" of this report is Pinkerton National Detective Agency operative John Conklin Fraser. Fraser arrived in Las Cruces by train after travelling all night from Santa Fe, where he had consulted with Governor Thornton.[37]

Fraser's investigative cover was that he was a representative of the Fraser & Chalmers Mining Machinery Company.[38]

The Investigation

Garrett immediately began working the case. He visited the crime scenes.[39] He discovered that there would be no easy answer to the questions: *"Who killed the Fountains? Where were the bodies?"* Colonel Fountain was such a prominent person – and the crime so shocking – that almost everybody had a theory. Colonel Fountain, who had come to New Mexico as a Union soldier during the Civil War, had developed many personal and political enemies, all of whom were potential suspects.

Typical of the reports Garrett was hearing was the following:

"A few days ago two men came to town and claimed they had seen the legs of Colonel Fountain sticking out of the sand, but on investigation, was found only a small bush they had seen in the distance." [40]

Fraser also began working the case. He interviewed mailman Barela and learned nothing new. His conversations with others led him to consider Colonel Fountain's political enemies prime suspects. Colonel Fountain was a Republican. The leader of the Democrats, and Colonel Fountain's bitterest personal enemy, was attorney Albert B. Fall.[41]

Garrett was taking a broader approach, speaking with many minor figures, most with criminal connections. Because he knew there was an $8,000 payoff for solving the killing, he was promising payments for information and eventual testimony in a trial. In short, he was searching for a snitch. (This strategy would backfire when those accused of the killings were put on trial.) Based on Governor Thornton's executive order, even if the snitch was involved in the crime, Garrett could promise immunity and a pardon:

"I further offer a full and complete pardon to any party connected with the commission of said crime – except the principle one – who is first to turn state's evidence, and furnish his testimony for the arrest and conviction of his associates." [42] *[Executive Order by Governor Thornton]*

On March 8, Garrett and Fraser met in El Paso for a long discussion. Garrett told Fraser his suspects were Oliver Lee, Jim Gililland,[43] and William McNew, all men who had been indicted for cattle rustling or brand changing by Colonel Fountain in Lincoln. In his report to Governor Thornton, Fraser wrote:

"I saw very plainly that he (Garrett) did not want me to go out and cause a stir by an open investigation. He told me that what he wanted me to do was to try and pull everybody off from the idea that Oliver Lee, Gililland, and McNew are the men and to stop them from talking so much." [44]

About a later meeting with Garrett, Fraser wrote:

> *"[I] called on Mr. Garrett at his room and had another talk with him; he is a man who says very little, so anything I learn from him is through questions."* [45]

Garrett had no interest in Fraser solving the crime. Garrett wanted – and intended – to do it himself.

By March 26 – less than a month after starting the investigation – Garrett was confident he had found his snitch – John "Jack" W. Maxwell, who had a ranch near Lee's.

Maxwell said he had visited Oliver Lee's ranch on February 1, the day the Fountains disappeared. He said Lee was not there. He said he spent the night at the ranch. He said Lee, McNew, Gililland, and a hired hand rode up to the ranch the next day, on fresh horses. He said he later saw, in a pasture about a mile from the ranch house, *"used-hard"* horses, suggesting the men had switched horses before appearing at the ranch house. [46]

Based on this evidence, Garrett signed a contract with Maxwell:

> *"Tularosa, N. M., March 26, 1896"*

> *"This is to certify that we, the undersigned, agree to pay John Maxwell two thousand dollars ($2000) in case he give us information that will lead to the arrest and conviction of murderers of Col. A. J. Fountain and son, the said $2000 to be due as soon as the conviction is had."*

> *"P. F. Garrett and C. C. Perry"* [47]

Pinkerton Investigation Terminated

Fraser stayed in Las Cruces for 20 days. His cover as a sales representative was blown after just a few days. In his almost daily reports to Governor Thornton, Fraser continued to criticize Garrett, implying he was unprofessional. For example, on March 18, Garrett set up a meeting between Fraser and Oliver Lee in Albert Fall's office, who was serving as Lee's attorney. The meeting was impromptu, and seeing the two men together prevented Fraser from interviewing Lee and Fall separately. [48]

In the interview, both Lee and Fall repeated disparaging stories about Colonel Fountain. Lee said that Fountain had offered him a $1,000 to assist in a case based on manufactured evidence. Fall said *"he did not like Colonel Fountain any more than he did a snake,"* then repeated a story in which he claimed Colonel Fountain had cold-bloodily murdered an escaping prisoner. To this, Fall added:

> *"...it was rumored that Mrs. Fountain had caught the Colonel in a compromising position with his own daughter just before he went away."*

> *"I got it from a reliable citizen, who got it from some one else...."* [49]

Fraser, like Garrett, had become convinced that Lee was the leader of the men who had killed Colonel Fountain – and was the man on the white horse at the killings. But unlike Garrett, who dismissed any involvement by Fall, Fraser felt that there was *"a master hand in this whole affair,"* above Lee, and that person was probably Fall. [50]

In explaining to Governor Thornton why he was leaving Las Cruces, Fraser said he had been handicapped by Garrett because:

> '...any information I have gotten from Garrett I have been compelled to draw out of him.... I believe he is thoroughly honest in his intentions, but may be a little careless and not consider certain points of much importance." [51]

He also intimated that a certain C. C. Perry, sheriff of Roswell, New Mexico, who Garrett was working with, was incompetent.

Governor Thornton wanted the investigation to continue, so the Pinkerton Agency assigned Operative William C. Sayers to the case.[52] Sayers began investigating various leads in Santa Fe and other New Mexico communities on April 15.[53]

Sayers had not made it to Las Cruces by May 12 when Governor Thornton abruptly terminated the Pinkerton Agency's investigation.[54]

Although Governor Thornton did not say so in his communication with the Agency, the reason for the firing was that all of Fraser and Sayers' reports were stolen:

> "The papers... were reports of [an] investigation into the Fountain murders, which had been held with the governor. The papers were stolen from the governor's office, and well-founded suspicion points toward a federal official with a notorious reputation (they are all rather notorious, but this fellow is exceptionally so) as the thief." [55]

It is uncertain who the newspaper was pointing to; probably it was Albert Fall.

Fraser and Sayers' reports to Governor Thornton are fascinating and show how criminal investigations were conducted in the 1890s by professional detectives. In the murder trial that eventually resulted, neither Pinkerton detective was called to testify, and no evidence obtained by either investigator was introduced.

Struggle to Become Sheriff

Governor Thornton had promised Garrett would be made county sheriff. This was a plum position. Besides a salary, a sheriff could collect and keep various fees and court expenses, such as the fee for serving a summons or the costs of taking a prisoner to jail. In his letter to his wife on February 25, 1896, Garrett had written:

> "...the Sheriff's Office of Dona Ana County... is worth $6,000 a year." [56]

Governor Thornton wanted to make Garrett sheriff for at least two reasons. First, he and other private citizens were paying Garrett's monthly salary and expenses while he was working privately; second, the authority of the sheriff's office would presumedly aid Garrett's investigation.

The current sheriff, Guadalupe Ascarate, a Democrat, had gained his majority through voter fraud (almost certainly engineered by Fall). His legitimacy was challenged by his Republican opponent, Numa Reymond. On March 20, the district court removed Ascarate and appointed Reymond sheriff.[57]

Prior to the court decision, Reymond had promised Governor Thornton that if he was awarded the sheriff position, he would appoint Garrett his chief deputy sheriff, and then resign, thus making Garrett sheriff.[58]

Garrett was in the courtroom when the Reymond ruling was issued. He happily, but prematurely, wrote his wife:

Numa Reymond. After initially balking, Numa resigned as Dona Ana Sheriff, permitting the appointment of Pat Garrett as his replacement. Undated photo. Courtesy Archives and Special Collections, NMSU.

"I have delayed writing you to see what turn affairs would take. Everything has gone so far as well as I could wish, the Sheriff's office of this county was turned over to me this morning, so I have decided we would locate here for awhile at least." [59]

Reymond unexpectedly balked. With the office in his hands, he refused to resign. He claimed his campaign expenses for his earlier run against Ascarate had cost him thousands of dollars, and he needed to recover the money.[60] In addition, Reymond claimed that he had already promised the chief deputy sheriff position to Oscar Lohman, so he could not appoint Garrett.

"Relying upon [Reymond's] promise and the undisputed understanding that he was to have the office, Oscar Lohman went to the court house and took possession...." [61]

It was suggested by Reymond, then, that Garrett:

"...be made outside deputy, to do the rough work, and Oscar Lohman [be designated] to run the office, keep the books, handle the funds and appoint policemen." [62]

Garrett categorically refused to accept such a proposition.

As Reymond was a Republican, the *Rio Grande Republican* newspaper strongly supported his position. The Democrats had lost Ascarate, but Garrett was a Democrat, so the *Independent Democrat* newspaper just as strongly supported him.

Rather quickly, a compromise was reached. Reymond resigned and left in a snit to visit his home country of Switzerland, complaining that he had spent over $16,000 seeking the sheriff's seat. Oscar Lohman gave up his claim and the parties supporting Garrett agreed that Garrett would serve for two months, after which the County Commissioners would meet and pick a sheriff.[63] (Oscar would later become Garrett's best friend in Las Cruces, and Garrett would name his next son after him.)

Garrett leaped into fulfilling the duties of county sheriff. He transported a man who had been declared mentally unfit to a mental hospital in northern New Mexico;[64] recaptured two prisoners who escaped from the county jail (and ordered an adobe wall built around the jail to prevent future escapes); [65] and investigated the death of a man who had been found in the desert a mile or so from Wildy Well.

The dead man had a scrap of paper in his pocket with the initials H. G. A. He was about 70 and his death was ruled accidental due to water deprivation:

"It is supposed the man lost his way, not knowing the country, and so missed the places where water could have been procured. It is pitiable to think of death resulting from such a lack, when water was so near." [66]

He also arrested and charged Luis Herrera with involvement in the Fountain murders. Herrera's white horse was found running wild with Fountain's buggy horses when they were eventually captured. After a few days, Herrera was able to prove an alibi and explain how he lost his horse, and was released.[67]

In July, Garrett was appointed Deputy U. S. Marshal, giving him legal standing for Federal cases and permitting him to make arrests in other counties.[68]

Garrett's ranch house on Eagle Creek, Lincoln County, New Mexico, bought
September 4, 1883. Elizabeth "Lizzie" Garrett was born here on October 9, 1885.
Undated photo. Courtesy IHSF.org.

Garrett's house in Roswell, New Mexico, next to the canal that he built while living
there. Dudley Poe Garrett was born here on June 8, 1887. Ann "Annie" Garrett was
born here October 2, 1889. The house is still standing. 2007 photo.

As the end of Garrett's agreed-upon period as sheriff approached, a majority of county commissioners made it known that they did not support his re-appointment. Garrett took immediate action, as explained by the Democratic newspaper:

> *"Mr. Garrett remembering that [Albert] Fall had some time previously informed him that the bonds of the county commissioners were void, because under the law a county officer could not be on another officer's bond, drove out to the Gold Camp where Fall was, returned with him the same night, and the next morning took him up to Santa Fe to see Governor Thornton and have the county commissioners removed."* [69]

Governor Thornton removed the two commissioners with questionable bonds and replaced them with two new commissioners. The removed commissioners were Republicans. The new commissioners were Democrats, giving the Democrats a majority on the commission.

> *"...the new board met, elected Vincent May chairman, declared the sheriff's office vacant by virtue of Reymond's abandonment and removal to Europe, and Pat F. Garrett was appointed to fill the vacancy."* [70]

Family Leaves Uvalde, Texas

Confident now of his income, Garrett was ready to move his family from Uvalde to Las Cruces.[71] His family consisted of his wife Apolinaria 35, daughter Adelaida "Ida" 14, daughter Elizabeth "Lizzie" 10, son Dudley Poe "Poe" 8, daughter Ann "Annie" 6, and two-month old Patrick Floyd, Jr.

Ida was born February 20, 1881, four months and 24 days *before* Garrett killed Billy the Kid, while Garrett and Apolinaria were living in Lincoln, New Mexico.[72] (That Garrett already had a daughter when he killed Billy the Kid is revealed here for the first time.)

Lizzie was born on October 9, 1885, while Garrett was living on a ranch on Eagle Creek, near Alto. She was named after Garrett's mother, Elizabeth Ann (as was Garrett's second daughter Ann). Lizzie lost her sight when four or five years old as a result of being treated for an eye condition with blue-vitriol (copper sulfate), a not uncommon practice then.[73]

Poe was born on June 8, 1887, in Roswell shortly after Garrett bought a ranch there. He contracted infantile paralysis (polio) while a child and was left with a bent spine and partial paralysis on one side.[74] He would often see himself described in newspapers as *"Garrett's hunched-back son."* [75] Poe got his name from John W. Poe, the deputy sheriff who was with Garrett when he hunted down and killed Billy the Kid.

Annie was born on October 2, 1889, also in Roswell.[76]

When Garrett first learned that his newly born child, Pat Jr., had an eye problem, he wrote Ida:

> *"It scares me to know the baby's eyes are sore. Tell your Momma to have the doctor to come and see him at once. I would not have such an accident to happen to him as happened to Lizzie for nothing in the world."* [77]

(Pat Jr. would lose his right leg due to an infected abscess when he was twelve.[78])

Elizabeth "Lizzie" and Poe Garrett, circa 1890. Lizzie was born October 9, 1885.
Poe was born June 8, 1887. Photo taken before Lizzie was blinded by an ill-judged
eye treatment and Poe contracted infantile paralysis. Never before published photo.
Courtesy IHSF.org.

Garrett married Apolinaria Gutierrez on January 14, 1880, in Anton Chico, about 60 days after the death of his first wife, Juanita Martinez. Juanita Martinez had died within a few days of the marriage ceremony.[79] (Many sources assert that Garrett's first and second wives were sisters. Not true. Juanita's parents were Albino and Feliciana Martinez. For more details, see the author's *"Billy The Kid's Grave – A History of the Wild West's Most Famous Death Marker."*)

Many of Garrett's letters to his wife are extant. Almost every letter contained a line that reflected his deep devotion to Apolinaria and his children:

"I have been awake for two hours woke at one o'clock I cant sleep so have got and lit my pipe. What a terrible thing it is for a man to be so poor that he is compelled to stay away from his wife and children this long...." [80]

"I never was so home sick in my life if we had money this would not be so.... Send me a kiss on one corner of your letter." [81]

"I love you and our babies better every day." [82]

On April 12, 1896, Garrett left for Uvalde. He had instructed his wife:

"We will leave all of our household effects there. Bring nothing but your clothing." [83]

On April 19, Garrett arrived back in Las Cruces by train with his family. He rented the McCowan house on Church Street.[84]

Ida Dies

On October 12, 1896, Ida Garrett died of ulcerated tonsillitis. She was 15 years and 7 months old.

"As she had been ill but little over a week, her death came as a shock to her many friends. The funeral services were held at the home, at five o'clock the same day. Beautiful flowers hid the casket and surrounded it." [85]

Ida's fellow students at the Loretto Academy in Las Cruces published a memorial to her which read in part:

"The highest praise we can bestow upon our dear one is that she was kind, gentle and patient in her sufferings – in a word she was loved by all.

"Our convent home is silent"
"The light from earth has fled;"
"Our hearts are throbbing sadly"
"Since "Our dear Ida" is dead." [86]

Garrett purchased a family plot in the Independent Order of Odd Fellows (IOOF) Cemetery in Las Cruces. He buried Ida under a gravestone that read:

"Farewell Forever to Ida"
"Daughter of Mr. and Mrs. P. F. Garrett"
"Born Feb. 20, 1881"
"Died Oct. 12, 1896" [87]

For more details on the Garrett IOOF family plot, see Appendix A.

Ida Garrett's gravestone in Garrett family plot in Las Cruces IOOF cemetery (see Appendix A). Undated photo. Courtesy Nita Stewart Haley Memorial Library and J. Evetts Haley History Center.

Hanging Jesus Garcia

On November 6, 1896, Garrett hanged Jesus Garcia.

Garcia was tried on October 9, and convicted of killing Isabella Montoya Garcia on July 26, 1896, at Loma Parda, New Mexico. Isabella was Garcia's third wife. [88]

Isabella was shot in the face and back while she was picking mesquite beans. The newspapers reported that Garcia had killed his first two wives too, one in Mexico and one in Arizona. [89]

Following his conviction, a petition signed by 500 territorial citizens was submitted to Governor Thornton, requesting that Garcia's sentence be commuted to life in prison. The request was denied. [90]

The hanging took place at 1:15 pm on the Las Cruces courthouse grounds:

"The prisoner for the past few days has been very nervous and had ate nothing for two days, nor had he slept but very little for some nights."

"Quite a large crowd, numbering several hundred, about one-fifth being women, were present. Sheriff Garrett and Deputies Brent and Rudesile escorted the prisoner to the scaffold...."

"After arriving at the scaffold, the prisoner's legs were pinioned, the black cap was drawn over the face, the rope was sprung and the body shot through the trap door, falling a distance of six feet, breaking the neck...." [91]

Elected Sheriff

Garrett's appointed term as sheriff ended with Reymond's term, making it necessary to win the office if he wanted to continue as sheriff – which he assuredly did.

Since Garrett's appointment, the political climate in Las Cruces had changed. The Republicans had gained popularity, while the Democrats had lost favor. It was obvious to Garrett that if he was to win the sheriff's office, it would have to be with Republican support. So Garrett made a deal with the Republican political powers. He renounced his Democratic affiliation and declared himself an Independent.

In turn, the Republican Convention nominated him for county sheriff. His address to the convention explained his situation:

> *"The closest attention was paid his speech, as every one realized the main issue of the campaign hung on the re-election of Mr. Garrett as sheriff. He first made clear his position with regard to the democrats of Las Cruces, who had at first heartily welcomed his arrival; saying he was the right man in the right place, etc. He said he had at the time thought it for the best when he co-operated with them for the removal of two county commissioners."* [92]

He said he was surprised when the Democrats turned against him.

Although Garrett did not say it, the audience knew the reason the Democrats turned on him – the suspects he was pursuing in the Fountain murders were powerful members of the Democratic establishment.

> *"Mr. Garrett, by his quiet wit and sarcasm made quite an impression upon his hearers.... He retired amid great enthusiasm."* [93]

The next speaker to the group was Colonel Fountain's daughter Maggie:

> *"Cheer after cheer greeted her.... She appealed to the voters on the especial behalf of Pat Garrett... as she believed the murderers of her father would soon be brought to justice at his hands."* [94]

The Republican newspaper was blunt in its opinion of the leader of the opposition and of the party's campaign tactics, writing:

> *"Other words beginning with the same letter as FALL: Foul foe, futile foister, faithless flockmaster, filthy filcher, fatal failure, fizzled fomenter, fearful fraud."* [95]

> *"The damn-ocrats are calling Pat Garrett a Texan down the river and here among the Mexicans, but out in the Sacramento mountains they are calling him too much of a Mexican, that he is married to a Mexican, etc. What contemptible double-dealing that is; but it won't win votes this year."* [96]

Garrett learned the results of the election on November 6 – the same day he hanged Jesus Garcia – he was the officially elected sheriff of Dona Ana County. The vote tally was 1,210 to 1,080, not close by the standard of the time.[97]

The election state-wide was a rout for the Republicans, with one exception – Albert Fall was elected to the Territorial Council as Dona Ana County's Eighth District Delegate.[98]

Patrick Floyd Jarvis Garrett, circa 1886. Never before published photo.
Courtesy IHSF.org.

Hard Working Sheriff – 1897-1898

Garrett began his two-year term as elected sheriff on January 1, 1897. His attempts to arrest the Fountain murderers were stalled. He was confident Oliver Lee, Jim Gililland, and William McNew were the three horsemen who *"had done the killing,"* but he needed evidence sufficient to convince a local jury.

Deputy John McLeod Killed

Two weeks after taking office, Garrett's deputy John McLeod was killed. McLeod had gone to Loma Parda to investigate a report of cattle rustling by a Francisco Duran. McLeod found Duran in possession of a butchered beef. Duran said he was given the beef by Rito Montoya. Montoya did not own any cattle, so McLeod arrested both on suspicion of cattle stealing.

While in Loma Parda, McLeod learned that a certain Domingo Baca had stolen a saddle. McLeod deputized two men and sent them to arrest Baca. They returned reporting that Baca refused to surrender. McLeod then deputized four more men, as Baca had an outlaw reputation, and all seven went to arrest Baca.

At Baca's house, McLeod saw Baca hiding behind an adobe wall. McLeod walked up to the wall and asked Baca to surrender:

> *"Baca replied by raising his gun and firing, striking McLeod in the side. McLeod pulled his gun and fired as he was falling. The deputies about the same time fired into Domingo Baca from the other side of the wall, riddling his body with bullets."* [1]

The 36-year-old McLeod died the next morning. His body was sent to his former home in Kansas for burial.[2]

Jesus Chacon Murderers Caught

In late March, Garrett solved a crime that was almost two years old. In May, 1895, Manuel Fuentes, Daniel Valderama, and husband and wife Jesus and Luz Chacon left El Paso for the Mogollon Mountains, near Silver City.

Theodoro Chacon, Jesus' brother, grew concerned about Jesus when his letters to Jesus were never answered. He travelled to El Paso to investigate. Theodoro found Fuentes wearing his Jesus's clothes, and Luz Chacon and Fuentes telling different stories about where Jesus was.

Based on Theodoro's oral evidence, Garrett began a search for Luz Chacon and Manuel Fuentes. They were located in El Paso and arrested. Brought to Las Cruces and interrogated, Luz Chacon revealed that:

> *"...Fuentes murdered her husband and compelled her to live with him. He threatened to murder both her and her brother, Daniel Valderama, if anything was ever said about the matter. She said that the body had been burned and the remains buried and gave the officers a description of the location where the foul deed was committed."* [3]

Fuentes agreed to take Garrett to the scene of the crime. There, the remains of Jesus' burned body were recovered. Buried with Jesus were his hat and the pistol used to kill him.[4]

On June 13, Fuentes escaped from the Las Cruces jail, made it to Mexico, and was never located again.[5]

Hanging the Murderers of Francisco Chavez

On April 2, 1897, Garrett attended the hanging of four murderers of Francisco Chavez. The murder of Chavez was a cold-blooded political assassination of a man who was in the opposite political party from the killers. Before Colonel Fountain and Henry's murders, it was the most sensational killing of a public figure in New Mexico history.

Five years earlier, on May 29, 1892, at about 10 in the evening, ex-sheriff Francisco Chavez was walking with Atilano Gold near his home in Santa Fe when he was hit by a *"volley of shots."* The shots came from behind a telegraph pole positioned at the entrance to a graveyard:

> *"Chavez stopped, turned toward the right and exclaimed as he reached for Gold with his right hand: 'The brutes have murdered me!' As he said this he fell, and at the same instant two or three more shots were fired."* [6]

An immediate investigation around the telegraph pole found the footprints of two men, but the shooters were gone. *"Several brass cartridge shells for a Colt's 45 revolver were picked up."* Doctor Sloan was brought to the site and quickly determined that Chavez was dead: [7]

> *"The body was lifted and conveyed to Chavez's room, scarcely 100 yards distant."*

> *"An examination of the body revealed the fact that four of the five shots had taken effect.... One ball had split the heart in two. Another ball passed through the liver. A third shot, evidently fired after the victim had turned, entered the groin. The victim's left hand was probably part way in his pantaloon's pocket and this ball also tore off a part of the thumb and forehand. A fourth ball went through the right ankle...."* [8]

Three years later, four men were tried for Chavez's murder: the bothers Francisco Gonzales y Borrego and Antonio Gonzales y Borrego, Lauriano Alarid, and Patricio Valencia. A fifth man who also was believed to be involved, Hipolito Vigil, was shot and killed while being arrested.[9]

The evidence against the men consisted primarily of eye witness testimony. One witness said he was present when the murder was discussed. A second testified that Francisco told him that he (Francisco) had fired the Colt pistol. He also said Francisco had paid Atilano Gold to lead Chavez to the spot where he was killed. A third witness testified he saw Francisco and Hipolito standing near the telephone pole at the moment of the murder, He stated he saw three other men loitering in the cemetery at the time of the killing.[10]

The defense called a series of friends and family members who testified that the accused were with them at the time of the murder.

In a spectacular move, the defendants' attorney, Thomas B. Catron, probably the most famous lawyer in New Mexico at the time, called *himself* to the stand as a defense witness to offer testimony refuting a prosecution witness's prior testimony.[11]

In spite of Catron's tricky legal ploy, the men were found guilty and sentenced to hang. After a series of appeals were denied, the hanging was set for April 2, 1897.[12] Garrett was present as an official witness.

> *"The four men walked with a firm step and mounted the scaffold without assistance. Each of them maintained a stolid indifference to the presence of death, and made no statement except to request the Sheriff to be particular about removing all traces of the cause of their death before turning their bodies over to their families."*

> *"Two and a half minutes after they had mounted the scaffold, the trap was sprung and the four condemned men paid the penalty of their crime. The necks of all except that of Valencia were broken. He was the lightest in weight and died from strangulation. His pulse, however, ceased to beat four minutes after the drop fell, while the pulse of Alarid, the heaviest of the number, beat for nine and one half minutes."*

> *"The bodies were cut down and placed in plain black coffins supplied by the county."* [13]

The next day Governor Thornton resigned his office, to be effective as soon as his successor was appointed. He had stated many times that his sole reason for accepting the governorship four years earlier was to clean up crime in New Mexico. With the execution of the Chavez murderers, he felt his job was done.[14]

Arresting the Killer of Vicente Sanchez

On June 7, Garrett arrested three men for killing Vicente Sanchez (misidentified in the newspapers as Vicente Chavez).

Sanchez and his partner Luis Montes were herding sheep along the Ruidoso River. On the day of the murder, Montes was at their camp when he heard one of their sheep-herding dogs barking followed by a series of shots. He rushed toward the shooting and found Sanchez dead. Sanchez had been shot once in the head and once in the neck.

It was just luck that enabled Garrett to make the arrests. He happened to be in the area when the murder was reported. At the scene of the killing he observed tracks that appeared to be those of the killer. The tracks led him to the camp of John Pruit, William W. Brazel, Jr., and Noah Barefoot, who he arrested for the killing.[15]

William W. Brazel, Jr., was well known to Garrett. His father William W. Brazel had a ranch on Eagle Creek, in Lincoln County, very close to the ranch that Garrett had bought in 1883.

In his testimony at his preliminary examination, Pruit said that he had been attacked by one of the herders' dogs, and had shot the dog in self-defense:

> *"Soon after I shot the dog, a man raised and shot at me, saying something at the same time he shot. Me not understanding in the language, I don't know what he said. When he shot at me I fell and then shot at him."* [16]

Pruit was indicted for murder. Brazel and Barefoot were released, as they were not with Pruit at the time of the shooting. Pruit was released on bond, but before he could be tried, he was killed in a gunfight in Texas.[17]

First Hint of the Coming Storm

On September 19, 1897, Garrett was served process papers (notice of a lawsuit) by the clerk of the Second Judicial District of the Territory of New Mexico.[18]

That serving was probably how Garrett first learned he was being sued by the Albuquerque Bank of Commerce for a $1,000 loan that he had co-signed on June 12, 1890 – *seven years earlier*.[19]

The 1890 note's co-signers were George Curry, Jno. F. Eubanks, and P. F. Garrett, in that order. The maturity date was six months (December 12, 1890). The interest rate was one percent per month beginning at maturity.

The money was pocketed by George Curry, although why he needed it is unknown. In any case, he chose to never repay the loan.[20]

At the time of the loan, George Curry was living in Lincoln and was working as a clerk for James J. Dolan, Billy the Kid's bitterest local enemy during the Lincoln County Wars. Curry was 29 years old.[21] Curry knew Garrett well, having *"met him many times,"* as he wrote in his autobiography.[22]

Curry may have been a poor clerk in 1890, but by 1897 he was an established public figure. He had been elected sheriff of Lincoln County in 1892. In 1894, he was elected to the New Mexico Territorial Senate. In 1895, he was appointed clerk of the Fifth Territorial District. In 1896, he was re-elected to the territorial assembly.[23]

Curry was one of the *"prominent New Mexicans"* at the meeting in El Paso on February 21, 1896, when it was decided to hire Garrett to pursue the Fountain murderers.[24]

Garrett was appalled to find the Albuquerque bank going after him for Curry's loan, even though as a co-signer he knew he was equally responsible for re-payment.

Garrett's response was to have his lawyer file a demurrer with the court, pleading for dismissal and alleging that there was no legal basis for the lawsuit against him.[25]

A Good Sheriff

From his first month in office, Garrett was recognized as a good sheriff. The *Rio Grande Republican* newspaper wrote:

> *"Sheriff Garrett's expenses in running the sheriff's office have been, on an average, $293.46 per month.... Formerly the sheriff's office cost the county from $10,000 to $18,000 a year. Quite a saving that, isn't it? The voters of Dona Ana county made no mistake when they elected Mr. Garrett sheriff of their county."* [26]

In July, 1897, Garrett was appointed by the court to handle the foreclosure sale of Patrick Coghlan's ranch at Three Rivers (Tres Ritos).[27] Coghlan had mortgaged his ranch in 1892 to Numa Reymond for $26,785.48, accepting the ruinous interest of 12 per cent per year.[28] By the time of the court foreclosure, the amount due Reymond was in excess of $43,000.[29]

George Curry. On June 12, 1890, Curry took out a $1,000 loan from the Albuquerque Bank of Commerce that Garrett co-signed. Curry never repaid the loan. Undated photo. Courtesy Leon Metz Papers, C. L. Sonnichsen Special Collections, UTEP.

Site of Garrett's Home Ranch House, located on the White Sands Missile Range.
Nothing remains at the site except a few scattered artifacts, and about 300 yards
above the site, a rock corral wall. 2007 photo.

Rock corral wall above Garrett's Home Ranch. View is to the east toward White
Sands National Monument. 2007 photo.

Garrett organized the court-ordered round-up and auctioning of Coghlan's livestock. The buyers, for $23,000, were William W. Cox and Oliver Lee.[30] With the money he received from the involuntary livestock sale, Coghlan temporarily staved off the loss of his ranch. (In 1906, after numerous further financial difficulties, he lost the ranch to Albert Fall.) [31]

Garrett also pursued his personal interests. He brought his race horses and their colts from Uvalde to Las Cruces by train car.[32] He constructed a race track for training his horses.[33] As he had no range land of his own, he made a deal with W. W. Cox to pasture his horses:

"W. W. Cox brought in a team of Pat Garrett's horses this week which have been ranging out at his place. They look fine, and Bill says he fed them 'three squares' a day." [34]

Garrett's best racer was named "Punch". In April, he began touting a race at San Marcial against Frank Selman's "Bay Jim." The purse was $200. The match drew wide attention in the territorial newspapers.[35]

On the day of the race, however:

"...Punch was not in condition, Mr. Garrett paid a [$100] forfeit and did not run." [36]

In July, after moving his family into a rented *"brick cottage,"* Garrett purchased a piano for his daughters.[37]

Garrett Buys a Home Ranch

On December 10, 1897, Garrett purchased what would become known as the Garrett Home Ranch from W. W. Cox. The Las Cruces newspaper noted:

"Sheriff Garrett purchased two watering places from W. W. Cox on the west side of the rincon and about two miles west of the Mormon mine. He has stocked the range there with some fine horses and a bunch of thoroughbred Holstein cattle." [38]

No deed has been found for this sale, possibly because Dona Ana County Deed Book where the deed likely was recorded is missing. The above newspaper announcement is an *important discovery* in Garrett's story, as many authors and historians have searched for the prior owner of Garrett's Home Ranch, with zero success.

Second Year Begins Well -1898

The good will that Garrett had accumulated in his first year led him to announce that he would run again as an Independent, and that he expected he probably would be endorsed by both the Democrats and the Republicans.[39]

In January, Garrett hired a full-time manager for his horse racing "studio" – John Burke.[40] With Burke handing the logistics, Garrett entered races throughout New Mexico. In March, his "seven stalls" of horses participated in a huge race in Albuquerque, in which there were:

"...more high-class horses... [then had] ever been attracted to New Mexico before." [41]

Oliver Milton Lee. Undated photo. Courtesy Leon Metz Papers, C. L. Sonnichsen Special Collections, UTEP.

Even Robert Fitzsimmons, now the world heavyweight champion, brought his *"stable of runners"* to the race.[42]

In the same month as the Albuquerque race, Garrett had a street fight in attempting to arrest a tramp:

> *"...the fellow resisted and pulled a knife.... He was promptly knocked down by Garrett, with a pistol, and taken into custody and charges were preferred against him for being drunk and disorderly. He gave his name as Walter Clifford and was sentenced to twenty days in the county jail."* [43]

Oliver Lee Marries

On January 7, 1898, Oliver Milton Lee married Winnie Rhode in Halletsville, Texas, Winnie's home town.[44] Being on the lam did not interfere with his wooing of Winnie.

Winnie Rhode was the sister of W. W. Cox's wife Margaret Zerilda Rhode.[45] Her brother was Print Rhode, a long-term friend of both Lee and Cox (see page 179).

Court Issues Judgment

On January 26, the Bank of Commerce obtained a judgment against Garrett in the Second District Court for $997.92, the amount due on the bank loan to George Curry that Garrett had co-signed in June, 1890.[46]

Garrett ignored the judgment.

Garrett Arrests McNew and Carr

On Sunday, April 3, Garrett arrested McNew and William Carr for the murder of Colonel Fountain and his son.[47]

Garrett planned this action carefully. He waited until he knew that McNew and Carr were in Las Cruces. Then he obtained bench warrants for the arrest of Lee, Gililland, McNew, and Carr from District Judge Frank Parker by submitting an affidavit that he could provide evidence of their guilt. The key assertion was based on Jack Maxwell's account:

> *"Patrick F. Garrett of lawful age being first duly sworn... upon his oath deposes and says..."*

> *"...that he can bring before the court a witness who saw Lee, McNew, and Gililland early on Sunday morning, February 2, 1896, being the very next morning following the supposed murder of Colonel Fountain and his son Henry. This witness will testify that he was at Oliver Lee's ranch at the time that Lee, McNew, and Gililland arrived there and that both the men and horses were in a very tired and worn out condition."* [48]

Because he knew that the four men would be warned of any grand jury's decision and slip into hiding before he could arrest them, Garrett did not go to a grand jury for indictments.[49]

Still counting on surprise, Garrett ordered a posse of 11 men to race to the ranches of Lee and Gililland and arrest them. But Lee and Gililland's informants were faster. Before the posse could get to the men's ranches, someone from Las Cruces had already alerted them. The posse searched for the men for three days before giving up.[50]

William W. Cox. Undated photo. Courtesy Archives and Special Collections, NMSU.

Geraldine Combs Gerber, Albert B. Fall, Anna Robertson, Isaac Rhode, Hal Cox, Jim Cox, Leonard Cox (on horse), Addison P. Center, and William W. Cox at San Augustine Ranch. 1900 photo. Courtesy Archives and Special Collections, NMSU.

San Augustine Ranch house today. 2005 photo.

Garrett included Carr in the arrests because he believed that Carr was one of the men who had shadowed Colonel Fountain during his trip home from Lincoln.

McNew-Carr Preliminary Examination

The preliminary examination to determine if there was sufficient evidence to hold McNew and Carr began April 9, in the Las Cruces courthouse.[51] Albert Fall represented the two men. When the session opened, Fall complained that his clients feared for their lives, because *"a considerable number of persons present were armed."* (This was facetious and brazen, as Fall was known to always carry a derringer in his vest pocket.) Judge Parker ordered:

> *"... all persons except the sheriff and three of his deputies should vacate the room if they were armed – none moved."* [52]

The first prosecution witness was Garrett's prize informant, Frank Maxwell. Maxwell testified that when he visited Lee's ranch February 1, the day Colonel Fountain disappeared, Lee and McNew were not there. He said the two men arrived early in the morning of February 2, on fresh horses, and that later that same day, he saw their worn-out horses stashed in a nearby pasture.[53]

But on cross-examination by Fall, Maxwell was a debacle:

> *"[Maxwell] admitted that he had told four or five conflicting stories to various friends of the accused men, but stated in explanation that he had been informed his life would be in danger if he testified against Lee and his friends, and that he told the various stories to avoid entanglements which might result in personal violence to himself."* [54]

Maxwell added that until his appearance in court, he had never sworn to any account of the events that he had told (hence, by implication, the non-court accounts were lies).

Fall then had Maxwell admit that he had been given a $2,000 contract to testify to certain facts.[55]

The prosecution called more than a dozen witnesses. Garrett took the stand briefly. The most damning prosecution witness may have been James Gould, who testified that he was at McNew's ranch on February 1, and McNew was not there that night.[56]

When the prosecution ended its case, the defense surprised those present by not calling any witnesses.

The judge ruled April 16. McNew was ordered held without bail for trial for murder. Carr was released due to lack of evidence.[57]

Shootout at Wildy Well

Following McNew's hearing, Lee told a Democratic newspaper that he did not trust Garrett – a known killer – with his life, and would not surrender to him. Garrett responded with a long letter to the *New Mexican Review* defending himself and swearing to enforce the law impartially, *"without favor to any faction or party, and let the chips fall where they will."* [58]

On July 9, Garrett's deputy Jose Espalin discovered through a surprise visit to Cox's San Augustine Ranch that Lee and Gililland were there. He made no attempt to arrest them; instead, he returned to Las Cruces and notified Garrett. Garrett put together a posse consisting of himself, Ben Williams, Kent Kearney, Clint Llewellyn, and Jose Espalin.[59]

At Cox's ranch, the posse discovered Lee and Gililland were gone, but their horse tracks were visible heading toward Lee's Dog Canyon Ranch. They followed the tracks to Wildy Well, owned by Lee. The well site included a windmill, furnace, steam pump, water tank, adobe house, and several smaller buildings and was used to pump drinking water for Cox's livestock. James Madison, a full-time Lee employee, lived at the site with his wife and four kids.[60]

The posse arrived at the well at about 4:30 in the morning. Deputy Williams described what happened next:

"We went into the house and searched it, but did not find the men there. However, we found two other men sleeping in the house. We asked one of them where Lee and Gililland were, and he said that he did not know, that they were not around there. Their horses and saddles being there, we thought that they could not be far away, so we began to search around the premises." [61]

A ladder leading to the roof of the house led Garrett to suspect that someone was hiding on the roof, which was surrounded by a low parapet:

"Garrett, Kearney and Espalin got on the roof of some low out-buildings. Llewellyn got behind a large water tank near by...."

"Kearney rose up and called to Lee and Gililland to surrender, and about the same time fired. Lee and Gililland raised their guns to shoot at the same time. Several shots were exchanged, all parties taking a part."

"During the fusillade Kearney received two wounds, one in the shoulder, breaking it, and as he was falling, received another bad wound in the thigh." [62]

Lee, through an employee, gave the *El Paso Herald* his version. He said he and Gililland were asleep on the roof in *"plain-view"* when the posse opened fire without warning. They woke to the impact of bullets striking around them. They had no choice but to grab their *"Winchesters"* and return fire.[63]

When the shooting stopped, it was obvious that Kearney was badly hurt and exposed to further shots. In Williams' account, someone on Lee's side offered a truce, which Garrett accepted so he could get Kearney to medical care. In Lee's account:

"I called out to Garrett, 'Don't you think you've got the worst of this?'"

"Garrett replied, 'He needs a doctor.'"

"...after some further talk I agreed not to fire on them while he and his men were leaving; but I told him I would keep them covered, in order to be on the safe side...."

"As the posse was leaving, I said, 'Now, Pat, I guess you will go away and tell a lie about this fight.' But he said he would not; that he would tell it just as it happened." [64]

Wildy Well, site of shootout between Garrett and posse and Oliver Lee and James Gililland. Persons unidentified. Undated photo. Courtesy Leon Metz Papers, C. L. Sonnichsen Special Collections, UTEP.

Wildy Well today. Located on Fort Bliss Military Base. 2008 photo.

Kearney was taken to Alamogordo. His wounds were assessed as serious, but not fatal. Asked about the fight, he said Lee and Gililland fired first, just after he called on them to surrender.[65]

Kearney died four days later, July 14, 1898.

Shootout Continues With Words

When Lee read what Deputy Williams had told the public about the shootout, he was enraged – the account hid the plain fact that, in Lee's mind, Garrett never had any intention of letting Lee surrender – that Garrett's plan, pure and simple, was to murder him.

He fired off a letter to the *Albuquerque Democrat:*

"...Pat Garrett, sheriff of Dona Ana county, in the presence of several reliable people, and before the shooting, said that if he ever got the opportunity, he would kill Gililland and Lee.... That is the class of men put in power to enforce the law...." [66]

Lee added that Garrett knew that Deputy Espalin was *"a man who could be hired to kill almost any man for money,"* and Deputy Williams was a killing *"maniac,"* and *"a bitter enemy of mine and has been for years."*

As evidence of the posse's murderous intent, Lee wrote:

"I had just awakened but had not discovered that we had visitors, when a shot was fired.... I saw Kearney fire the second shot and about the same time Garrett and Espalin rose and fired, Garrett about the same time saying 'throw up your hands Lee.'" [67]

Lee was charging Garrett with attempted murder because he was not given a chance to surrender before he was fired upon. Lee added the following fascinating detail:

"After some talk.... I agreed to not shoot them, and they at once came from cover, having to walk to their horses, about a hundred yards distance, in plain view with their backs toward us, while Gililland and I had them covered with our guns...."

"After getting their horses, they rode off in the direction of Turquoise [train] station, which is about two miles distant from that point, and Garrett wrote me a note and sent [it] to the ranch by a section man. The following is a copy, I retain the original:"

"'Lee, how is Kearney? There is no telegraph here. If he is still alive and you think he has a chance of getting well, I will send to La Luz for a doctor. [signed] Garrett'" [68]

It was very strange that Williams' account of the shootout implied by omission that the posse took Kearney with them when they retreated. Instead Lee explained that:

"[Garrett only] returned in about four hours. After looking at Kearney's wounds, I advised that he not be moved until a doctor had dressed his wounds, and I think it one of the most inhuman acts I ever heard of, to move a man in his condition."

"Just think of it! The man had his shoulder shattered by a ball and thigh bone broken near the body. Garrett had that man loaded into a wagon, hauled two miles, then loaded into [a train] car and shipped thirty miles, knowing that the least jar or movement caused almost unbearable torture to the wounded man and also lessened his chances of recovery." [69]

Lee had considered moving Kearney into the house, but decided it would cause Kearny *"too much pain."*

Garrett responded in the *El Paso Daily Times:*

"I read the letter, but I do not consider it necessary for me to go to the newspapers to contradict lies from such a source...."

"The reporter reminded Sheriff Garrett that Lee claims it was too dark for him to recognize the sheriff's party...."

"'All bosh,' said Sheriff Garret in his quiet way. 'Lee reached his house only two hours ahead of my party and when we arrived there it was broad daylight. Lee knew we were there fifteen minutes before the fight commenced, because a woman screamed when we entered the house where we expected to find Lee. He says, too, that he was in his bed asleep when we fired on him. That is also untrue, for he was five feet from his bed lying on his stomach holding his gun in readiness when we discovered him on top of his house.'"

"It is true that Kearney, my deputy, fired first, but it was after Lee had been called to surrender...."

"I thought that probably Kearney had fired too quick and I asked him, Kearney don't you think you shot too soon. He replied, 'No sir. Lee was raising his gun to shoot when I fired.'" [70]

The *New Mexican Review* weighed in on Garrett's side:

"In [his] communication Lee makes several statements, among them that Garrett had said that he would kill Lee. Whether or not Garrett ever said so is very doubtful, for Garrett is a very closed mouthed man. Then Lee tries to make it appear that Kearney was killed by moving him. Be that as it may, there is nothing whatever in Lee's conduct to entitle him to further recognition as anything else than an outlaw."

"When Garrett's posse came up he should have given up, and not tried to dictate terms to the law. A man who tries to override law should be hunted down like a mad dog." [71]

Lee shot back with a second letter:

"If you are interested in the welfare of the people of this county you will surely abstain from championing the cause of an assassin...."

"I believe you know of your own knowledge that Garrett is an infidel, believing in neither God or hereafter, so that no oath that you could administer to him would be held sacred...."

"If I am not killed before the next election in this county and if a square man, one that cannot be hired to commit murder, is elected, I will at once surrender to him and answer to the courts of this territory any charges that may be brought against me...."

"So long as Garrett is sheriff, I cannot surrender without my life being in danger and as I have no intention of committing suicide, I will just stay at home." [72]

Lee's accusation made public what was said privately about Garrett, that he was a non-believer in God (see page 147).

The "letter" shootout between Garrett and Lee attracted nation-wide attention, causing the *Rio Grande Republican* to observe:

"In the states, an outlaw, dodging the officers of the law, would not think of writing letters to the press to excuse his crime. In Texas, if the whereabouts of an escaped murderer was known, he would be arrested.... But in New Mexico, Oliver Lee, after killing an officer of the law... retires to his ranch and sends the papers a graphic description of the fight he made and tells why he will not be arrested by this or that officer." [73]

Hunting Lee and Gililland

The newspaper exchange did not stop Garrett from ordering out a posse whenever he had any information on the whereabouts of Lee or Gililland.[74]

Ironically, Lee and Gililland were in a position analogous to that of Billy the Kid, following the Kid's escape from the Lincoln County Jail. Lee and Gililland, like Billy, were supported by many friends and allies, who supplied them with food and shelter, and warned them whenever Garrett was out searching for them.[75]

Lee's biggest supporter was Eugene Manlove Rhodes, the future Western writer, who provided Lee and Gililland a long-term hideout at the H. G. Ranch, in northern Dona Ana County, where Rhodes was working as a cowhand.[76]

Striking Bean and Suing Bull

On August 11, Garrett was in the May Brothers' store in Las Cruces when he encountered Sam Bean. Bean had just published a letter in the *Independent Democrat* in which he wrote that Garrett had murdered Billy the Kid, and intended the same for Lee and Gililland.

When Garrett confronted Bean, Bean began berating Garrett, making sarcastic remarks about how incapable Garrett was of ever catching Lee and Gililland. Garrett lost his temper and struck Bean three times in the face. The men had to be separated by a third person.[77]

Bean was a hugely respected Las Cruces citizen. He had first entered New Mexico in 1845 when it was part of Mexico, and was a veteran of the Mexican-American War. He was 80 years old.[78]

The *El Paso Times* reported that:

> *"...Garrett, when he regained his composure, deeply regretted that he had struck Bean."* [79]

Garrett might have been sorry that he hit Bean, but he was mad as hell at the *Independent Democrat*. On October 6, Garrett obtained three indictments for libel against editor Carlton E. Bull. The indictments were for publishing Lee's two letters on the Wildy Well shootout and Bean's letter calling Garrett a murderer. The indictments charged that Bull:

> *"...unlawfully, wickedly and maliciously intending to injure, vilify and prejudice one Patrick F. Garrett, and to deprive him of his good name, fame, credit and reputation, and to bring him into great contempt, scandal, infamy, and disgrace...."* [80]

With these indictments in hand, Garrett arrested and jailed Bull. Bull bonded-out almost immediately.[81] Post haste, Bull decided Las Cruces was not for him. He resigned as newspaper editor and moved to Temple, Texas.[82]

Bull returned to Las Cruces a year later for the libel trial. He was represented by Albert Fall. When the trial session opened, Fall:

> *"...moved to quash the indictment on the ground that there is no criminal libel law in New Mexico. Judge Leland sustained the motion and Mr. Bull was discharged."* [83]

Running for Re-Election

On August 26, Garrett notified the public that he intended to run for a second term as sheriff.[84] Although Garrett no longer expected to run unopposed, he was expecting an electoral *"landslide."* [85]

The election was a continuation of the war between Garrett and Lee:

> *"Friends of Oliver Lee put forth every effort to defeat Garrett on the grounds that he had endeavored to assassinate Lee... and during a fight that resulted, Lee was compelled to kill Deputy Kearney in self-defense."* [86]

The center of the opposition was the *Independent Democrat*. The newspaper published a series of mocking one-and-two-liners, including several that did not make much sense, but after Garrett's libel charges, stayed away from the explicit charge of murderer. Examples from one issue:

> *"Who told a lie? A republican."*
> *"Who's afraid of Lee's little gun? A republican."*
> *"Why is the republicans' sheriff afraid of Lee's little gun?"*

> *"Why should you vote for a person who cannot himself keep the peace?"*
> *"Garrett has not made a good sheriff. Garrett has made a good sheriff. A bird sat on a limb. Another bird sat on a limb."* [87]

On November 8, 1898, Garrett beat his opponent Jefferson J. Sanders by 385 votes, the largest electoral majority received to that date by a Dona Ana County sheriff candidate.[88]

Chapter 3 | Second Term – 1899-1900

Lee and Gililland Surrender

Lee and Gililland were ready to give themselves up – but only under their terms.

An event that influenced their decision was the creation of Otero County. On January 30, 1899, the territorial assembly made a new county out of parts of Dona Ana, Soccoro, and Lincoln Counties. The new county was named after the sitting governor, Miguel A. Otero. (He had opposed the idea of the new county until it was proposed that the county be named after him.[1])

The effect of this legislative action, from Lee and Gililland's point of view, was to move the site of the disappearance of Colonel Fountain and his son into the new county, putting the jurisdiction of the Fountain cases into the new county's court. And it had another big benefit – the new county would have its own sheriff, someone other than Garrett. Some sources assert that the creation of Otero County was the brainchild of Albert Fall for just these reasons.[2] (This is not true. On the last day of the previous territorial assembly, Fall and Curry sponsored and passed a bill prohibiting the creation of the new county.[3])

The territorial press began to speculate that Lee and Gililland had just been given a get-out-of-jail-free card:

> "The question now naturally arises: Has the New Mexico assembly legis-lated Lee, et al, out of a possible job – in the Territorial penitentiary?"[4]

> "[It was soon revealed that] there were no provisions made in the bill creating Otero county for the removal of pending cases, the same must be tried at Las Cruces. The new sheriff of Otero county [would] have no jurisdiction over the Lee case and Pat Garrett will retain the warrant for the arrest of Lee and Gililland."[5]

With the Otero County option ruled out, Lee opened surrender negotiations directly with Governor Otero. He obtained extraordinary concessions. Lee and Gililland would be permitted to surrender to District Judge Parker, they could have two armed body-guards with them, at no time would they be placed in Garrett's custody, and they would be jailed in the Socorro County Jail, not the Dona Ana County Jail.[6]

On March 13, 1899, Lee telegrammed Judge Parker that he and Gililland were com-ing to Las Cruces to surrender:

> "They wore full beard and old clothes and many who had known them for years did not recognize them when they met."[7]

They were accompanied by two heavily-armed bodyguards, Eugene Manlove Rhodes and James Simpson.[8]

They boarded the south-bound Santa Fe to Las Cruces train at Alamen. To Lee and Gililland's dismay, they discovered that Garrett and Texas Ranger Captain John R. Hughes were on the same train in the smoking compartment with a chained prisoner.

Colonel Albert J. Fountain. Undated photo. Courtesy Archives and Special
Collections, NMSU.

"Lee started into the smoker but first looked through the glass over the door and seeing the ranger captain did not enter." [9]

The four men settled in the *"rear of the same coach which [was] partitioned off from the smoker."* At one point during the trip, Garrett walked past Lee and Gililland, but gave no indication that he recognized them.[10]

"When the train reached Las Cruces, Deputy Sheriff Ben Williams was at the depot and asked Captain Hughes if Lee and Gililland were on the train. The two men were not in sight as they had got off the train on the opposite side to surrender to Judge Parker, who was there awaiting them." [11]

Judge Parker immediately deputized Rhodes and Simpson as special officers and authorized them to accompany Lee and Gililland.[12] Interviewed, Lee stated:

"All the long and continued talk about us is all stuff. It was exaggerated and manufactured." [13]

Lee repeated his assertion that surrendering to Garrett would have meant his death. He said that while on the run he had never left New Mexico. This latter statement was untrue – he had travelled to Texas 14 months earlier to court and marry Winnie Rhode.[14]

After delivering his prisoner to El Paso, Garrett returned to Las Cruces. Learning that Lee and Gililland had surrendered and were in Judge Parker's custody:

"He (Garrett) called upon Messrs Lee and Gililland, shaking hands cordially with Lee." [15]

In a court appearance before Judge Parker that afternoon, Lee and Gililland were indicted for the Fountain murders and ordered transported to the jail in Socorro until they could be arraigned.[16]

Twelve days later, Lee and Gililland were brought from Socorro to Las Cruces for their arraignment. Fall, acting as their attorney, entered a plea claiming that Otero County alone had jurisdiction. Judge Parker denied the plea. Judge Parker then granted Fall's request for a change of venue on the grounds that his clients could not get a fair trial in Las Cruces. He ordered the trial moved to Hillsboro, the county seat of Sierra County.

At the end of the hearing: *"Papers were served by Sheriff Garrett on Lee and Gililland in the court room... for $50,000 damage by Fountain's widow for the death of her husband."* [17] *[This suit was later dismissed for lack of evidence.]*

Geronimo Parra

Why were Garrett and Captain Hughes on the train?

In October, 1898, authorities in El Paso learned that Texas' most-wanted man, Geronimo Parra, was in the territorial penitentiary in New Mexico. In 1893, Parra had been sentenced to seven years in the New Mexico pen for a series of robberies. During Parra's trial, no one discovered Parra was wanted in Texas for the murder of Texas Ranger Charles H. Fusselman. Fusselman was ambushed and killed on April 17, 1890, while pursuing a gang of cattle rustlers led by Parra.[18]

Texas authorities appealed to Governor Otero to release him into their custody, so he could be tried for Fusselman's killing. After some negotiations:

Rock house on Rock House Ranch bought by Garrett on October 24, 1899. Wayne Brazel leased the ranch for five years on March 11, 1907. The ranch house was built about 1885. Persons unidentified. Photo circa 1900. Courtesy Archives and Special Collections, NMSU.

Rock house today. Site located on White Sands Missile Range. 2018 photo.

"The governor [said] Texas authorities could have Parra any time they wanted him, as his time was practically up, owing to good behavior." [19]

Captain Hughes and Garrett were assigned the task of transporting Parra from the penitentiary in Santa Fe to El Paso. In Santa Fe, Captain Hughes was asked what he thought would happen to Parra. He replied that he did:

"...not believe Parra [would] hang and the fact that he has been one of the main stays of the Christian Endeavor society at the penitentiary for two years will certainly be considered in the judicial determination of the prisoner's future course." [20]

By coincidence, Garrett and Captain Hughes were transporting Para to El Paso on the same day Lee and Gililland boarded the train to surrender to Judge Parker.

Some writers have suggested that Garrett did recognize Lee when he walked past him, but was too scared to confront him. This is contradicted by contemporaneous statements of Garrett, Hughes, and Lee.[21]

In El Paso, Parra was sentence to hang for Fusselman's murder. His hanging on January 5, 1900, was the last in El Paso.[22]

Garrett Buys the Rock House Ranch

On May 24, 1899, Garrett purchased the Rock House Ranch from David Wood for $200.[23] The ranch was named after a two-room, rock cabin built on the property in 1885.[24] Included in the sale was Sinking Spring, a watering hole located about a mile from the cabin.

The Rock House Ranch was located in the middle of Bear Canyon in the southern San Andres Mountains. It was 30 miles due north of Garrett's Home Ranch (see satellite image on page 130).

Garrett had known David Wood since at least 1881. Wood was the deputy sheriff of Dona Ana County when Billy the Kid was tried in Mesilla and sentenced to hang for murdering Sheriff William Brady. Wood was also one of the six men selected to escort Billy to Fort Stanton, where Billy was turned over to Garrett, who then took him to Lincoln to hang.[25] Billy's death sentence specified that he hang in Lincoln County, where the alleged crime had occurred.

(Billy escaped from the Lincoln County Courthouse where he was jailed on April 28, 1881. He killed Deputies James W. Bell and Robert Olinger during the escape. Billy was killed by Garrett just before midnight on July 14, 1881, in Pete Maxwell's bedroom at Fort Sumner – See *"Billy the Kid's Grave: A History of the Wild West's Most Famous Death Marker"* by the author for details.) [26]

Hillsboro, New Mexico

The venue change for the Fountain murder trial meant that the trial would take place in Hillsboro, the county seat of Sierra County, about 80 miles from Las Cruces.

Hillsboro was founded in 1877 when gold was discovered in the nearby mountains. At the time of the trial, Hillsboro was in freefall, the gold having played out. The population dropped from its boom-town high of about 1,200 in 1888 to about 500 in 1899 (the

Hillsboro courthouse. Undated photo. Courtesy Center for Southwest Research and Special Collections, UNM.

Aerial view of Hillsboro, New Mexico. X marks courthouse lot. 1976 photo. Courtesy Historic American Buildings Survey, Library of Congress.

Hillsboro courthouse today. 2008 photo.

Sadie Orchard's stage. The line ran between Hillsboro and Lake Valley. Persons unidentified. Circa 1900. Courtesy Geronimo Springs Museum.

county population was less than 3,200.) [27] Transportation into and out of the town was by stagecoach or horse. The closest train service was 18 miles away.[28]

"A limpid stream flows through the same gulch in which most of the houses are situated."

"The county courthouse stands upon an eminence overlooking the town. It is built of brick and stone and is large and commodious." [29]

There were three hotels in town, the Orchard Hotel, Ocean Grove Hotel, and Union Hotel (the Union was the best). The Orchard and Ocean Grove Hotels were owned by James and Sadie Orchard. Sadie had been a famous madam before marrying James in 1895.[30]

The Orchards ran the town's only stage line. Sadie was the line's main stage driver. The fare to the train stop at Lake Valley was $2.00.[31]

Although there was no telegraph line into Hillsboro, there was a private telephone line between the town and Lake Valley. In anticipation of the excitement to be generated by the Fountain murder trial, which already getting attention from newspapers from New York to California, *El Paso Herald* City Editor John Sneed leased the telephone line and had it converted to a telegraph line. His contract with the owner specified that:

"... only Sneed or such persons as were authorized by him could send news-paper reports over the short line." [32]

Pre-Trial Celebrities

In days before their scheduled trial, Lee and Gililland were afforded amazing free-dom of movement. As ordered by Judge Parker, they were jailed in Socorro rather than Las Cruces. But they were permitted to come and go from the jail at their discretion. For example, on April 27, they were allowed to travel to El Paso for *"personal business."*

"They were supposed to be the strict custody of Deputy Sheriff Cook, but while here they were permitted to roam about town at will." [33]

They were interviewed by the *El Paso Herald,* which opined that Lee was *"a man of superior intellect and higher education."*

"Where did you spend your time during the time you were supposed to be a fugitive?"

"'I wouldn't like to say,' replied Lee. 'That's a matter that ought not to be made public.'"

"Do you expect to come out all right at Hillsboro when the trial comes off?"

"'I haven't the least uneasiness about that on earth.'" [34]

When Judge Parker learned of the El Paso trip, he issued this statement: [35]

"The action of the sheriff of Socorro county in bringing Lee and Gililland to El Paso and turning them loose upon the streets after they had been refused bail, was entirely without the knowledge of consent of Judge Parker or the dis-trict court." [36]

Fountain Murder Trial – Opening

Thursday, May 25, 1899

Three years, three months, and 24 days after Colonel Fountain and Henry's mysterious disappearance, the trial for their alleged killing finally began on the second floor of the Hillsboro courthouse. In the days leading up to the opening, large groups of supporters of the two sides began to arrive in Hillsboro. Because of the limited hotel lodging available, Fountain supporters set up a camp on one side of town and Lee and Gililland supporters set up camp on the other side.

The prosecution team consisted of Richard P. Barnes, district attorney for Grant and Sierra Counties, William B. Childers, U. S. District Attorney for New Mexico, and Thomas B. Catron. The defense team consisted of Albert Fall, Harry M. Daugherty, and Harvey B. Ferguson.[37] Catron was considered a highly competent attorney who was the equal of Fall. Fall was famous throughout the territory for his extraordinary courtroom prowess.

The trial opened promptly at 9 a.m., Judge Parker presiding. The prosecution team immediately surprised everyone present. They announced two shockers:

First, they were dropping the prosecution of McNew without prejudice, meaning they could re-file the charges against him at a later date; and second, they were prosecuting Lee and Gililland *only* for the killing of young Henry Fountain.[38]

The reasoning for the second decision apparently was that they felt the jury would be more sympathetic to the killing of a child, and also, they could prosecute Lee and Gililland for the killing of Colonel Fountain if the result of this trial went against them.

With the charges against him dropped, McNew was let out of jail.

Fall, as he had in the preliminary examination, claimed that Lee was under imminent threat of assassination. When not in court, the two defendants were kept in a small, one-room jail on Main Street. Judge Parker ordered that Lee could have two heavily armed bodyguards with him at all times, including in the jail.[39]

The prosecution then asked for a continuance. Prosecution witness Jack Maxwell had ignored his subpoena and had not shown up. Garrett, who had arrived the day before, immediately left Hillsboro looking for him.[40] The judge granted a continuance until 10 a.m. the next morning.

The press reported:

> *"The delay in the case has certainly been very unfortunate in one respect at least. It seems to have given Lee and Gililland an opportunity of turning a great deal of public sentiment in their favor."* [41]

Friday, May 26

Garrett and Maxwell were not present. Judge Parker refused a further continuance. The trial proceeded with the selection of the jury. As in a capital case today, potential jurors were questioned as to whether they:

> *"...were opposed to capital punishment... or had read newspaper reports of the case and had therefrom formed an opinion."* [42]

Thomas B. Catron, lead attorney for the prosecution in the Lee/Gililland trial, circa 1900. Courtesy C. M. Bell Studio Collection, Library of Congress.

When the venire – the pool of potential jurors – was exhausted, only 11 men had been selected. Judge Parker ordered that a second pool of potential jurors be gathered from bystanders and persons on the streets of Hillsboro:

> *"At precisely ten minutes of three o'clock, after many challenges by both sides, the last juror ran the gauntlet and took his seat in the jury box."* [43]

The jurors selected were: Thomas Maher, Henry Patrick, Oscar Greeley, Prajedes Torres, Tomas Chavez, Thomas Ingils, Louis Kruse, A. Bentley, Abel Chavez, August Reingardt, John E. Wheeler, and R. A. Nichols. [44]

Because some jurors spoke only Spanish, an interpreter was appointed.

Fountain Murder Trial – Testimony

Monday, May 29

Garrett and Maxwell were still not present. One of the prosecution team expressed their concern to the press:

> *"[Maxwell] is considered the most important witness for the territory and without his evidence the prisoners will readily prove an alibi."* [45]

Judge Parker announced that because he was expecting a long trial, the court would hold both day and night sessions.

The first witness called was ex-Governor Thornton. He testified to offering a reward for solving Colonel Fountain and his son's killing (not unusual in a murder case), and that he had seen some of the forensic evidence of the killing.

The next several witnesses provided testimony showing that Fountain was followed from Lincoln. They described finding Fountain's abandoned buggy and following tracks from the buggy to a campfire, and from there toward Lee's Dog Canyon Ranch. At a certain point, *one set of tracks split off from the others and went to Wildy Well.* One man followed that track. The other tracks continued toward Lee's ranch, until they were effaced by a herd of cattle driven over the tracks.

A map drawn by Carl Clausen showing the routes the searchers had taken was introduced by the prosecution as an exhibit (see page 54).

The indictments of Lee and Gililland obtained by Fountain from the Lincoln County grand jury were introduced as exhibits.[46]

Tuesday, May 30

The newspapers reported that Garrett had located and arrested Maxwell. In El Paso, on their way to Hillsboro, Maxwell was interviewed by the *El Paso Herald*:

> *"...there is no truth whatever in the reports that I was afraid to go to Hillsboro.... I have been sick for a couple of weeks...."* [47]

Witnesses provided details on the formation of the search posses and the evidence of murder, such as the pool of blood found near where Fountain's buggy had left the road.[48]

Colonel Fountain's son Albert was called. He testified he was in the first search posse. He confirmed previous testimony about evidence found at the murder site. At Fountain's buggy, they found:

MAP OF THE SCENE OF THE FOUNTAIN DISAPPEARANCE.
Drawn By Fountain's Son in Law, Carl Clausen, and Used In the Court Room.

Map drawn by Fountain's son-in-law of scene of Fountain's disappearance and submitted as evidence in Lee/Gililland trial:

(A) Where buckboard was found
(B) Dry camp, where fire was built
(C) Route of big horse led by Fountain
(D) Route of white horse driven by Fountain
(E) Route taken by mounted men leading one of the horses driven by Fountain (Black Mare)
(F) Where trail ran into road leading from Dog Canyon to Lee's Well and where cattle were met by posse
(G) Single houseman going through 2nd pass to Lee's Well (Wildy Well)
(H) Where mail carrier met Fountain, Feb 1, '96
(K) Blood was found on edge of road
Scale: 1 inch equals 12 miles.

El Paso Herald, June 1, 1899

"An old suit of my father's and the little boy's coat and hat and two shawls. My father's cartridge belt was also found on the seat of the buggy, but his rifle was gone [it was never found]." [49]

Wednesday, May 31

A week after the trial opened, Maxwell was finally present. Called to the stand, Maxwell repeated his story about Lee not being at his ranch on the day of the disappearance, how Lee and Gililland came in the next day, and his finding the exhausted horses in a distant field at Lee's ranch later that day.

But, as before in the preliminary examination, Maxwell's credibility was severely damaged by Fall's cross examination. Maxwell admitted to using multiple aliases, to having given contradictory accounts of his story, and to the $2,000 contract with Garrett for his testimony if Lee was convicted.

The *El Paso Herald* noted:

"...[Maxwell's] evidence proved more damaging to the territory than to the defense." [50]

Thursday, June 1

Gililland's brother-in-law Riley Baker testified to various incriminating comments that Gililland had made about the killing, including *"the bodies [will] never be found,"* but these statements were put in doubt by Fall's cross examination.[51]

Humphrey Hill, who had spoken to Colonel Fountain at La Luz the day before Fountain disappeared, was called. Catron asked him to relate their conversation. Fall objected. The jury was removed and Catron and Fall argued over admission of Hill's testimony for more than an hour:

"The three attorneys on either side were given ample opportunity to display their legal knowledge and oratorical powers.... Each talked long and earnestly...." [52]

Judge Parker ruled the conversation inadmissible – a victory for the defense.

Friday, June 2

Garrett took the stand:

"His entrance into the court room... created a stir among the spectators." [53]

He testified that his first investigative action on arriving in Las Cruces was to visit the murder scene:

"I found blood where we supposed the murder of Colonel Fountain took place.... A bloody spot indicated at once that murder had been done. The ground was soaked and the blood had spurted." [54]

He described the reasons for obtaining warrants for Lee and Gililland, and tracking them to Wildy Well. He described the shootout, saying:

"Mr. Lee and Mr. Kearney shot at about the same time, but Mr. Kearney shot first...." [55]

James R. "Jim" Gililland, shortly before he died August 8, 1946. Courtesy Center for
Southwest Research and Special Collections, UNM.

Garrett testified that he had offered Maxwell the $2,000 contract, and produced a copy that was entered as an exhibit.

Fall opened the cross examination by asking Garrett who hired him as an investigator. Garrett answered Governor Thornton. When asked who was paying him, Garrett said the *"Masonic Lodge."* Fall asked how Garrett became sheriff. Garrett:

> *"...startled the listeners... by saying that Attorney Fall had gone with him to Santa Fe and got the two county commissioners removed so he (Garrett) could be appointed sheriff."* [56]

The cross continued:

> *"Fall: 'What was the condition of affairs when you went to Cruces?'"*
> *"Garrett: 'You fellows had been shooting at one another and cutting up.'"*
>
> *"Fall: 'What fellows?'"*
> *"Garrett: 'You, Lee, Williams, and others.'"*
>
> *"Fall: 'With the present evidence in your possession, why did you wait two years to procure warrants for the defendants?'"*
> *"Garrett: 'You had too much control of the courts down there.' (laughter)"* [57]

Garrett was excused. Dr. Francis Crosson, a physician and chemist, was called. He testified that he tested a sample of the blood found by the searchers, even tasting it, and determined it had all the characteristics of human blood.

On cross, Crosson admitted that there was no definitive test for human blood:

> *"Fall: 'Will you undertake before this jury to taste samples of human blood, dog blood, or rat's blood and tell which is human blood?'"*
> *"Crosson: 'O, I don't know.'"* [58]

Saturday, June 3

Captain Thomas Branigan, a recognized expert in trailing, *"minutely"* described the tracks he found at the killers' campfire.

> *"The next day, he said, he saw one of the set of tracks on top of a house at Lee's ranch. They were made by Oliver Lee. Saw another set of tracks in Las Cruces a short time later. They were made by McNew."*
>
> *"Brannigan [Branigan] also described following a train of horsemen toward Lee's ranch until a large herd of cattle was encountered, which passed along the direction in which the trail was going, completely obliterating it."* [59]

Fall's cross of Branigan, as reported in the *El Paso Herald*:

> *"...was tedious and long drawn out.... On a few points witness was harassed unmercifully...."* [60]

Monday, June 5

Before the session opened, the prosecution issued the following statement to the press:

> *"All newspaper reports, including Associated Press, sent from here about the trial of Lee and Gilliland are gross misrepresentations of evidences and*

facts generally. We ask you to publish this daily until the trial is over or we notify you that misrepresentations have ceased." [61]

Major W. H. H. Llewellyn was the major witness called. He testified to finding the buggy and the killers' campfire, and seeing a child's tracks at the campfire, all made by a child's right shoe. He testified that while following the horse tracks from the campfire, a herd of Lee's cattle *"came into the trail"* and trampled the tracks.

Llewellyn also testified that he was with Captain Branigan in Las Cruces:

"...when William McNew passed along and Captain Brannigan measured his tracks and compared them with a pair of tracks around the camp fire." [62]

He said the two sets of tracks matched.

When the time came for cross, Llewellyn said he felt ill, so Judge Parker adjourned for the day.[63]

Tuesday, June 6

Court began with Fall's cross of Llewellyn:

"Fall: 'You testified twice that the track in Las Cruces was not the same as any of the three near the blood.'"
"Catron: 'He did not.'" [64]

Fall accused Catron of *"posting"* the witness – signaling what he should say – to which Catron took personal offense, demanding an apology. Fall said he would gladly apologize to the court, but not to Catron.

The prosecution then rested its case.

Fall moved for an immediate jury verdict of not guilty. Judge Parker denied the motion and adjourned the court until the next morning.[65]

Wednesday, June 7

The first witness for the defense was George Curry, now the sheriff of Otero County. (He was appointed as the first sheriff of the new county on March 28, 1899.)

Prior to his testimony, Curry gave an interview to the press announcing that he knew who had killed Colonel Fountain and Henry:

"...I can tell who planned the killing and who vainly lay in wait for Col. Fountain once before he was killed. Miller, one of my former prisoners, who was pardoned out of the penitentiary by Gov. Thornton, made a confession to me which I have kept secret, having no occasion to divulge it till now." [66]

Curry said Ely "Slick" Miller and two men he did not identify had made a pact to kill Colonel Fountain and several other cattlemen. Miller was arrested before the murders could be carried out, but the other two men executed the plan without him (Miller).

"Curry said that Miller told him that the bodies of Col. Fountain and his son are buried in the white sands on the San Augustine plains." [67]

When Curry took the stand, Fall asked if he knew who had killed the Fountains. Catron objected. The jury was sent out. After hearing the arguments of both sides, Judge Parker ruled Curry's account of Miller's confession inadmissible.

Curry testified that Maxwell had once told him that he was at Lee's ranch the night that the Fountains disappeared, and Lee, Gililland, and McNew were all there.

On cross, Catron got Curry to admit that he owed Lee a *substantial* sum of money.

Joe Morgan testified that he saw the defendants at Lee's ranch the day of the murder.[68]

Thursday, June 8

The defense called Albert Blevin, a Texas and Pacific Railroad fireman, who worked near Lee's ranch. Blevin testified:

"...he was with Lee and Gililland at Lee's ranch, 60 miles from the murder scene during the very time Colonel Fountain and son are said to have been killed." [69]

He said he was with the defendants for two days, and Maxwell was there the whole time. He said the cattle that supposedly had obliterated the tracks were simply under contract to be delivered to Lee's ranch on that day.

Blevin was cross examined by Catron:

"The prosecution held the witness nearly three hours vainly trying to confuse him." [70]

When the cross ended, Fall called Oliver Lee's mother, who testified that her son was home on the day of the alleged murder.[71]

Fall then called Lee to the stand. Lee said that he was at his personal residence at his Dog Canyon Ranch on February 1, the day the Fountains were supposedly murdered. He said he didn't even learn that he was suspected until two days later:

"He then went to Las Cruces, found a warrant issued and offered to surrender and stand trial then but was refused. An extra issue of a Las Cruces paper advocated mob law and openly accused him of the Fountain murder." [72]

Catron objected to the introduction of the newspaper, but Judge Parker allowed it in as opinion, not as fact. In an editorial comment encouraging lynch law, the newspaper opined:

"In the early fifties in this western country the sturdy pioneers had a mode of treating criminals which, though perhaps not law, was justice. Men of Dona Ana, it is impossible at the present time to have the law carried out. Justice is in your hands." [73]

Fall next asked Lee about the shootout at Wildy Well. Lee repeated the story he had told in his letters to the newspaper, that he was asleep on the roof when the firing started:

"Kearney fired twice and Garrett fired before I fired." [74]

Lee said his response, which led to Kearney's death, was self-defense.

When the session ended, the defense announced that they were releasing half of their witnesses as they were confident that Lee and Gililland's alibis were proved.

June 9, Friday

Testimony began with Lee under cross examination by Childers. Childers demanded to know who had told Lee that Garrett planned to kill him. Fall objected, saying to answer the question would put the source's life at risk. Judge Parker ruled that Lee must answer.[75]

Lee said it was Albert Ellis, a black barber at Las Cruces.

(In his letters to the newspaper, Lee had written, *"Pat Garrett... in the presence of several reliable people... said that if he ever got the opportunity, he would kill Gililland and Lee."*)

Childers then asked:

> *"Childers: 'Did you know Charles Rhodius and Mark Coffelt?'"*
> *"Lee: 'Yes'"*

> *"Childers: 'Did you have anything to do with killing them?'"* [76]

Fall strenuously objected. The jury was removed while the two sides argued.

Fall admitted that Lee had killed Rhodius. Lee had been indicted for the killing, but the indictments were later dropped; therefore, the killing was inadmissible. Childers argued that the indictments could be brought into evidence to impeach the moral character of a witness. After hearing both sides, Judge Parker ruled the evidence inadmissible.[77]

The only witnesses to the Rhodius/Coffelt incident were the winners. The story told by Lee, and eventually accepted by authorities, was that on February 12, 1893, Lee, McNew, and Thomas Tucker rode up on Rhodius and Coffelt driving a herd of cattle to El Paso. Lee told Rhodius that several of cows in the herd were his. An argument followed, at the end of which, Rhodius drew his pistol and fired at Lee. Lee fired back, killing Rhodius. McNew then shot Coffelt, who he said had *"pulled on him."* [78]

Saturday, June 10

The defense opened by calling their last witness, Archie Prentice "Print" Rhode (Print was the brother of Cox's wife, Winnie Rhode). His testimony was explosive. He said he had foiled a plot to murder Lee by bombing his house.

> *"On July 11, 1898, a day before the fight in which Kearney was killed at Lee's [Wildy Well], Llewellyn had supper at my house. In the presence of my wife, he said he would do anything to 'do' these men [the defendants]."* [79]

Rhode said Llewellyn then pointed to a wagon that contained dynamite and said:

> *"...when he heard Lee was at home, they would go there, invite the women out, and throw dynamite into the house."* [80]

> *"If they didn't come out he would throw the dynamite in [anyway] and blow 'em up."* [81]

Barnes, for the prosecution, began his cross of Rhode oddly:

> *"Barnes: 'Did Llewellyn seem to have his senses that day, the day he did all that talking?'"*
> *"Rhode: 'About as much senses as he ever had, I guess.'"*

"The witness caused much hilarity in the court room by his droll answers. The jury, counsel, and audience were kept laughing a large part of the time." [82]

When Rhode stepped off the stand:

"The spectators almost broke forth in cheers. The sympathy of the local community, particularly the ladies, is now with the defendants." [83]

The defense called Garrett to the stand. He was asked about his financial interest in the case. The prosecution objected to the questions, which were ruled inadmissible.

Barnes called Llewellyn as a rebuttal witness to Rhode's murder-plot statements. But to the great surprise of everyone present, Llewellyn was not in the courtroom, and *"no messenger was sent for him."*

Branigan and others were put on the stand by the prosecution to rebut Rhode's story. Their statements were that Llewellyn had neither told Rhode of a murder plot nor was there ever such a plot.[84]

When Barnes finished his rebuttal, Ferguson told the jury that the prosecution had neither established a *corpus delicti* (proof that there had even been a crime) nor had they cast even a shadow of doubt on the truth of the defendant's alibis.

The defense then rested, without putting Gililland on the stand.[85]

Sunday, June 11

Court opened with an argument between the attorneys over the proper charge to the jury. The prosecution wanted it to include murder in the first, second, and third degree, as well as acquittal. Defense wanted only first degree murder and acquittal. Judge Parker ruled in favor of the prosecution.

Barnes made the summation of the case for the prosecution.

"He laid great stress on the spot of blood, referring to it as the central point in the case." [86]

Barnes then went through the chain of events presented by the prosecution witnesses. Only one hypothesis explained them all:

"The defendants had murdered the child." [87]

Barnes's speech was "flowery" and contained many literary quotes that *"probably went over the heads of the jury."*

"The interpreter had a hard time to translate some of the fancy work.... In speaking of Mrs. Lee... he remarked that she but laid 'a wreath of maternal duty on the alter of maternal love.' This was too much for the interpreter, and counsel had to explain." [88]

Ferguson made the closing summation for the defense:

"He took up the witnesses for the prosecution one after the other and tried to discredit them. Mr. Ferguson's style is one that compels attention. He held the interest of the jury and of the audience very closely from the beginning to the end of his speech. He talked straight to the jury as to individuals, and once called Juror Chavez by name." [89]

Ferguson was especially hard on Maxwell. Could anyone doubt that he was offered $2,000 to give false evidence to convict Lee and Gililland?

> *"The prosecution had unlimited money, they had Mr. Garrett, they had a Pinkerton detective, they had all the machinery of the territory at work to convict these men; was it likely that they would have employed the man Maxwell as a 'detective?' Hardly."* [90]

He attacked the blood spot evidence, the cornerstone of the prosecution's case:

> *"To convict in this case you have got to be sure that that blood was the blood of the boy Fountain."* [91] *[The trial was for Henry's muder, not his father's.]*

Ferguson also attacked the track evidence, saying it was *"impossible to identify a man by his boot tracks in sand."* [92]

Ferguson then asserted that there was no evidence at all against Gililland. The prosecution had only presented *"three irresponsible men, two of them jailbirds,"* to repeat supposedly self-incriminating statements they assert were spoken by Gililland. And further, all three men were known enemies of Gililland.

As to the shooting of Kearney at Wildy Well, Ferguson said:

> *"Sheriff Garrett by his evidence that Kearney fired the first shot in that fight of July, 1898, lifts all burden from Lee for the killing of Kearney."* [93]

Lee and Gililland were not given an honest chance to surrender – they were fired upon while asleep.

Ferguson concluded by saying that no fair-minded man would convict Lee and Gililland of killing Henry Fountain.

That evening, Oliver Lee's wife and new baby arrived in Hillsboro:

> *"The scene of greeting in the little adobe jail was pathetic but brief. Lee forbid his wife and child from attending the court room...."* [94]

Monday, June 12

Childers opened the session with his rebuttal to the defense's summation. He began by reaffirming the strength of the blood evidence. It had every characteristic of human blood and no evidence was introduced that any animal of any kind was killed at the site.

> *"The murder of Col. Fountain at the time accounts for the blood being there; its presence cannot be accounted for on any other theory."* [95]

Childers turned next to the tracking evidence:

> *"Mr. Ferguson has told you that it would be impossible to measure or iden- tify horse or man tracks.... You well know that the trailing of horses and men is an everyday occurrence in this country and that to men familiar with the track- ing of individuals or parties by such means the work is easy and certain."* [96]

As regards the Maxwell contract, it was not unusual:

> *"It is all right to pay a man money as a detective to secure evidence in a case or to put in shape to use that which is in his possession. When the governor*

offers a reward for a fugitive, it is the same thing." [97]

He added it would be protecting criminals if money could not be used to secure evidence.

Childers attacked the alibi offered by the defendants' witnesses by pointing out their reasons to lie, and by reasserting the testimony of those who said Lee was not at the ranch the day of the killing.

Regarding Lee's supposed fear of assassination, he asked, if it was true:

"Why did not the defense call him [the barber, Ellis] to testify?" [98]

In concluding, he said:

"To hold that you cannot convict of murder because the body cannot be found is to condone murder.... It is so easy in this country to waylay a man and conceal his body where it cannot be found." [99]

Tuesday, June 13

Daugherty started the closing argument for the defense. In a very long address, he repeated the points made by Ferguson in his summation. He said the defense had sixty witnesses subpoenaed, but only called ten, because that was all they needed to prove Lee and Gililland's truthful alibis.[100]

After Daugherty concluded, Fall reluctantly took up the argument. He originally had not intended to give the closing address, but, at Lee's fervent plea, he agreed to do so.[101]

After reaffirming the defense's evidence, Fall turned to his main argument – the trial was not at all a criminal trial – it was political persecution disguised as a criminal prosecution:

"In many streams there is a point at a sharp bend in the course where the water pauses in its onward flow and forms an eddy. Around the edges the slime gathers, and the froth, and logs, and dead leaves, and all manner of floating filth. The moss and ferns grow dank, and the shadowy places are haunted with creeping things. Snakes come out in the sun on the slimy logs, and if they are disturbed in their retreat, they sting in the heel the man who is so foolish as to venture there. Dona Ana county is just such a dead eddy." [102]

Fall's concluding words were greeted with applause by the onlookers.

Catron began the closing argument for the prosecution. He addressed first Fall's political accusation.

"I do not know what your political belief is, gentlemen of the jury, and I care less. It was alleged... that political animus against the democrats is responsible for the bringing of these men before the bar of this court." [103]

Catron said this charge was absolutely untrue, that these men were in court only because of the facts. He then reviewed the evidence showing their guilt. He concluded:

"Consider your [decision] just as if some one sacred and dear to you had been destroyed as this man and this child were destroyed. I leave the case with you." [104]

Fountain Murder Trial – The Verdict

Catron finished his address to the court at 10:30 p.m., June 13. Judge Parker then read his charge to the jury. The charge was extensive, addressing 28 points. Judge Parker explained the applicable territorial law, the requirements for the three degrees of murder, the necessity to carefully scrutinize all of the evidence, and the meaning of *"guilt beyond a reasonable doubt."*

Judge Parker then dismissed the jury and closed the session. *It was 11:20 p.m.*

Fall waited until the jury men were in their sleeping quarters, then he hunted up Judge Parker and *demanded* his client's right to have the jury begin immediate deliberations. Judge Parker, bizarrely, agreed.

The jury was reassembled – and returned from deliberation in just eight minutes with a verdict:

"After they were in the court room, it was found that most of the attorneys were absent and the court took an informal recess until they could be sent for."

"At exactly one minute before midnight, Foreman Bentley handed the verdict to the clerk and it was read...."

"'We find the defendants, Oliver Lee and James Gililland, not guilty.'"

"Immediately the people in the court room rose in mass, cheered and clapped and stamped...." [105]

Lee and Gililland were acquitted of the murder of Henry Fountain. But they were not free. Judge Parker ordered them jailed without bond until their trial for the killing of Kearney.

Fountain Murder Trial – Aftermath

Immediately following the announcement of the verdict, Hillsboro authorities arrested John McCutcheon, the publisher of the *El Paso Graphic.* He was charged with contempt. He had taken the side of Lee for three years, and during the trial published a number of obviously made-up articles asserting that Colonel Fountain and his son were still alive. (The charges against McCutcheon were later dropped.) [106]

Prosecutor Childers was interviewed the morning after the trial. He complained about the numerous untrue reports sent out by newspapermen during the trial. For example, he said, all the reports of hostile bands of armed men marching in the streets of Hillsboro ready to fight each other were false. Also false:

"...was the statement that the women of Hillsboro presented the defendants with flowers." [107]

El Paso Herald City Editor Sneed sued the Associated Press for using – without his paid permission – the telephone line that he had converted to a telegraph line to send out press reports. He won the case, getting $65 dollars in damages. [108]

Based on press reports, no observer of the trial seems to have been surprised by the verdict. The *El Paso Herald* opined:

"No arguments of counsel could make the case of the prosecution, which seemed so inconclusive, any stronger." [109]

The *Santa Fe New Mexican* opined:

"...a sufficient explanation for the acquittal of the defendants is that the death of the boy they were accused of murdering could not be proved by the prosecution." [110]

Garrett, too, after hearing the closing arguments, knew the trial was not going to produce a conviction. Acquittal meant that he would not receive the large sum he had been promised for a conviction. It was a stinging personal failure. He was the person responsible for gathering the evidence necessary to obtain convictions. And he was the person who had made the decision to sign the $2,000 contract with Maxwell for his testimony, which turned out to be a legal millstone around the necks of the prosecutors.

Based on the trial details available today, the prosecution *did not* meet the standard of proof beyond a reasonable doubt. (The prosecution made a mistake in trying the defendants for Henry's murder rather than Colonel Fountain's, as the blood evidence did not prove *Henry* was dead.)

McNew, following the dismissal of his case, had stayed in Hillsboro to support Lee and Gililland. The next morning, just after returning to El Paso, McNew's five year old son Oliver McNew was in a horrific accident.

The McNew family was riding in a taxi hack (horse-drawn buggy) when young Oliver accidentally opened the vehicle's door just as the hack crossed in front of a trolley car:

"...the boy pitched out and a minute later his legs were ground and crushed by the iron wheels of the street car.... The child's agonizing screams could be heard two blocks away.... Seven men took hold of the [street car] and by sheer force lifted it up and removed the child." [111]

Oliver recovered, but was permanently disabled.

The trial of Lee and Gililland for the killing of Kearney was scheduled for September, 1899. Just before the trial, they:

"...received notice from Judge Parker that their case... [would] not be reached at this term of the court.... This action is taken on account of the great number of cases... on the docket." [112]

When the indictments against the two men expired, the case was dropped; as was the civil lawsuit for wrongful death filed by Mrs. Fountain.

No one was ever tried for the murder of Colonel Fountain.

What Happened to the Bodies?

That Colonel Fountain and Henry's bodies were never found reveals shrewd planning by the killers.

So what happened to the bodies? Over the years, most speculation has centered on three theories. One theory is that the bodies were burned up in the firebox powering the steam boiler at Wildy Well. The second theory is that the bodies were taken to Lee's ranch and disposed of there. A third theory is that the bodies were disposed of by burying them in the mountains.

Oddly enough, supporting all three of these theories are confessions attributed to a Gililland.

Wildy Well Firebox

Katherine D. Stoes, in a personal note, wrote:

"[Will] Isaacks told me that Gililland told him just before he died... that the men drew straws as to the cremation of the bodies in the furnace of the steam boiler of Wilde Well.... McNew drew the short straw." [113]

Katherine was the wife of Henry Stoes, a member of the Fountain search posse. A historian and author, Katherine spent years researching the Fountain disappearances.

The map shown on page 54, an exhibit in the Fountain trial, shows that the tracks of one horse were trailed to Wildy Well. The person on that horse, if what Will Isaacks said was true, would have been McNew. On arriving at Wildy Well, he would have put the bodies in the furnace of the steam engine.

Dog Canyon Ranch

A second theory is that the bodies were taken to Lee's Dog Canyon Ranch. Lee was an extremely cautious man, who had many acrimonious enemies. To ensure that he could never be trapped inside his ranch house, he dug an escape tunnel from the house to an outbuilding.

This tunnel is depicted in a rough drawing made by Henry Stoes (see page 8). The existence of the tunnel was confirmed by archeological evidence in 1985. [114]

In this theory, the bodies were temporarily hidden in Lee's tunnel and disposed of later. The main evidence for this theory comes from Gililland's sister, Lucy Gililland, who had good reason to inform on or to slander her brother.

Lucy was married to Robert H. Raley when McNew shot Raley in front of the Colthrop Hotel in Orogrande on September 23, 1915.

McNew was charged with first degree murder of Raley. McNew's murder trial began on April 13, 1916. Lucy testified that on the day of the killing she and her husband received a note from attorney J. L. Lawson asking them to telephone him. They rode to the hotel by buggy to make the call (they had no home phone). Both got out at the hotel, with Raley carrying a shotgun:

"As Raley was about to enter the [hotel] gate, a shot was fired and she [Lucy] saw her husband totter.... As she bent over him, a second shot was fired...."

"After the second shot was fired, [she] said she heard McNew call out to her: 'Get away from here, Lucy, or I'll hurt you too.'" [115]

The first bullet killed Raley instantly. After the body was collected by the coroner, Lucy said that her brother, James Gililland, somehow obtained Raley's clothes:

"The clothing was burned by her brother [that same night]. The note was in the pocket of Raley's shirt... when the clothing was burned." [116]

Testimony by both sides established that Raley and McNew were fierce enemies who had threatened each other numerous times. Several witnesses for Raley testified that McNew had offered them $500 to $1,000 to kill Raley.

Lawyer Lawson testified that he did not write Raley a note, so the prosecution argued the note was a *"decoy note"* intended to draw Raley to the hotel to be killed.

McNew did not testify. Testimony by a witness called by his lawyer established that McNew had shot Raley as alleged (confession by proxy), and that he had indeed shouted the warning to his sister Lucy.

In his instructions to the jury, presiding Judge Colin Neblett said if the circumstances of the shooting were:

"...such as to cause an ordinarily prudent man to believe that there was imminent danger to his life or imminent danger of great bodily harm... such circumstances furnishes as complete a defense for the defendant as if the danger actually existed."

"...it is not essential to the right of self defense that the danger should in fact exist...." [117]

The jury acquitted McNew on the ground of self-defense.

The burning of the Raley's clothes made Lucy and her brother unforgiving enemies who never spoke to each other again. On October 27, 1915, she wrote a letter to Albert Fountain, Jr., in which she said:

"I write this in great fear. One of the men who killed your father and little brother has just killed my husband. If I had done my duty on the stand (although it would have ruined my brother) it is possible my husband would still be alive. There is great danger here as long as the three [Lee, Gililland, and McNew] live." [118]

Lucy was said to have told friends privately that she was working at Lee's ranch at the time of Fountain's disappearance. One morning when she went to feed Lee's pigs, she found them:

"...rooting up from a shallow grave near the fence the remains of Henry Fountain; as the swine tore into the boy, she went into shock." [119]

A gruesome end, if true.

Expedition to locate Fountain bodies. The markers are visible in the center of the photo. Left to right: Arthur J. Fountain III (grandson of Colonel Fountain), Albert J. Fountain IV, Henry Fountain, Carlos Madrid, Frank Burris, Jim Flanagan, Stuart B. Tracy, Robert H. Armbrust, Jack Weisenhunt, and Mirdon M. McGee. December 25, 1950. Courtesy Karl Laumbach and Albert J. Fountain IV.

Mountain Burial

In early 1950, Albert J. Fountain III was summoned to a lawyer's office. There, Albert was introduced to Jack Spence, who presented him with a small, silver lapel pin.[120] The pin was probably made especially for Colonel Fountain. It was triangular in shape, with a Mason's square and compass positioned above three chain links representing the Independent Organization of Odd Fellows (IOOF). Using family photos, Albert was able to identify the pin as one that Colonel Fountain always wore. And further, the family was certain that Colonel Fountain was wearing the pin when he left home on his fateful trip to Lincoln.[121]

Spence told Albert the following story:

"...about five years [earlier] a dying man in Truth or Consequences confessed to a friend... that he had been one of three cattle rustlers who had ambushed Fountain and his son and killed the older man first and then later the boy."

"According to the dying man, the boy and the buggy were taken with the body of the dead man on a circuitous route to the Oscura Mountains where, after considerable debate among the three men, the youngster was also killed and the two bodies buried." [122]

The friend of the dying man later abandoned his anonymity and publicly identified himself as Butler "Snooks" Burris. He also identified the dying man as James Gililland.[123]

Burris claimed that besides confessing to the murders, Gililland told him where Colonel Fountain and Henry's bodies were buried. The almost inaccessible location was in a *"steep, long canyon, with rugged rock walls"* in the Oscura Mountains. It was marked by a *"man-made pillar of stone."* [124]

On November 25, 1950, an expedition of 12 men travelled to the purported location of the burials. There they found:

"...a high headstone, about 2 1/2 feet tall. Two smaller rocks [stood] about midway between the headstone and an almost square "footstone" such as was commonly used in old western burials."

"The canyon in which the markers were discovered matched exactly with a description of the site given by the informant [Burris]." [125]

"But when the grave was opened... it appeared that it had never been opened before. The immediate ground under the markers was excavated and clearly showed strata lines that would indicate no other shovels had ever touched the spot." [126]

The reaction of the men of the expedition varied. Some felt they were in the wrong location; others that the bodies were never buried at that spot.

Of these three theories, the first seems the more credible. It was known apparently by the posses that Lee had a tunnel leading from his house to an outbuilding, as Stoes' map indicates. That knowledge would have made hiding the bodies at the Lee's ranch risky. The fact that no tracks were found by the posses leading into the mountains casts serious doubt on the mountain burial theory.

Garrett with daughter Pauline. Circa 1901. Never before published photo.
Courtesy IHSF.org.

Pauline Juliet Garrett Born

On September 11, 1899, the Garretts' sixth child was born in Las Cruces: Pauline Juliet Garrett.[127]

Killing Norman Newman

On July 23, 1899, the governor of Oklahoma offered a $500 reward for the arrest and conviction of Norman Newman, charged with brutally killing John White, his ranching partner. Newman had just escaped from jail in Greer County, Oklahoma.[128]

Oklahoma Sheriff George Baylock trailed Newman *"across the Panhandle of Texas and all over southern New Mexico."* He finally located him working as a cook at Cox's San Augustine Ranch (Newman may have been a distant relative of Cox). Sheriff Baylock went to Las Cruces and swore out an arrest warrant. Garrett, Deputy Jose Espalin, and Sheriff Baylock then rode to Cox's ranch and entered the ranch house without announcing themselves. They found Newman washing dishes in the kitchen.

When Garrett attempted to arrest him, Newman fought:

> *"...all over the kitchen and out through a French window onto the porch. After being knocked down several times and losing the greater portion of his clothing, which by the way, was the clothing of the man he had murdered, he finally escaped back into the house...."* [129]

There Newman was shot twice by Deputy Espalin, killing him instantly.

W. W. Cox was extremely upset that Newman had been shot inside his house. He had family in the house and his wife was pregnant.[130] A number of authors have expressed doubt that the man shot was actually Newman. However, when the body was returned to Oklahoma:

> *"...all who had known the murderer in life recognized him at once. He even had on the boots and pants he wore [when he escaped].... About noon, Newman's sister... came in and identified the body."* [131]

Robbery at Rincon

On October 15, 1899, robbers broke into the Rincon post office, stealing stamps and coins. They also gained access to the nearby saloon, where they took jewelry and *"three dozen quart bottles of liquor."* Garrett and Deputy Williams left for Rincon to locate and arrest the robbers. It was believed that:

> *"three men in the guise of miners who had been prowling about town the greater part of the day [were] responsible for the robbery."* [132]

The men succeeded in getting to Mexico before they were caught.

Bowman Bank Robbery

Garrett began the second year (1900) of his second sheriff term dealing with another robbery. 1899 and 1900 were banner years for those in the robbery business in the American West.

On February 12, 1900, Garrett cashed a $50 check at the Bowman Bank of Las Cruces. He was the fifth person to do business in the bank that morning.[133]

Downtown Las Cruces, circa 1905.

Interior Bowman Bank. Woman may be Miss Otto. Photo circa 1900. Courtesy
Gordon Steele.

At 2:00 pm that afternoon:

> *"...two strangers rode into town quite hurriedly....They appeared to be cowboys about 30 years old, had on white hats pulled down over their eyes, boots and spurs, one mounted upon a light buckskin and the other on a dark roan horse."* [134]

This was their second trip to Las Cruces. The first was four days earlier. As they were approaching downtown that time, one of them *"had his horse taken away from him by someone who claimed it."* They surrendered the horse and, riding double, returned to their camp in the Organ Mountains, east of town.[135]

This time, however, events went as planned. They tied their horses at the hitching post and walked into the Bowman Bank:

> *"Mr. J. G. Freeman, the assistant cashier, and Miss Otto, the stenographer, were the only persons inside."*

> *"One of the robbers asked Mr. Freeman if he could cash a check, at the same time drawing two six shooters. Mr. Freeman, thinking it was a joke, was slow to throw up his hands... but the click click of a gun made him realize the situation."* [136]

The second man emptied the cash drawer, overlooking *"a lot of silver dollars."* He then forced Mr. Freeman to open the safe, *"where most of the money was kept."* He pocketed the money he found. He opened a package belonging to a depositor that contained gold jewelry, *"but underestimated the value and threw them down."* He missed several pieces of diamond jewelry wrapped in paper.[137]

> *"He then asked for a package that came by express and was delivered to the bank this forenoon which Mr. Freeman produced and which was taken intact."*

> *"This package is supposed to have been money sent to pay off the employees of the Modoc and Torpedo mines. How the robbers knew this package had come is a mystery unless they were watching and saw it delivered to the bank by the agent of the Wells Fargo Co. Express."* [138]

Holding their guns on Freeman and Otto, the gunmen backed out the door, mounted their horses, and *"quietly rode by the way they entered town."*

Alerted by Freeman:

> *"Mr. Solignac grabbed his six shooter and got to the corner in time to get two shots at a range of two or three hundred yards, which only made them [the robbers] hasten their speed until they turned out of sight."* [139]

Garrett immediately deputized two posses to pursue them. He led one posse in the direction indicated by witnesses. Deputy Williams led the second posse south, on the assumption that the robbers might head for Mexico.

Garrett returned that night after a fruitless search. Based on new witness information, early the next morning, Garrett took his posse toward Bear Canyon, northeast of town. They quickly picked up the robbers' horse tracks. In the foothills, they located *"a saddle, coat, and hat, and a short distance farther, a worn out horse."* Garrett deputized William

Cravens and asked him to take the horse to Las Cruces. From where the abandoned horse was found, tracks of a single horse led to a camp, where one man was arrested. Tracks from that camp led to the town of Organ, where two brothers were arrested.[140]

Meanwhile, Williams had arrested three El Paso *"boys,"* who, after a day in jail, proved their innocence and were released.[141]

The next morning Williams went after the abandoned horse, which had not been brought to Las Cruces. Williams found it and took it to Garrett's Home Ranch, where it was identified as one of the robbers' horses. At Garrett's ranch, Williams met Cravens. When asked why he had not returned the horse to town as ordered, Craven's evasive answers seemed suspicious, so Williams arrested him.[142]

Before leaving Las Cruces, Williams had examined the saddle and recognized it as one he had personally seen sold to Print Rhode a few years previously. He rode to Rhode's ranch and asked him about the saddle. Rhode said he had sold it to a man named Wilson. Williams asked Rhode if he would recognize the saddle if he saw it again. Rhode said no. Williams arrested Rhode on suspicion of being an accessory to the robbery.[143]

There the investigation stalled. Cashier Freeman, on seeing the three men Garrett had jailed, swore they were not the robbers. They were released.[144]

Then, Garrett got a break. On March 17, Sheriff James Blair arrested James Brooks in Cochise, Arizona. Brooks had stolen a horse and saddle in Hanover, New Mexico, and Sheriff Blair had tracked him to Cochise. On the return trip to New Mexico:

> *"Brooks grew confidential and said that Wilson, accompanied by one J. Wilbur, had come to Arizona to persuade him to assist them in holding up and robbing Bowman's bank in Las Cruces. Brooks refused...."* [145]

Sheriff Blair reported this confession to Garrett, including the information that Wilbur owned a house in San Antonio, Texas.

Deputy Williams took the train to San Antonio and obtained arrest warrants for Oscar J. Wilbur and William Wilson. On March 19, Williams and San Antonio Deputy Will Green warily approached Wilbur's house. Their idea was to surveil it to discover how Wilbur's arrest could be accomplished safely. They observed two men leave the house:

> *"Deputy Williams thought that he recognized Wilber and Wilson, but he was not sure on this point, so the officers passed the two men, then turned back and overtook them."* [146]

Williams called to Wilson, saying he was under arrest:

> *"The two officers and the two men reached for their pistols instantly. Wilson did not get his gun all of the way out of his scabbard before Williams covered him with his pistol. Deputy Sheriff Green was not quite so quick. Wilbur got his gun out of his scabbard first, but Green drew a bead on his man first, and then Wilson and Wilber both surrendered their weapons and were taken to the county jail."* [147]

When Wilbur's house was searched, they found two Winchester rifles, two Colt's pistols, and:

> *"...a large quantity of deadly 44-calibre dum dum bullets. There were also two long, newly made money sacks, stitched with brass rivets."* [148]

After initially denying it, Wilbur confessed to the crime while being transported to Las Cruces. He said the man with him in the bank was Wilson, and that Cravens and Print Rhode had aided them before and after the robbery.[149]

On April 11, Wilbur and Wilson had their preliminary hearing. Both pleaded not guilty and were ordered held for trial.[150]

Their trial began April 20. The lawyers for the defense were Albert Fall and John Franklin. The prosecuting attorneys were Major W. H. H. Llewellyn, S. B. Newcomb, and Herbert B. Holt.

> *"The two principals, Oscar J. Wilbur and William Wilson, both pleaded guilty. The sentence was held for consideration by the judge."*

> *"The case of Print Rhode and William Cravens was called as accessories.... Both pleaded not guilty...."* [151]

The first witness for the prosecution was Cashier Freeman, who described the robbery. Then Wilbur was called to the stand. Wilbur testified that he, Wilson, and Brooks had planned the robbery, but Brooks backed out after a disagreement. He said that he and Wilson met with Rhode and Cravens, who agreed to help them:

> *"Wm. Cravens came to their camp with Rhode and brought horses. Cravens agreed to come on with them and stay outside of town and throw any one off the trail if they were pursued."* [152]

The first attempt to rob the bank was foiled when a man in Las Cruces recognized his horse and made Wilson surrender it to him.

Four days later Rhode and Craven brought them the horses they robbed the bank with:

> *"In making their escape one of their horses gave out about four miles from the mountains. They then rode the one left until he also gave out."*

> *"The second day after the robbery Rhode came to their camp early in the morning and later in the day Craven also joined them, when they divided the money, giving Rhode and Cravens $100 each.... the whole amount was $1,136."* [153]

Fall began his cross examination of Wilbur by moving that his testimony be stricken. The court declined:

> *"...Fall then put him [Wilbur] under a fire of questions in which he admitted that he had turned state's evidence in the hopes of shortening his term in the penitentiary...."* [154]

The next witness testified that he had seen the two robbers go into the bank, but had not seen their faces. Juan Carbonier testified to seeing Wilson riding his (Carbonier's) horse on February 8, and making him surrender it.

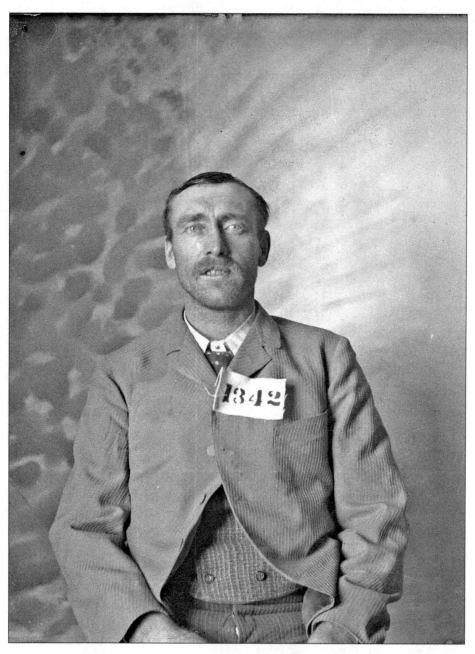

William Wilson, sentenced to 10 years in the state penitentiary for his part in the Bowman Bank robbery, February 12, 1900. 1900 photo. Courtesy 1970-006 New Mexico Department of Corrections Records, State Archives of New Mexico.

Oscar J. Wilbur, sentenced to 5 years in the state penitentiary for his part in the Bowman Bank robbery, February 12, 1900. Pardoned after six months. 1900 photo. Courtesy 1970-006 New Mexico Department of Corrections Records, State Archives of New Mexico.

Garrett testified about finding the saddle and horse, and deputizing Cravens and asking him to take the horse to Las Cruces.

Williams testified to arresting Cravens and Rhode. He testified to recognizing the saddle as Rhode's, which was introduced as an exhibit. He testified to arresting Wilbur and Wilson in San Antonio.

Wilson was called and testified to committing the bank robbery, but denied that Rhode and Cravens were involved in any way.[155]

When the prosecution rested, Fall called Cravens to the stand. He denied any involvement, declaring:

> *"He did not take any horses to Wilber and Wilson, nor have any talk with them about robbing the bank."* [156]

Print Rhode was called. He said he had known Wilson for eight years, and, maybe, had sold the saddle to him years earlier. He admitted that Wilbur and Wilson had stayed at his ranch house the day before the robbery. He said that at their request he had loaned them an alarm clock, because they wanted to get up early. They left at daybreak and were not riding horses.

Following the closing arguments, the jury deliberated for 30 minutes, then found Rhode and Cravens not guilty.

The court sentenced Wilson to ten years in the penitentiary, and Wilbur to five – in recognition of his cooperation with the prosecution.[157] After serving six months, Governor Otero granted Wilbur a pardon.[158]

National Aspirations

The day after the successful prosecution of Wilbur and Wilson, Garrett announced he would not pursue a third term as sheriff, but would instead run for the Territorial Council as a Republican.[159]

Garrett quickly decided on a higher goal – the office of Delegate of the Territory of New Mexico to the United States House of Representatives. His candidacy was widely welcomed by the public. One newspaper opined, in an opinion Garrett probably did not appreciate:

> *"If elected Pat would probably be known in Washington as the tall killer of the Rio Grande."* [160]

1900 was a good year to run for office as a Republican. The President of the United States was a Republican – William McKinley – and Republicans were ascendant in New Mexico.

The Dona Ana County Republican Convention met September 24 and nominated Garrett as their candidate for the U.S. House of Representatives. They elected Garrett and five others as delegates to the Territorial Republican Convention. The main issue for the Dona Ana County Republicans was the construction of the Elephant Butte Dam.[161]

Garrett jumped into campaigning. Two days after his selection he spoke at the Albuquerque State Fair:

"[Garrett] was the hero of the day.... lots of people went home satisfied because they had seen the tall giant who killed 'Billy the Kid.' He is dead earnest for the delegate nomination...." [162]

The Territorial Republican Convention opened October 3 in Santa Fe. As is often the case in politics, the convention was tightly controlled by an "old guard." When the time came to put forward the nominations for delegate to the U. S. House, Bernard S. Rodey of Bernalillo County gave a passionate, flowery speech in which he nominated Solomon Luna of Valencia County. Every mention of the name of Luna was *"greeted with thunderous applause."* He ended by affirming that:

"Mr. Luna is a man whom the office sought, rather than the man the office." [163]

J. Francisco Chavez, of Valencia County, then arose and said that he was speaking for Luna, and Luna *"did not want the nomination for personal and private reasons best known to himself."* Luna then spoke and said that he appreciated the nomination, but he could not accept it, and he withdrew his name.

The convention adjourned until the following day. Although the convention did some business the next morning, it did not return to the nominations for House delegate. In the afternoon the leaders of the convention caucused. When they returned to the convention, they announced that they had selected Bernard S. Rodey as their candidate for House delegate. Thomas B. Catron then moved that Rodey's nomination be ratified by acclimation, which was done.[164]

These events – orchestrated by party bosses – must have reminded Garrett of his run for the New Mexico Territorial Council in 1882. His term as sheriff of Lincoln County had just ended – during which he had captured and killed Billy the Kid, after the Kid had escaped from jail by killing two guards. Garrett was the most famous lawman in New Mexico, probably in the American West, and acclaimed as a man of *"remarkable nerve and cool courage."* [165]

When he announced his candidacy as a Democrat for the Council (in 1882), he expected to be supported by the leaders of the party, who had strongly supported his election as sheriff previously. But the *"old regulars"* chose to support one of their own for the office, David M. Easton.

Undeterred, Garrett announced he would run as an independent. The Democratic leaders responded by mercilessly attacking Garrett as *"ungrateful:"*

"One year ago last July, D. M. Easton and J. J. Dolan circulated in Santa Fe a subscription paper for Garrett's benefit, raising $1,150 and paying the same to him in person. [His] opposition to Mr. Easton... is easily explained. Mr. Garrett, as is well known, is an illiterate man; the newspaper notoriety he received from his success in killing the 'Kid' has upset his brain...." [166]

Garrett responded to this attack, which was signed "X," with a public letter. He admitted that Easton and others had supported him for sheriff, but that did not mean that he had *"sold"* himself to them. He denied being ungrateful. He denied flattery had disturbed his brain. As to being illiterate, he wrote:

"X claims that it is well known that I am very illiterate. If this be true, I claim that it is more my misfortune than my fault, and I must say that it does not look very generous in X to blame me for faults over which I have no control." [167]

The *Rio Grande Republican* published Garrett's letter, but added the following mocking comment:

"[Garrett's] very letter is sufficient proof of both of X's charges. We have thrown the mantle of editorial charity around his errors in spelling and punctuation; but the wording is just as he wrote it." [168]

On September 19, 1882, Garrett met W. M. Roberts in LaRue's store in Lincoln. Garrett accused Roberts of being "X" and writing the letter signed by that letter. Robert denied it. Following an exchange of angry words, Garrett:

"...drew a long 45 caliber revolver and without a word beat Roberts over the head with it several times, inflicting some deep gashes, and knocking him quite insensible." [169]

Garrett replied in the *Mesilla News* that he only *"took [Roberts] by the collar, shook and struck him."* He denied pistol-whipping and knocking Roberts down.[170]

The election was held November 3, 1882. Garrett placed third, 307 votes behind the Republican winner, Harvey H. Whitehill of Silver City, but 70 votes ahead of the fourth place finisher, Easton.[171] The *Silver City Enterprise* greeted Garrett's loss with:

"The defeat of Pat Garrett is one of the gratifications that roll upon us like sea waves upon the bathers of the beach." [172]

With the 1900 House Delegate election, Garrett took his nomination defeat like a loyal soldier. He campaigned across the territory for the Republican candidates. In Carlsbad, campaigning with Rodey on the eve of the vote, the local newspaper noted:

"Pat Garrett... spoke next and was better received than the former speaker [Rodey], because Mr. Garrett said to begin with that they couldn't expect him to say much – and he didn't." [173]

Rodey won the seat against the Democratic candidate Octaviano A. Larrazolo by a large majority.[174]

Garrett "Killed"

On August 20, 1900, Garrett took out a personal life insurance policy for $1,000 from the Sovereign Camp of the Woodmen of the World. The beneficiary of the policy was Garrett's wife, Apolinaria. The Sovereign Camp of the Woodmen of the World was a fraternal organization founded in 1883, much like the International Organization of Odd Fellows (IOOF) or the Benevolent and Protective Order of Elks (BPOE).[175]

What motivated this decision by Garrett? Of course, Garrett knew how dangerous a job he held, but it was nearly over, his term expiring December 31. If he had been prescient, however, he might have known that in a mere 19 days he would be reported as having been killed by a man named Claude Barbee.

On August 21, Claude Barbee killed Deputy Kinney Hamilton. Deputy Hamilton was chasing Barbee for having stolen a horse at a revival meeting at Angus, New Mexico. Hamilton found Barbee at Eugene Manlove Rhodes' ranch in northern Dona Ana County. When asked to surrender, Barbee drew a pistol and fired:

> "Barbee's bullet entered the stomach of Hamilton, who pitched forward with a cry for mercy on his lips...." [176]

Barbee then fired three more shots into Hamilton's body. The Tularosa coroner refused to make the trip to Rhodes' ranch to examine the body, so Hamilton was buried next to the corral where he was killed. Two years later his body was washed away by a heavy rain. [177]

Garrett dispatched two deputies to find and arrest Barbee. Through some sort of confusion, it was reported in the *El Paso Herald* the next day that Barbee had killed Garrett and Deputy Williams. [178]

Barbee was not caught until almost four years later when he was recognized living in Bisbee, Arizona. He was arrested and brought to New Mexico. While awaiting trial for murder, he escaped, and was never found again. [179]

Juan Telles Killed

On December 23, 1900, Garrett faced his last serious crime. In what was probably a personal tragedy, his deputy Carlos Telles killed Juan Telles (no relation).

> "The shooting occurred in front of a [Las Cruces] saloon at about 2 a.m. Several parties heard the shooting and when they ran to the door they saw a man running down the street. One of the men ran after him and caught Carlos Telles a block or two past the cemetery." [180]

Carlos had no gun when caught, but a search of the area located a pistol in the cemetery with two fired shells.

The cause of the dispute was Juan's seduction of Carlos' daughter. Both men had threatened each other previously.

Carlos was charged with murder. At his trial, six months later, Carlos was defended by Albert Fall. Fall argued that Carlos had shot Juan in self defense. The jury returned a verdict of guilty of second degree murder and sentenced Carlos to 35 years in the penitentiary. [181] Carlos was pardoned on the basis of good behavior by Governor Otero on May 26, 1903. [182]

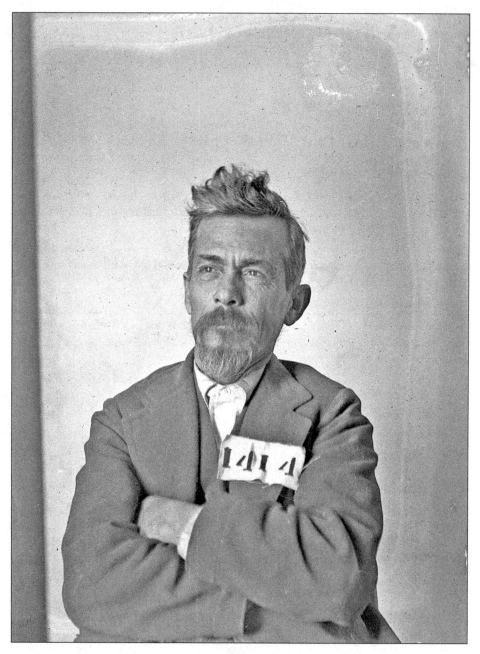

Carlos Telles, sentenced to 35 years in the state penitentiary for killing Juan Telles. Carlos was one of Garrett's deputies at the time. Carlos was pardoned after serving two years. 1901 photo. Courtesy 1970-006 New Mexico Department of Corrections Records, State Archives of New Mexico.

Chapter 4 | Return to Private Life – 1901

Garrett greeted 1901 with optimism. While it was true that his nomination as House candidate had been defeated without a floor vote, he had proved himself a hard-working and reliable Republican. As two-term sheriff of Dona Ana County, he had served impartially and honestly – and had not enriched himself like most prior sheriffs.

He expected – with good reason – future opportunities in the public sphere, and the political support of the New Mexico Republican Party.

Financial Troubles Renewed

As soon as he was a private citizen, the Albuquerque Bank of Commerce renewed its efforts to make Garrett repay the loan he had co-signed with George Curry in 1890. The bank apparently delayed enforcement action until Garrett was no longer sheriff, because as county sheriff he would be responsible for enforcing any court-ordered legal judgment in the county – which he probably would not do against himself.

The Bank of Commerce engaged Henry D. Bowman, owner of the Bowman Bank, as its agent to collect this loan. Bowman inquired if the Bank of Commerce would settle for less than the amount due. Bank of Commerce Vice President and Cashier W. S. Strickler replied:

> *"I wired you in reply this morning that the judgment now amounted to something over thirteen hundred dollars and that our attorneys advised against taking any less than the full amount of our claim, as they now state they will have no difficulty in collecting it."*

> *"We have been disposed to be quite liberal with Mr. Garrett in this matter but he has apparently given so little attention to it, that we feel now that we should go ahead and have every dollar that is due us."* [1]

When Bowman informed the Bank of Commerce that he had been unable to collect even one dollar from Garrett, the bank replied:

> *"In this connection can you not tell me privately as to what Garrett has? Would it be worth while for us to run any more garnishments down that way?"* [2]

After several more letters to Bowman, including a request to discover whether Garrett was seeking a loan from another bank, the Bank of Commerce dropped it efforts against Garrett for repayment – for the moment. [3]

Meeting President McKinley

On May 5, 1901, a committee of *"the most influential citizens of the territory, led by 'Hon. Pat Garrett,'"* met with President William McKinley in El Paso. [4]

President McKinley was on a 10,000-mile, *"western tour"* of the United States to celebrate his re-election. It had begun in Washington D. C. on April 29 and would end in San Francisco. He was travelling in a sumptuous, nine-car presidential train. *"No better train ever started,"* noted one newspaper. The president's car, "the Olympia," was 70 feet long with five private rooms, sitting room, dining and observation room, and presidential bedroom.[5]

President McKinley met Garrett and his committee members in the Olympia:

"After the introduction the committee explained to the president that they were very desirous of getting New Mexico into the union of states.... They had prepared data of every nature on the territory, mentioning at length the increase of population, the cattle and agricultural resources, mining and railroads...." [6]

President McKinley listened respectfully, but *"made no promises"* on supporting New Mexico statehood.

The committee then turned to a distressing political grievance: the *"removal"* of Governor Otero.[7]

Prior to the appointment of Otero as governor, Thomas B. Catron was the undisputed boss of the Republican Party in New Mexico. Otero, although a Republican, clashed with Catron almost from his first day in office.[8]

In the previous year's territorial convention in which Rodey was elected U. S. House candidate, Otero had supported Rodey, and Catron had opposed him. (Although there is no record of a public statement to the effect, Catron probably supported Garrett.) [9]

Otero's term as governor would end June 7, 1901. He was campaigning for reappointment.

By bringing up the issue of Otero's removal – meaning no reappointment – with President McKinley, Garrett was aligning himself with Catron, who was orchestrating a territory-wide campaign to block Otero's reappointment.[10]

McKinley's response was that:

"[He] could not consider such a matter while on his trip." [11]

Six weeks later, June 15, 1901, Otero was reappointed Governor of New Mexico.

Mining Interests

From his first term as sheriff, Garrett had pursued various mining interests, none of which had produced significant wealth. On June 3, Garrett joined with Henry D. Bowman of Bowman's Bank and numerous other investors to create the Franklin Mining Company of El Paso and Las Cruces.

"The company owns five valuable claims on the great Organ lode near Las Cruces.... For various reasons these claims have been lying idle...." [12]

There is no evidence that Garrett made anything from this investment.

President McKinley Assassinated

September 6, 1901 – President McKinley stepped into the Temple of Music, at the Pan-American Exposition, in Buffalo, New York. He had spent most of the morning touring Niagara Falls with a group of supporters. Waiting for him was:

"...a vast crowd [that] had assembled long before the arrival of Mr. McKinley." [13]

A man stood near the edge of the crowd, next to a young girl. He held his hat in his left hand. His right hand was wrapped in a white handkerchief.[14]

As President McKinley approached, shaking hands with the members of the crowd, the man stepped toward him:

"[The man] reached out the apparently bandaged hand to meet the extended hand of the President.... Then came the awful truth. [The man] did not accept the proffered hand of the President, but quickly pressed his own right hand near the President's clothing and the click of a revolver was heard twice." [15]

"The first bullet entered too high for the purpose of the assassin.... On receiving the first shot President McKinley had lifted himself on his toes with something of a gasp. His movement caused the second shot to enter the abdomen." [16]

The shooter was Leon Frank Czolgosz, a 29-year old, self-avowed anarchist.

As Czolgosz attempted to fire a third shot, James Parker knocked the gun from his hand. Parker, an African American, also had been waiting to shake the President's hand.

Immediately, a group of men jumped Czolgosz. President McKinley seeing Czolgosz being roughed up, said:

"Let no one hurt him." [17]

At first, President McKinley did not realize he had been hurt. He was helped to a chair:

"...where he removed his hat and bowed his head in his hands.... His waistcoat was hurriedly opened, the President meanwhile admonishing those about him to remain calm....

"'But you are wounded,' cried his secretary; 'let me examine.'"

"'No, I think not,' answered the President. 'I am not badly hurt.'" [18]

President McKinley was rushed to the nearby Exposition Hospital:

"Six doctors were at the President's side within thirty seconds after his arrival.... The first news that came from the operating room was that one bullet had been extracted, that this wound was superficial and by no means serious." [19]

The second bullet had gone completely through the stomach.

"The hole made by the entrance of the bullet was small and clean cut, while that on the other side of the stomach was large and ragged."

"As a consequence of the perforation the stomach fluid had circulated about the abdominal cavity."

"A five-inch incision was made and through that aperture the physicians were enabled to turn the organ about so as to suture the large bullet hole.... The anesthetic used in the operation was ether." [20]

The intestines were gently pulled though the incision and examined, with no sign of damage found. The second bullet could not be located. On learning of this fact, Thomas

Edison put together *"the most improved X-ray apparatus which could be constructed,"* and rushed it to Buffalo.[21]

While the president was being operated on, Czolgosz was taken to the main police station where he confessed, expressing sullen satisfaction with his action. He said he had been inspired by "Red" Emma Goldman's anarchist lectures and writings, but had acted alone.[22] Emma Goldman was arrested and accused of being a co-conspirator with Czolgosz. She was freed when no proof of her involvement was found. She refused to condemn Czolgosz for his action.[23]

Eight days after he was shot, on September 14, at 2:15 a. m, President McKinley died of infection from his abdominal wound.

Twelve hours later, Vice-President Theodore "Teddy" Roosevelt, Jr. was sworn in as the twenty-sixth President of the United States.

Justice was swift for Czolgosz. His trial began 9 days after President McKinley's death. The trial was held before the New York Supreme Court. The presiding judge was N. Y. Supreme Court Judge Truman C. White. Czolgosz's appointed defense attorneys were Loran L. Lewis and Robert C. Titus, both ex-justices of the N. Y. Supreme Court. The prosecuting attorneys were Thomas Penney and Frederick Hallar.

When the trial opened, Czolgosz was asked if he had heard and understood the charge:

> *"'I plead guilty,' said the prisoner, in a low voice...."*
>
> *'"Of course that can't be entered,' said the District Attorney."*
>
> *"A plea of innocent was entered by Czolgosz's attorneys."* [24]

The law for first degree murder in New York did not permit a defendant to enter a plea of guilty. Czolgosz did not testify in his own defense.

On September 25, Czolgosz was convicted of first degree murder. Before sentencing, Czolgosz was asked if he wished to make a statement. He said that no one had helped him and no one knew of his plan in advance. He concluded:

> *"I did it all myself."* [25]

Czolgosz was sentenced to die in the electric chair.

Czolgosz was executed October 29, 1901. His body was placed in a black coffin. After the coffin was lowered into a grave at the Auburn Prison cemetery, sulfuric acid was poured over the body to force rapid decomposition. A guard was placed over the grave for 12 hours to prevent vandalism or relic hunting. (His brain was saved for future study.) [26]

Unexpected Opportunity

On August 5, 1901, Garrett was interviewed by the *El Paso Herald* about his political aspirations. He replied that he was *"practically out of politics."* [27]

On September 23, Albert Fall wrote Garrett and offered him a job as receiver for a ranching operation for which Fall was handling the tax auction. Garrett's job would be to manage the orderly sale of the ranch's livestock. Fall wrote:

"Get in here tonight as I am in a big rush – I want to fix up papers. You will not have to live at the ranch, as you can employ Lee Moore who is there at $30 per month and you will be allowed at least $76 per month...." [28]

Garrett took the job. One week later he obtained the necessary receiver's bond from the United States Fidelity and Guaranty Company of Baltimore, Maryland, for $5,000.[29] (Garrett held this appointment until October 7, 1902, when the case was finally settled.) [30]

On November 9, another unexpected opportunity fell into Garrett's lap. Moses Dillon, the collector of customs at El Paso was removed from the office by President Roosevelt. Dillon was charged with numerous violations of the civil service law. [31]

Garrett excitedly seized on the idea of getting the collector position.

"A remarkable looking man attracted the attention of people in the lobby of the Shoreham last evening. Standing six feet five inches high, straight and slender of build – with not an ounce of superfluous flesh on a frame which nature molded for strength and endurance...." [32]

That man, of course, was Garrett. He and Albert Fall had traveled to Washington D.C. to lobby for the collector job for Garrett. This was the second time that Fall had gone to extraordinary lengths to obtain a highly desirable position for Garrett. The first time was in 1896 when Garrett was appointed Don Ana County sheriff to replace Numa Reymond. This time the effort was particularly surprising, considering that Fall had harshly examined Garrett during the Fountain trial, and Fall was the person most responsible for Lee and Gililland's acquittal. Nevertheless, Garrett and Fall were still close friends.

On December 12, Garrett and Fall met with President Roosevelt at the White House concerning the collector job. Earlier that morning Governor Otero, Delegate Rodey, and General Lew Wallace had visited with President Roosevelt about appointing Garrett to the position. General Wallace was the governor of New Mexico when Garrett was hunting Billy the Kid, and had known Garrett then.[33] New Mexico Delegate Rodey, in his letter of recommendation to Roosevelt, wrote:

"I unhesitatingly pronounce him [Garrett] an extraordinarily and well balanced able and sensible person.... He is an active energetic man whose word is his bond." [34]

The next day, Garrett's appointment was announced in the newspapers – catching the El Paso Republican establishment by surprise. The pushback was immediate:

"'Garrett not being from Texas,' said a prominent local politician this morning, 'hardly gives him as good a right to the place as a local man.'"

"Today business men of this city taken at random were asked if they preferred to see a local man rather than an outsider in the position of collector, and every one answered in the affirmative."

"Today numerous telegrams are being sent to the president requesting him to defer action until Texas can be heard from." [35]

Roosevelt wavered, letting it be known that the position was not yet decided.[36] Then, on December 16, he sent Garrett's name to the U. S. Senate to be confirmed.[37]

The El Paso Republicans continued the fight there:

"Charges against Garrett were filled before the committee on finance, alleging gambling. Garrett replied to Representative Spooner of the committee that he did not know the difference between a straight-flush and four-of-a-kind." [38]

On December 18, Garrett's appointment was confirmed by the U. S. Senate.[39] Garrett gained the job – he also gained many influential enemies in El Paso that would in the future do everything they could to oppose him.

On December 25, Garrett arrived back in El Paso. The next morning he was interviewed by the *El Paso Herald*:

"For the people of this city I have the kindest of feelings....The fight for this office has been fair and above board and I was fortunate enough to win out."

"In regard to the charges made against me at Washington I want to say that the president considered the source from which they came more than he did the charges themselves. They had no weight whatever with the president in this matter."

"I owe my appointment in a large measure to Judge Fall of this city. He rendered me considerable valuable assistance and I owe him a debt of gratitude."

"About the last remark President Roosevelt made when we parted was, 'Mr. Garrett, I am betting on you,' and I replied, 'Mr. President you will win the bet.' That was just before I left him to start for Texas."

"I consider President Roosevelt to be the greatest man this country has ever had." [40]

While Garrett was talking, Fall was standing beside him. Fall was asked about the main charge that was made against Garrett by his opponents:

"The county owed Garrett about four thousand dollars for money he had expended in the discharge of his duties. Later he made a collection of three thousand dollars of the county money and, as his attorney, I advised him to keep it. Then I went to the district attorney and asked him to make a charge against Garrett that the matter might be settled up."

"This was done and the result was that Garrett was allowed to keep the money and the county commissioners ordered that the remainder be paid to him. To do this a special tax has been levied and as soon as it is collected he will be paid about eight hundred dollars which is due him."

"There was no breaking of the law on Garrett's part as the money was his legitimately and he took that means of collecting it. His action was sustained by the courts and a settlement made of the matter." [41]

The New Mexico legislature passed a special act authorizing the funds necessary to repay Garrett, but Governor Otero vetoed the bill, perhaps because of Garrett's political opposition to Otero's reappointment as governor seven months earlier.[42]

Chapter 5 | Collector of Customs – 1902-1903

Zero-Tolerance

Garrett was sworn in as El Paso Collector of Customs on January 2, 1902. He made the following appointments:

"Chief deputy, Numa Buchoz, of El Paso, salary $2,000 per annum; cashier, Harry B. Lane of Las Cruces, N. M., salary $1,500; collector of the sub-port at Columbus, N. M., Morgan Llewellyn, son of Major Llewellyn of Las Cruces, N. M., salary $3.50 per day." [Garrett's salary was $3,000] [1]

When Morgan Llewellyn resigned 20 days later, Garrett appointed Albert Fall's father collector at Columbus.[2] (When Fall's father resigned in 1903, Garrett appointed Fall's brother to replace him.) [3]

In his first public announcement, Garrett said there was a large amount of smuggling taking place between El Paso and Mexico:

"The articles smuggled are purchased at stores in Juarez and generally consist of souvenirs and goods of that kind. They are concealed about the person and brought across to this side."

"The inspectors will take great care to see that this practice is stopped...." [4]

Garrett's first attempt to stop the smuggling was a disaster. On January 18, he ordered that all street cars coming from Juarez be stopped and the passengers searched.

"At one time about five hundred people, some say a thousand, were waiting to be searched and complained bitterly at the delay.... The government found a considerable amount of goods that were being smuggled into this country, all of which were confiscated." [5]

The public outcry caused Garrett to try a different plan:

"...the customs office had a corps of officers on the other side watching the stores where purchases were being made. Those at the bridge were kept informed by telephone of this and when anyone came along [that had been observed in a store], they were searched." [6]

This plan, too, had to be rescinded, with Garrett going back to voluntary declaration.

In February, Garrett intercepted a shipment from Juarez of statues showing a boy getting spanked. Garrett refused them entry on the ground that they were obscene:

"I wouldn't permit such a thing in my home or office, and that is enough." [7]

The shipper appealed the decision to the Treasury Department. Garrett was required to ship a sample to the department, but used express rather than mail because of Post Office obscenity regulations. The Treasury Department upheld Garrett's decision.[8]

Garrett Mortgages Ranches

On April 8, 1902, Garrett mortgaged his Home Ranch, Rock House Ranch, 30 head of cattle, and 150 head of horses to Martin Lohman for $3567.50. The interest rate was 12 percent per year.[9]

Martin Lohman was not a bank. He lent money as a side business to his general merchandise store.

Why Garrett wanted the money badly enough to mortgage his ranches and livestock – particularly at such a ruinous interest rate – is unknown. As collector, he was making $3,000 a year, an excellent salary.

Mary Lohman Burns to Death

On April 16, Garrett learned that the four-year-old daughter of Oscar Lohman was killed when she accidentally set fire to her dress while playing with matches.[10]

Garrett would name his next child Oscar Lohman Garrett.

Corralitos Calf War

"WAR BETWEEN GARRETT AND MEXICAN CATTLEMAN"

Garrett woke up to this front page headline on the *El Paso Daily Times* on April 23. The previous day the Corralitos Company had moved 1,048 calves through the port at El Paso. The duty on calves under one year was $2.00 per head. The duty on calves over one year was $3.75 per head.

(The Corralitos Company was a 1.5-million-acre Mexican ranching and mining corporation, owned principally by American mogul William Randolph Hearst.) [11]

Garrett supervised the assessment himself and ruled that the shipment contained 820 head that were older than one year (yearlings). Those he assessed at $3.75 per head.[12]

Corralitos Company manager Britton Davis was outraged. He had declared only four percent of the calves in the shipment as yearlings, and he was not used to having his declarations challenged. He rounded up several cattlemen who told Garrett that he was mistaken in his assessment. Garrett responded by saying that he had the right to tax the cattle based on his judgment of their fair value:

> "There is nothing to the matter except this: The Corralitos company offered at the custom house 1,048 head, 48 of which they said were over one year of age and 1,000 calves.... They were turned into the corral and Inspector Dwyer and myself classified them and we made them 820 head over one year.... I made my classification according to my best judgment after a long experience with cattle." [13]

Garrett agreed to allow a second inspector to make an assessment when the cattle reached their final destination, Denver, Colorado. That inspector concluded there were 282 head older than one year.[14] Garrett responded:

> "Now that this second classification has been made, it is of little import, as I shall not recommend its acceptance by the department, but shall stand by my own classification."

> *"[The company] seemed to think it was a question of revenue alone... it is to protect the cattlemen on this side that we have acted."* [15]

On May 23, a second shipment of Corralitos Company cattle passed through the port. The company declared 388 calves and 100 yearlings. Garrett and Inspector Dwyer ruled there were 186 calves and 316 yearlings.[16]

It was now war between Garrett and Mexican cattle producers. The Corralitos Company appealed to the New York Board of Appraisers. They also began organizing political resistance to Garrett among the many disgruntled members of the El Paso Republican establishment who strongly resented Garrett's appointment.

On July 7, Garrett travelled to New York to argue his case before the Board of Appraisers. The Corralitos Company sent two business managers and numerous *"affidavits of cattlemen and cattle importers"* supporting their position.[17]

While in New York, Garrett visited a shooting gallery on Coney Island:

> *"...giving a free exhibition of the way they shoot in Texas. Within half an hour the ex-sheriff had collected a box and a half of cigars, all there was on hand, after breaking every clay pipe in sight and making a record for bull's eyes that never has been equaled on the island."* [18]

On his return to El Paso, Garrett told the *El Paso Herald* that he was confident the board would rule in his favor.[19]

On September 2, the Board of Appraisers ruled against Garrett, ordering him to accept the calf and yearling numbers that had been declared by the Corralitos Company.[20]

Three weeks later, Garrett filed an appeal of the board ruling.[21] On April 14, 1903, the appeal was denied.[22]

This fight and loss was a disaster for Garrett. Before he became collector, Mexican cattle importers were cheating on their import duties by claiming yearlings as calves. It is highly likely the previous collector was accepting bribes to ignore standards. Garrett was too honest to go along with that practice. But the difficulty he faced was that without honest documentation of when a calf was born, it was not easy to judge its age. As a general rule, a larger calf is an older calf, and that was the standard that Garrett was applying.

Craig Diamond Case

This case started with the arrival in El Paso of Professor James J. Craig with his wife the former Mrs. Martha A. McHatton on August 4, 1902, from St. Louis, Missouri. Professor Craig – who was really Harry Silberberg, swindler and con man – publicized himself as a world-renown palmist. He was able to *"read the destiny of your life from the lines of your hand."*

Craig claimed falsely that he had:

> *"...just completed a tour around the world, where he read the palms of the greatest eastern potentates.... The professor, though a young appearing man, has lived some twelve years with the great Hindoo palmists and knows their science from its inception."* [23]

Harry Silberberg, alias James J. Craig, of the Craig Diamond Case. *San Francisco Examiner,* May 19, 1904.

In addition, Craig claimed he was:

> *"...an expert in criminology, and has read the hands of all the famous criminals of the world."* [24]

On November 12, Craig pawned $33,000 worth of diamond jewelry with the El Paso firm of Silberberg Brothers for $5,900 (no relation). [25]

The jewels were on display in the store window for one day when they were confiscated by Inspector Dwyer at the order of Treasury Agent Joseph F. Evans. Agent Evans alleged that the jewelry had been brought into the United States without being declared and therefore an import duty was due on them.[26]

Mrs. McHatton quickly filed suit claiming the diamonds were hers and asking for a divorce from Craig, who, she asserted:

"...had married her through hypnotic influence and secured her money, at the same time having another wife in the city...." [27]

By this time, Craig had left El Paso for Mexico City, Mexico. To determine if duty was owed on the jewels, Garrett went to Mexico City to interview Craig. Craig *"refused point blank to make any statement whatever."* [28]

The case of who owned the jewels and whether duty was due on them occupied the courts for three years. By the time of the final determination, October 12, 1905, the story of the jewels was known.[29]

The jewels had been given to Miss Suzette Maynard by a New York banker boyfriend. She later married Shirley R. Tuck. Mrs. Maynard-Tuck was persuaded to travel to London, England, with Craig, where the jewels were pawned. After the couple's return to the United States, Craig left Mrs. Maynard-Tuck and began a relationship with Mrs. McHatton. Craig convinced Mrs. McHatton to travel to London with him to redeem the jewels. She paid the London pawn broker $10,000 cash, and in return was given a (bad) check for $10,000 by Craig.

(The first person Craig tried to get to go to London with him was Mrs. Susan E. Barber, the former Mrs. Alexander A. McSween of Lincoln County Wars' fame. She travelled as far as New York with Craig before backing out.) [30]

Craig and Mrs. McHatton returned to the United States with the jewels concealed in Mrs. McHatton's clothing. They married in St. Louis. When they reached El Paso, Craig convinced Mrs. McHatton to pawn the jewels with Silberberg Brothers.

The whole time Craig and Mrs. McHatton were traveling to London and back they were shadowed by Mrs. Maynard-Tuck.

The court ruled that the jewels belonged to Silberberg Brothers, accepting that Mrs. Maynard-Tuck had given up her claim to the jewels by accepting a $1,200 payment from the Silberberg Brothers. The court ruled also that the jewels:

"...being of American manufacture were not dutiable and it was not necessary to declare them upon entry as the customs laws only require merchandise to be declared." [31]

Garrett was ordered to turn the jewels over to Silberberg Brothers.

The case was followed nation-wide. When the jewels were sold by the Silberbergs, they were put on public display as the *"Craig Diamonds."* [32]

Harry Silberberg never returned to El Paso. By October 23, 1903, Silberberg was in St. Paul, Minnesota, where he secretly married Miss Bonnie Hinkle, defrauding her step-father out of a large amount of money. Although arrested, he got out of jail by pretending to have consumption. An unidentified *"veiled lady"* (probably Mrs. Maynard-Tuck) smuggled leeches to him in jail, which he put *inside* his throat, thus creating what appeared to be tuberculosis hemorrhages.[33]

Later known variously as the *"King of Confidence Men,"* the *"Genius of Chicanery,"* the *"Wolf of Society,"* and *"The Great Lover,"* Silberberg continued to run cons around the world until at least 1921. (In 1921, he was in Europe pretending to be a high official of the War Finance Corporation with the authority to issue loans in exchange for a ten percent commission.) [34]

Fighting Removal Efforts

Garrett's strict customs enforcement, even for tourists bringing low-value souvenirs and curiosities from Juarez, produced numerous complaints and appeals to the Department of Treasury. These reports produced a rebuke from Secretary Leslie M. Shaw, who already considered the appointment of Garrett a mistake. Knowing that his enemies were working hard to get him dismissed – and that they already had the sympathy of the Secretary – Garrett, on February 8, 1903, wrote directly to President Roosevelt, presenting his side of the issue:

"At the time of my appointment to office, your instructions to me were that you expected a clean, honest administration, which you seemed to have reason to doubt had previously existed...."

"I feel very much humiliated by the reprimand of the Secretary, especially as I am totally ignorant of any irregularities or mismanagement of the affairs of my office."

"It has been and is my ambition to treat all persons doing business with this office with the utmost courtesy, and if in any case it has not been done I certainly do not know if it." [35]

Garrett concluded:

"...the Secretary's letter comes to me as a severe shock, especially as I know of no foundation for it." [36]

Garrett knew he had a gruff public manner, and had been working to improve it by reading *"Modern Eloquence,"* edited by Thomas B. Reed. *"From one to three volumes [of the ten volume set] are constantly on his desk."* [37]

On February 24, the *El Paso Herald* revealed that I. A. Barnes was circulating a petition to remove Garrett as Collector. The newspaper quoted the response of one El Paso businessman:

"Mr. Garrett is above all conscientious.... The Corralitos cattle people have been after him ever since he got into office... and the Juarez merchants are also after him, because he enforces the law and does not allow the importation of goods duty free. It hurts their business and they howl." [38]

On March 6, the *El Paso Herald* announced that Barnes was trying to get Garrett's job, using his influence with the Roosevelt Administration, especially with Secretary Shaw.[39] Three weeks later, Barnes was appointed by Shaw as a special agent to investigate the customs service along the Texas border.[40] His first official action was to travel to Mexico to consult with the cattle interests who claimed Garrett was mistreating them.[41]

Roosevelt Visits New Mexico

Having won the presidency by assassination, President Roosevelt knew that if he was going to get elected on his own merits, he needed to introduce himself to the country. So on March 15, 1903, he announced a 69-day, 13,500-mile trip to 22 states and two territories:

> *"[It would be] the most prolonged tour ever undertaken by an executive of the United States.... It will extend from east to west in a zig-zag line...."*

> *"No ladies will accompany the party, nor will any of the members of the cabinet. The train will probably consist of four cars...."* [42]

The trip was not planned to be all work. President Roosevelt intended to spend 16 days *"recreating"* in Yellowstone Park.

President Roosevelt left Washington D.C. on April 1. On April 30, Garrett *"was summoned by the president in a special letter forwarded from Yellowstone Park just as the chief executive was leaving there."* [43]

President Roosevelt's train pulled into Santa Fe on May 5. He was greeted with a 21-gun salute. Garrett was at the station as part of the official reception committee. After spending the morning giving a speech and participating in a parade, Roosevelt boarded his train about noon with Governor Otero and Garrett as his special guests. The two men were escorted to the dining car for lunch with the President. Garrett was seated on President Roosevelt's right and Governor Otero on his left. [44]

Governor Otero and Garrett disembarked at Albuquerque, President Roosevelt going on to Arizona.

Asked what he had talked to the President about, Garrett said: *"The president is greatly interested in the west and likes the western people and ways."* He said they discussed the future water needs of New Mexico and the benefits of building storage reservoirs.

> *"He is greatly interested in irrigation for the west and will do all that he can to help it along."* [45]

Fisticuffs

Three days after his return to El Paso, Garrett got into a fist fight with George M. Gaither. [46]

The origin of the fight was the forced hiring of Gaither as a *"special appraiser of cattle."* [47] Secretary Shaw had instructed Treasury Agent Evans to monitor Garrett, in the hopes of obtaining damning information – and forcing Garrett to hire someone who could easily spy on him was the ideal way to pursue that.

On March 9, Garrett hired Gaither for 30 days, as ordered by Agent Evans.

On April 7, Garrett fired Gaither. Garrett notified Secretary Shaw of his action:

> *"As [Gaither's] term of office expires to day, and his services are of no further value for the purpose for which he was appointed, I respectfully request my action be approved and authority be granted to pay him."* [48]

Gaither responded to the firing by telling people that Garrett had promised to hire him beyond the 30-day trial period, and that Garrett had thereby failed to honor his word.

On May 8, Garrett and Gaither met in downtown El Paso for the first time since Gaither's firing. Reported one witness:

> "I saw two men standing immediately in front of the... Turner building.... A second later both men began to strike at each other, and a lively fight ensued...."

> "Mr. Gaither accused Mr. Garrett of having told him, Gaither, a lie.... Garrett replied that Mr. Gaither was a son-of-a-bitch, or more accurately, I believe he said 'a damn son-of-a-bitch....'" [49]

Agent Evans, who was present, told it this way:

> "I saw Collector Garrett approaching, walking rapidly, and when he reached us he accosted Gaither by asking him if he had said that he Garrett had promised to appoint him to office for 60 or so days, to which Gaither replied that he had said as much, when Garrett using vile language and in wrath called him a God d-d liar, and Gaither struck him." [50]

Gaither's version:

> "Mr. Garret came up to me and said, 'Did you tell Buchoz that I said the position you had was permanent?'"

> "I said, 'No, I did not, but said that you promised, with the assistance of Colonel Evans, if possible to make it permanent.'"

> "Thereupon Mr. Garret said, 'You're a God damned liar.'"

> "I immediately struck him and we commenced fighting." [51]

Barnes was thrilled by the fight between Garrett and Gaither. He gathered all the critical statements he could and forwarded them to Secretary Shaw, then asked Garrett if he had any statement to make in his own defense. Garrett replied, in part:

> "...I have no moral objection to making a statement of facts in the case, but having been tried and adjudged upon malicious statements, without an opportunity to present my case, I have to respectfully decline to accede to your request." [52]

Both Garrett and Gaither were fined $5.00 for the fight by the justice of the peace.

Smelter Case

On July 11, customs employee Vance Fulkerson announced his resignation to the press. Fulkerson was stationed at the ore smelter owned by the American Smelting Company. His job was to collect the customs duty on lead ore imported from Mexico. (There was no duty on any other type of ore.) [53]

Before his resignation, Fulkerson had approached Garrett and told him he had evidence that the operators of the smelter were cheating on their tariffs. He said he would provide proof of the fraud if he was appointed to the committee charged with investigating the crime, members of which by law received a reward if fraud was uncovered.[54]

The Treasury Department ordered Fulkerson to turn over the evidence, refusing his request to serve on the investigating committee. Fulkerson was asked his response by the *El Paso Herald:*

> *"I have nothing whatever to say. I am out of the service and that ends the matter...."*

> *"'Would you give your evidence in the matter if the department should reconsider and decided to appoint you on the investigating board?' he was asked."*

> *"I am out of the service, I say, and as far as I am concerned the matter is ended."* [55]

Hoping that illegal acts on Garrett's part would emerge, Barnes threw himself into the smelter investigation. Instead, a woman came forward charging Barnes with inappropriate behavior. In addition, it emerged that Barnes had lied about his job qualifications. He was forced to resign on September 1.[56]

An audit led by Garrett showed that Fulkerson had been stealing customs collections. When confronted by Garrett, Fulkerson admitted he had been stealing for two years. He was indicted, but before he could be arrested, he fled to Mexico. Following his extradition from Mexico, he pled guilty to embezzling and was fined $1,000.[57]

Treasury Agent Evans was also taken down by the smelter case. After Fulkerson was indicted, but before he fled to Mexico, Evans accompanied Fulkerson and his brother to the Bank Saloon, a place to which he was apparently no stranger. On this night, Evans lost his entire $200 paycheck. He then wrote a $1,000 check to cover additional losses. When the saloon owner tried to cash the check, it proved to be worthless.[58]

When the details of this event became known, members of the public came forward and charged Evans with being:

> *"...in company with the Fulkersons a great deal of late, buggy riding and knocking about the city."* [59]

Evans tried to make up his bad check, but was only able to come up with $500. Charged with behavior unbecoming of a treasury agent, Evans was forced to resign, ending a 30-year career with the Treasury Department.[60]

The committee investigating the smelter found no irregularities in the payment of duties.[61]

Personal Affairs – 1903

On June 17, 1903, Garrett received a letter from Thomas B. Catron. The first paragraph read:

> *"On February 20, 1901, I loaned you, as you will remember, $500, which you stated then you would be able to repay in about two weeks. I know the reason why you failed was because the Governor vetoed the bill of which you secured the passage in order to get your fees paid, and of course, under the circumstances, it was perfectly satisfactory for me to wait on you until you might be better provided in order to make the payment."* [62]

Catron added that he *"very much needed the money now."* He said he was paying a bank 12 percent interest on the money. It seems unlikely that Catron would borrow money to loan to Garrett – more probably this story was a pretext to ask for interest, which he said amounted to another $140. In a magnanimous concession, he told Garrett that if he could not pay the full 12 percent interest, to send the amount of interest *"you think you should pay."*

Garrett did not reply. Catron sent Garrett three more letters. Each letter admonished Garrett for not replying to the previous letter and added more interest to the $500 loan. On September 24, Catron wrote:

> *"You certainly must recognize that you are not treating me right when you decline any of my letters.... I am actually in need of that money, and very much in need of it.... I am sure you can raise the money if you try to do so."* [63]

In his third letter, Catron threatened legal action.

Why Garret was so pathetically bad at managing money is a mystery. Oral accounts say he spent much of his time gambling. But if that was true, he surely would have taken out IOUs – and there is not a single mention of such an action in any primary source.

On July 22, Garrett was burglarized while asleep in the El Paso rooming house where he was living (his family was living on the Garrett Home Ranch):

> *"Entrance was effected through a window in the sitting room where a light was burning brightly.... [The burglar] took the customs collector's coat and trousers off a chair and threw them out of the window...."*

> *"He appears to have been very considerate, for after going through the clothing on the outside of the house, he threw down a small book that contained passes and receipts.... He also left the trousers after taking a pocket knife and the watch...."* [64]

On September 10, Garrett took out a $5,000 life insurance policy with the New York Life Insurance Company. The annual premium was $276.75. Why he decided to do this at this time is unknown. Perhaps it was required for some business venture in which he was about to invest. Given Garrett's constant money shortage, it is unlikely he continued to pay the premium for long. [65]

On December 19, Garrett sold his horse Patchen, *"a noted pacer,"* to Sheriff Hubble of Albuquerque for $500. Perhaps Garrett repaid Catron with this money. [66]

Oscar Lohman Garrett Born

On December 30, 1903, Oscar Lohman Garrett was born. The *El Paso Herald* announced:

> *"Customs Collector Pat F. Garrett is keeping quiet today, but will be celebrating as soon as he comes down town, his wife having presented him with a pretty baby daughter this morning. This makes the collector the father of six bright children."* [67]

The newspaper got the sex of the child wrong. Oscar was named after Garrett's best friend in Las Cruces, Oscar Lohman.

Chapter 6 | Collector of Customs – 1904-1905

Garrett began his third year as customs collector with the satisfaction of seeing his professional enemies defeated. Both Treasury Agent Evans and Special Customs Agent Barnes, who had been charged by Treasury Secretary Shaw with scrutinizing Garrett's job performance, had lost their jobs – because of misconduct – exactly the kind of wrong-doing they had been seeking against Garrett.

But all was not well. The financial obligations Garrett had shoved into the background were charging forward.

For instance, on April 8, 1904, Garrett renewed his mortgage with Martin Lohman. Garrett had neither repaid any of the principal nor paid any of the interest.[1]

On April 24, 1904, the Bank of Commerce re-filled its complaint against Garrett for not repaying the $1,000 loan to George Curry that Garrett had co-signed.[2] The sheriff of Dona Ana County, Jose R. Lucero, served the summons on Garrett on September 6, 1904.[3]

Garrett made no legal response to the Bank of Commerce suit. On September 7, 1904, the Bernalillo District Court ruled that the bank could recover $1,733.18 from Garrett. Furthermore, it ordered this judgment would bear annual interest of 12 percent until recovered.[4]

Sinaloa Land Deal

In late April, Garrett, *"accompanied by some eastern capitalists,"* taking leave as customs collector, traveled to the Mexican state of Sinaloa to investigate a land deal.[5] Garrett was leading a *"syndicate"* of twelve El Paso businessmen who were attempting to buy a 3,000,000-acre block of Mexican timber and farm land. Garrett's partner El Paso Judge Seymour Thurmond told the *El Paso Herald:*

> *"We have not at yet concluded whether we will put the property on the market or retain it and reap the benefits of its development. ...Mr. Garrett and my associates are all business men and may not be in position to devote their time and attention to the property for the purpose of development...."* [6]

On his return to El Paso, three weeks later, Garrett told the *Herald* that *"the trip was a very enjoyable one,"* and that he felt:

> *"...greatly improved physically as a result of the rest and recreation attached to the journey."* [7]

On August 19, the *Herald* reported that Garrett and his partners had forfeited the right to the land *"on account of having failed to put up the necessary funds...."* [8]

Apolinaria and Elizabeth "Lizzie" Garrett, circa 1930. Never before published photo.
Courtesy IHSF.org.

Elizabeth Garrett Begins Career

Garrett's 18-year-old daughter Elizabeth graduated from the Texas Institute for the Blind on June 9, 1904. She had been a resident student at the institute since she was six years old. An experimental eye operation a year earlier, which Garrett traveled to Austin to attend, had failed to restore her vision.[9]

At the graduation ceremony, Elizabeth received three certificates of proficiency: piano, vocal, and pipe organ.[10]

Three weeks later, Elizabeth gave a public concert at the Women's Club in El Paso.

"Deprived of her sight, her parents determined to develop other sources of pleasure for her. She was given an eleven year course in music." [11]

In September, Elizabeth performed at the Texas Building at the World's Fair in St. Louis, Missouri.[12]

Thus launched into the public's eye, Elizabeth had an illustrious career. She gave concerts from New York to California. She performed for audiences ranging from president to prisoners. After a concert at the Sing Sing Correctional Facility, one of the prisoners, V.M. 67616, honored her appearance with a poem, which read in part:

"Fools, they!!"
"They call her blind!"
"They call her blind, yet could she lead"
"A thousand souls – sick men"
"From cold gray stones...." [13]

In 1914, Elizabeth wrote "OH FAIR NEW MEXICO," which became the New Mexico State Song. During World War I, she participated in a war department program teaching soldiers blinded in the war techniques of coping with their handicap. In 1923, she became a close friend of Helen Keller, often accompanying Keller on her lecture tours.[14]

Elizabeth was one of the first recipients of a Seeing Eye (TSE) guide dog.[15] During World War II, Elizabeth volunteered for the USO, giving concerts in Army and Navy hospitals.[16]

In a late interview, when asked what advice from her father most helped her to live her life, she said:

"Think your way out, daughter, and keep your head clear, above your heart." [17]

(Elizabeth died October 16, 1947, in her hometown of Roswell, New Mexico. She hit her head on a concrete banister after stumbling on a church step during a storm. She died before she could be taken to a hospital. She was 62 years old.) [18]

Seeking Reappointment

On November 8, 1904, President Theodore Roosevelt was elected president for his first full term. Along with thousands of other Americans, Garrett telegraphed President Roosevelt his congratulations. Expecting no reply, he was:

"... agreeably and pleasantly surprised to receive a note from Mr. Roosevelt thanking him for his congratulations and wishing him all possible success." [19]

A week later, Garrett announced that he was seeking reappointment as collector:

"'I will be an applicant for the place again,' he said, 'and if the only fight they make on me is regarding my citizenship, which is in New Mexico, I do not think it will have any effect, for Mr. Roosevelt is thoroughly conversant with the boundaries of all customs districts....'" [20]

The *El Paso Herald,* in response, noted:

"It is almost certain that there will be a fight on for both the post office and the collectorship... and that neither of the present incumbents will be reappointed without fighting for it." [21]

Rough Riders Reunion

The presidential train pulled into San Antonio, Texas, in the late evening of April 6, 1905. The train carried President Roosevelt and his chosen travelling companions, who had left Washington D.C. three days earlier.

President Roosevelt was in San Antonio to attend the seventh annual reunion of his Rough Riders, the 1st United States Volunteer Cavalry, which Roosevelt had raised seven years earlier to fight in the Spanish-American War:

"The President's train was run on a siding near the station, where it will remain until to-morrow.... The train is guarded by a detail of city policemen, and as the President will be astir early to-morrow, every precaution will be taken to permit him to secure a good night's rest." [22]

The next morning, at a wildly ebullient welcome-to-San Antonio ceremony, President Roosevelt was greeted by thousands of well-wishers. One of those well-wishers was Garrett, who was there with his El Paso friend Thomas "Tom" Powers:

"Captain Garrett's towering form finally caught the eye of Secretary Loeb... he hailed him and gave orders at once which admitted Captain Garrett and Mr. Powers to the president's car...."

Before Garrett was recognized, however, he was stopped several times on suspicion of being a dynamiter, for he carried under his arm the package containing 500 Mexican cigars which El Paso Consul Mallen had sent by him to the president.

"'How are you, Pat,' said the president as he grasped the hand of Captain Garrett. The greeting took place on the rear platform of the car and when the large hat set on Captain Garrett's head, fully two feet above the head of the president was seen to come off... a large cheer went up from the crowd." [23]

(Garrett had been appointed to the rank of captain by Texas Governor John Ireland during a brief term as leader of an independent Texas Ranger company in 1884.)

Seventh annual Rough Rider reunion, April 7, 1905, San Antonio, Texas. Garrett is second from the left. President Roosevelt is fourth from left. Tom Powers is second from the right. Others unidentified. Courtesy Leon Metz Papers, C. L. Sonnichsen Special Collections, UTEP.

Following meeting the crowds at the train, and after reviewing the troops stationed at Fort Sam Houston, President Roosevelt made his way in a procession to the fairgrounds, where the Rough Riders were camped:

"The proceedings after the [President] entered the fairgrounds were informal. The Rough Riders pressed around the President and the secret service men moved away." [24]

Garrett and Powers were invited to dine with the president at the camp site. They were seated at the president's table opposite President Roosevelt.

"During the general conversation... one of the Rough Riders came to the president for his autograph. He took the book but remarked that he had no

fountain pen. Mr. Powers was standing near the president and at once tendered Mr. Roosevelt one. In taking it, he said:"

"'Why Mr. Powers, you are just like all Texans; you are at all times fixed in case of need.'" [25]

During the socializing, the press took a photograph of President Roosevelt, Garrett, and Powers visiting together (see photo page 103).

Garrett had introduced Powers to President Roosevelt as a *"cattleman."* The truth was that Powers was an avid horseman (like Garrett), the owner of the Coney Island Saloon in El Paso, and a famed gambler. In 1892, he was involved in the killing of Colorado City, Texas, Marshal Gooch in front of the Senate Saloon:

"Marshal Gooch, who had been drinking, drew a pistol, and when George Bell and Tom Powers attempted to disarm him, he opened fire on them. About a dozen shots were exchanged, four taking effect in Gooch, two of which were fatal." [26]

Bell and Powers were not indicted as the killing was ruled self-defense.

Due to the public distribution of the photo, President Roosevelt learned that Powers was not an uncontroversial cattleman, but someone with a darker history, someone who the president would prefer not to be associated with in the public mind.

When news of Garrett's privileged meeting with President Roosevelt became known in El Paso, observers were convinced that Garrett would be reappointed collector. The *El Paso Times* reported the story of the visit under the headline *"PAT GARRETT HAS A CINCH."* [27]

Jarvis Powers Garrett Born

On July 28, 1905, Apolinaria and Garrett had their eighth child, born in El Paso.[28]

The baby was named Jarvis Powers Garrett. Jarvis came from Garrett's side of the family – it was his mother's maiden name. Powers came from Garrett's friend Tom Powers.

Garrett Visits Billy the Kid's Grave

In early October, 1905, Emerson Hough, a hugely popular Western writer, sought out Pat Garrett to interview him for an article on Billy the Kid. The two men became good friends. Garrett agreed to take Hough on a personal tour of sites in New Mexico associated with Billy and other New Mexican gunmen.[29]

On October 14, Garrett and Hough left El Paso for New Mexico, by horse-drawn wagon. They planned to feed themselves by hunting and fishing, and to spend the nights camping wherever *"night overtook them."* [30]

In report on the trip in the *El Paso Herald*, Hough wrote:

"We carried a plentiful supply of provisions and our culinary imple-ments consisted solely of a frying pan and coffee pot. We cooked our meals just where we happened to camp...."

"As for company, we did not care very much for that, as we had enough to think about as we rode along, going from place to place. There were some days when we did not see a human being...."

"One thing we were after was to find the old government trail. It is twenty years since it was used and it is now all grown over...." [31]

On October 25, 1905, Garrett and Hough reached Fort Sumner:

"...old Fort Sumner, once a famous military post... offered nothing better than a scene of desolation, there being no longer a single human inhabitant there.... We were obliged to search for some time before we could find the site of the Maxwell house.... Garrett finally located the spot, now only a rough quadrangle of crumbled earthen walls."

"'This is the place,' said he, pointing at one corner of the grass-grown oblong. 'Pete Maxwell's bed was right in this corner of the room and I was sitting in the dark and talking to Pete, who was in bed. The Kid passed John Poe and Tip McKinney, my deputies, right over there on what was then the gallery, and came through the door right here.'"

"Twenty-five years of time had done their work in all that country, as we learned when we entered the little barbed-wire enclosure of the cemetery where the Kid and his fellows were buried. There are no headstones in this cemetery, and no sacristan holds its records. Again Garrett had to search in the salt grass and greasewood. 'Here is the place,' said he at length. 'We buried them all in a row. The first grave is the Kid's, and the next to him is Bowdre, and then O'Folliard. There's nothing left to mark them.'"

"So passes the glory of this world. Even the headboard which once stood at the Kid's grave – and which was once riddled with bullets by cowards who would not have dared to shoot that close to him had he been alive – was gone...."

"Garrett looked at them in silence for a time, and turning, went to the buckboard for a drink at the canteen. 'Well,' said he quietly, 'here's to the boys, anyway. If there is any other life, I hope they'll make better use of it than they did the one I put them out of.'" [32]

Garrett and Hough may have been surprised that Billy's grave no longer had a marker, but the grave had actually been unmarked for over 15 years at the time of their visit.[33] (For a detailed history of the re-locating and re-marking of Billy's grave, see my book *"Billy the Kid's Grave – A History of the Wild West's Most Famous Death Marker."*)

Fight for Reappointment

As early as May, 1905, the Republican leadership of El Paso declared they would not support a second collector's term for Garrett. They were supporting Alfred L. Sharpe, El Paso's representative to the Texas House. Sharpe had won their loyalty by sponsoring and passing a law banning public gambling in Texas.[34]

Sharpe got the jump on Garrett for the job by leaving for Washington D. C. on December 4 to lobby President Roosevelt for the position. Upon learning of Sharpe's action, Garrett left for D. C. the next day:

Emerson Hough, author of *"The Story of the Outlaw: A Study of the Western Desperado."* Undated photo. Courtesy Leon Metz Papers, C. L. Sonnichsen Special Collections, UTEP.

"Garrett asserted before he left that he felt no uneasiness about being reappointed, but concluded to go to Washington to watch his opponent." [35]

Garrett took Powers with him to D. C., a questionable decision – just as it had been to take Powers to the Rough Riders Reunion.

Sharpe met with President Roosevelt on December 11. Garrett met with the president the following morning.[36]

Roosevelt decided he didn't want to reappoint Garrett – but he didn't have the guts to tell Garrett. Instead, he announced that he no longer considered the El Paso collector's position a personal appointment. This term, the appointment would be the responsibility of the Secretary of the Treasury Department. He knew, of course, that Treasury Secretary Shaw had opposed Garrett's initial appointment, and had organized the investigations of Garrett's job performance by Barnes and Evans.[37]

Secretary Shaw immediately announced that he favored Sharpe for the position.

Garrett tried to save his job by soliciting endorsements. He received them from all of his employees and many El Paso citizens:

"It is said that the banks all signed the endorsement and that a number of business men and most all the Democratic county officials also signed it."

"...Tom Powers, proprietor of the Coney Island saloon and gambling house, who is in Washington with Garrett, wired to his friends to get all the endorsements possible and they got to work [too]." [38]

However numerous and favorable Garrett's endorsements, Shaw remained unmoved:

"The Secretary was not content with opposing Garrett's reappointment and letting it go at that. He went to the President and made a personal matter of it. He told Mr. Roosevelt that he would not 'stand for' Garrett's continuance in the service." [39]

On December 15, it was announced that Garrett would not be reappointed. The newspapers reported that Garrett's loss of the collector's position was due to Powers:

"The trouble with Garrett, it is said, is that he offended the president by taking a professional gambler and saloon keeper with him to the Rough Riders' reunion at San Antonio last spring." [40]

"It's no use doing any more; the Powers incident at San Antonio is what finished Pat,' said one of his closest friends today." [41]

"The ditching of Garrett is no indication that the president has lost his liking for Rough Riders with notches in the handles of their guns; it merely shows that he draws the line at having such men, after he has appointed them to office, bring saloon keepers to his table." [42]

Emerson Hough sent President Roosevelt a bizarre letter of "support" for Garrett that was patronizing and insulting:

"I wish I could lessen your very just annoyance at the San Antonio incident. The San Antonio men did not protect the President as a public man so much as they might have done."

> *"At the banquet at the Menger Hotel in the evening there was present Billy Sims, a gambler in San Antonio.... [Sims] and his men killed Ben Thompson.... I believe... Powers [has] a cleaner record than that."*

> *"Garrett is here with me now, but I am not writing at his request.... I do so because he is sick and broken-hearted... over the loss of your confidence in him.... As you know, these big outdoor men are childlike in some respects. Garrett's earlier training left him largely in ignorance of the term strict business and this is the real apology for any shortcomings on his part."*

> *"If you can reappoint Pat Garrett, you will save his self-respect...."* [43]

Attached to Hough's letter to President Roosevelt was a one-page biography of Garrett. It continued Hough's back-handed praise of Garrett:

> *"A man of little book education, but well born and of high sense of honor."*

> *"Occasionally goes into saloons, but does not loaf there and does not frequent gambling places, open or private.... [I] know that he is not a drunkard and not a gambler."* [44]

The press noted Garrett's devastated emotional state also:

> *"Garrett... has been dejected ever since he had a talk with the President a few days ago...."* [45]

> *"He saw the President, but came forth with a gloomy countenance."* [46]

Pressed to comment on the Powers controversy, Garrett responded:

> *"...that he did not blame the President in the least for not reappointing him, and, in fact, felt inclined to indorse his action, when it was considered that the President could do little less in the face of the opposition raised by Secretary Shaw."*

> *"I have a good ranch in New Mexico... and I will go there for a time. Just what my future plans will be I do not know.... I simply take my medicine. Secretary Shaw opposed my reappointment, alleging that the people of my locality were not in favor of my holding the office any longer, and that he had received many letters from citizens stating that they did not want me to be re-appointed. I suggested that a man should have opportunity to defend himself before sentence was passed, but Secretary Shaw declared that he had already formed an opinion."*

> *"President Roosevelt did not intimate that he was displeased with my official conduct, and stated that the presence of my saloon friend at the Rough Riders' banquet at San Antonio, in his honor, had nothing to do with the case."* [47]

Garrett's impartial facade – and talk of a *"good ranch,"* which was really not so good – hid the desperate financial straits that Garrett was in as a result of losing the collector's appointment.

On December 20, Sharpe was confirmed by the U. S. Senate as El Paso Customs Collector. As a courtesy – and to reduce *"the pain of parting from his salary"* so suddenly – Sharpe permitted Garrett to continue in the collector's job until December 31.[48]

Tom Powers' Coney Island Saloon, El Paso, Texas. The saloon closed in 1918. Undated photo. Courtesy El Paso Public Library, Border Heritage Center, Aultman Collection.

Tom Powers with two of his Appaloossa show horses, circa 1908. Courtesy Leon Metz Papers, C. L. Sonnichsen Special Collections, UTEP.

Martin Lohman, private banker who held the mortgage on Garrett's ranches until he sold the mortgage to W. W. Cox. 1905 photo. Courtesy Center for Southwest Research and Special Collections, UNM.

Chapter 7

Financial Woes Deepen – 1906

On January 15, 1906, Garrett wrote to Albert Fall from his Home Ranch:

"I have got into a fix where it seems impossible for me to get along without using the $50 I was to send to you, if you will forgive me for this I will send it to you in a few days. I have written to two of my friends who owe me telling [them] the situation and asking them to send you some money at once."

"Be patient with me and I will try and never do [unreadable] again." [1]

Whether Fall was repaid as promised is unknown.

Finstad Ranch Murders

The Finstad ranch murders case offered Garrett an escape – at least temporarily – from likely financial disaster.

On December 18, 1905, a gang of bandidos attacked Ole E. Finstad's ranch house near Diez, State of Chihuahua, Mexico. Inside the house were four men: Finstad, Louis "Shorty" G. Coughener, C. W. McMurray, and Robert W. Rutherford. McMurray and Rutherford were visiting from a nearby ranch:

"The men had just finished their supper and were feeding seven little puppies [when there was a knock on the front door]. McMurray was the first to go to the door and he was shot through the eye and killed instantly."

"Rutherford followed and was immediately engaged in a battle with a bandit who carried a machete. While they were fighting, and after he had given Rutherford a death stroke, another bandit shot Rutherford in the heart." [2]

Finstad ran out the front door past Rutherford's body as it fell, but was struck on the head by Rutherford's killer. He ran into a corral and managed to hide in a hay stack.

"'Shorty' attempted to escape by a rear door, but ran into a bandit with a gun at that opening. The bandit shot him in the face and left him for dead." [3]

"The bullet entered his head near the nose and left through the cheek." [4]

The bandits stayed at the ranch for an hour, trying to open Finstad's safe, to no avail.[5]

When the Mexican police arrived, they arrested Finstad and Coughener. The two men, although the crime's victims, were also witnesses, and the Mexican legal system mandated that all witnesses to a crime be arrested until the trial court had a chance to examined the facts of the case.[6]

Several days after their arrest, Mexican authorities charged Finstad and Coughener with murdering McMurray and Rutherford, rejecting their explanation that bandits killed the two men.[7]

The bodies of McMurray and Rutherford were shipped to El Paso, and with them came the widow of Rutherford and more news of the event. The Mexican court theory that McMurray and Rutherford were killed by Finstad and Coughener appeared refuted by reliable evidence. The *El Paso Herald* called for Garrett – now that he no longer was collector – to investigate the case.[8]

Garrett accepted the challenge and travelled to Mexico on funds provided by Mrs. Finstad.[9] After his investigation, which included meeting with the governor of Chihuahua, Garrett returned to El Paso and told the press:

> *"I find that all of the officers of the state of Chihuahua believe that Finstad and Coughener committed the murders and all efforts of the imprisoned men's friends to convince them to the contrary are unavailing."*

> *"There is not a particle of evidence to sustain the theory to which the Mexican officials so tenaciously cling, and I believe that two men were never more unjustly charged and imprisoned than are Finstad and Coughener."*

> *"I have talked with [Finstad] and Coughener separately and their stories match to the slightest detail."* [10]

Convinced that only high-level U.S. government intervention could free the men from the Mexican court's false charges, Garrett contacted President Roosevelt in a letter dated January 21, 1906, who, in response, agreed to meet with him:

> *"As the president is known to have great faith in Mr. Garrett's judgment in such matters, it is expected that some important news in reference to the now noted case will be forthcoming from Washington."* [11]

On February 2, 1906, Garrett accompanied by a Dr. G. B. Calman met with President Roosevelt in the White House:

> *"[The president] called in secretary of state Root and assistant secretary Bacon, and to them in the presence of the president, Mr. Garrett and Dr. Calman made their statement of the case."*

> *"'I believe the president and the secretary of state were both impressed with the innocence of the two Americans,' said Mr. Garrett today, 'and I believe that they will now look further into the case than they have already done.... There is no doubt in my mind of the innocence of the two imprisoned men....'"* [12]

Dr. Calman had performed an autopsy on McMurray and Rutherford's bodies after they arrived in El Paso. His formal opinion from his examination was *"that the killing was the work of Mexican bandits."* [13]

As a result of Garrett's efforts, the U. S. government formally asked the government of Chihuahua to conclude the case quickly – which it did, convicting the two men of murder on March 15, 1906, and sentencing each to twelve and a half years in prison.[14] Garrett was present at the trial, but was not allowed to offer evidence.[15]

(On May 24, 1909, after Finstad and Coughener had served almost four years, the Mexican Supreme Court – accepting the Americans' explanation of the event – reversed their conviction and ordered the men released.) [16]

Seizure and Replevin

Following his praiseworthy actions in the high-profile Finstad case, Garrett probably was feeling hopeful about future financial opportunities.

Then, on May 25, at 6:30 in the morning, Dona Ana County Sheriff Jose R. Lucero with several deputies rode up to Garrett's Home Ranch. Sheriff Lucero had an execution order from the Second District Court to seize all of Garrett's personal property.

The seizure order was issued on behalf of the Albuquerque Bank of Commerce, which had won its lawsuit against Garrett for his failure to repay the loan made to George Curry in 1890 that Garrett had co-signed. The amount of the debt with interests charges and court fees was now $1733.18.[17]

Garrett was not at the ranch, which was probably planned. The seizure order was served to Garrett's wife Apolinaria and son Poe, who were present.[18]

Sheriff Lucero seized:

- 60 head of horses, more or less, with their increase
- 60 head of cattle, more or less, with their increase
- The Garrett Home Ranch, situated about one and one-half miles southwest of Gold Camp, with all the houses, fixtures, stables, and improvements thereon, containing roughly 160 acres, more or less
- 1,800 feet of pipe used to pipe spring water to Garrett's Home Ranch house and corrals
- The Bear Canyon Ranch [Rock House Ranch], with all the houses, fixtures, and improvements thereon [19]

Sheriff Lucero left a deputy at each ranch to stop Garrett from re-occupying the ranches. [20]

What could have been more mortifying?

The man who had replaced Garrett as sheriff of Dona Ana County was seizing all of Garrett's property for failure to repay a loan – just as Garrett himself had done numerous times as sheriff. There was no more public sign of financial failure than having your property auctioned off on the public square in front of the county courthouse. A man who just months earlier was consulting with the president of the United States on national matters was now exposed to the public as incapable of managing his own personal financial affairs.

The next day, May 26, W. W. Cox filed an affidavit in the Dona Ana courthouse affirming that he now owned the mortgage on Garrett's ranch and livestock properties issued by Martin Lohman on April 8, 1902. Cox had purchased the mortgage from Lohman on April 3, 1905 for $3,000. Cox wanted to insure that his claim against Garrett's assets was legally recorded.[21]

On June 5, Garrett wrote the lawyer for the Albuquerque Bank of Commerce and made a settlement offer. The terms Garrett offered are unknown. The lawyer replied:

"I have submitted [your offer] to the bank for its consideration and the bank says that they do not feel that they are called upon to accept [your] proposition.... They take the position that you were given every consideration and

show to settle this indebtedness and have failed to do so and that it has run along and interest accumulated until it amounts to quite a large sum...."

"In regards to Currie [Curry], Currie being in the Philipine [sic] Islands, to send the judgment there to sue him the bank thinks would be very troublesome and they do not know that he has anything except his salary from the government, which cannot be reached on execution, even if a judgment could be obtained there." [22]

Garrett's offer was probably that he was willing to pay a bit, but the bank should seek the majority from the man who had benefited from the loan 16 years earlier – George Curry.

Curry had resigned his position as sheriff of Otero County in 1899 and joined the U. S. military in the Philippines, which was occupying the Philippines following the Spanish-American War. After several years service, he was appointed the Governor of the Philippine Province of Camarines, then the Chief of Police of Manila. In May, 1906, Curry was Governor of the Province of Isabela.[23] (A year later, Curry would be appointed Governor of New Mexico.) Clearly, Curry was capable of repaying the loan if he had chosen to or had been forced to.

On June 23, Garrett made his legal response. Attorney Herbert B. Holt, acting for Garrett, filed a writ of replevin against Sheriff Lucero asserting that certain property seized by the sheriff was exempt from seizure because it was legally the property of Apolinaria Garrett, Garrett's wife. The exempt property claimed was:

- One bay stallion, unbranded, about 16 hands high, weighing about 1100 pounds, called 'Gray', of the value of $150.00
- One sorrel mare, unbranded, about 15-1/2 hands high, weighing about 1000 pounds, called 'Skip', of the value of $50.00
- One dun mare, about 14-1/2 hands high, weighing about 875 pounds, branded O on the jaw, of the value of $50.00
- One Jersey cow with suckling calf, of the value of $40.00, branded O on the jaw [24]

At the same time, Garrett filed a bond in replevin with the court for $580.00, guaranteed by sureties Martin Lohman and Albert J. Fountain, Jr.[25]

Replevin derives from English Common Law. A writ of replevin asserts that one's personal property has been taken unjustly by the state or another person. Replevin is a response to seizure – it can be filed only after the specified property has been taken.

The person filing the writ of replevin must submit a personal bond to the court equal to the value of the disputed property. Once the writ and bond have been filed, the person that took the property will be ordered to return it, and it becomes the duty of the court to determine if the property was justly seized.[26]

The court issued an order to Sheriff Lucero to return Apolinaria's property on the same day in which the writ of replevin was filed.[27]

On July 6, Sheriff Lucero published the first of two notices of the public sale of Garrett's seized property in the *Rio Grande Republican* newspaper, as required by law. The date of the sheriff's sale was set for August 4, 1906.[28]

On July 11, attorney Holt notified the Bank of Commerce by letter that the Garrett Home Ranch was Garrett's homestead (residence). As a homestead, it was exempt from seizure for personal debt. The letter also informed the bank that:

> *"[The Rock House Ranch] does not belong to me [Garrett] and did not belong to me at the time of said levy and for sometime prior thereto."* [29]

Although the letter does not name him, Garrett is claiming that the Rock House Ranch is owned by his 19-year-old son, Poe. The May 24, 1899, bill of sale of the Rock House Ranch showed that the property was bought by Garrett. Whether Garrett had truly sold or given the ranch to Poe, or whether he was just claiming it in response to the seizure, is unknown, as no deed of sale to Poe is recorded in the county records office.

On July 28, the Albuquerque Bank of Commerce filed an appraisement of the value of Garrett's Home Ranch with the court, as required by law. Two independent appraisers – *"disinterested householders of the neighborhood of the Garrett ranch"* – valued Garrett's Home Ranch at $225.00 and his spring and the pipe laid to it from the ranch at $250.00.[30] There should also be an appraisal of the Rock House Ranch as part of the court order, but no such document is in the court records.

On August 4, as publicized, Sheriff Lucero:

> *"...at the court house door of said County of Dona Ana, between the hours of ten o'clock in the forenoon and three o'clock in the afternoon of said day, [did] publicly sell, at auction, to the highest bidder, for cash, all the right, title and interest of the said Patrick F. Garrett in and to the [property listed below]:"*

> *"A possessory right in and to what is known as the Garrett Home Ranch and the improvements thereon situate, containing 160 acres, more or less."*

> *"Also one spring of water situate about 1800 feet northwest from the residence of said Garrett and the pipe therefrom laid to convey the water of said Spring to what is known as the Garrett Home Ranch."*

> *"A possessory right of the said Garrett in and to what is known as his [Rock House Ranch] and the improvements thereon."* [31]

The only bidder – and the buyer – was the Albuquerque Bank of Commerce. The bank paid $500.00 for each ranch.

Note that the sheriff auctioned and the bank bought a *"possessory right."* A possessory right gave the bank the right to occupy and evict Garrett, but did not invalidate any prior liens on the properties. New Mexico law at the time gave Garrett a one year grace period before the bank could force him off the ranches, as noted in the certification of the sale:

> *"I hereby certify that the said Bank of Commerce became and was the purchaser of all the right, title and interest of the said Garrett in and to the said property, and that upon the expiration of twelve months from the date of said*

sale, the said Bank of Commerce will become entitled to receive the deeds for said property." [32]

On August 17, Dona Ana County treasurer Oscar Lohman auctioned off half of Garrett's livestock – 15 horses, 10 colts, 14 cows, and five calves – at the courthouse door for failure to pay $1,000 in past due property taxes.[33] The sale brought in $456.50. The same day, Cox renewed the mortgage on Garrett's remaining livestock.[34]

Sheriff Lucero charged the county $383.18 in expense costs to handle the auctioned livestock. These expenses included $55.95 to pay four men to round up the livestock and $213.60 to herd and pasture the livestock from June 10 to August 4.[35]

Oscar Lohman had caught the Bank of Commerce sleeping with his tax sale. The bank had seized the livestock along with Garrett's ranches and expected to sell them as part of its loan recovery. Lohman claimed priority for the tax lien. The bank sued, alleging that Lohman had sold the livestock *"without proper authority of law."* [36] The case was eventually dismissed.

Dead Man Found

On August 21, Garrett found a dead man about two miles from his Home Ranch, Celso Diaz, an *"old wood hauler of the Organ mountains:"*

"Two burros were found tied together with a rope and the other end of the rope was fastened to the dead man's leg. It is supposed that while handling the burros... they stampeded and Diaz was in some way caught in the end of the rope and thrown and dragged to his death."

The burros had drugged the body about a mile:

"The body was black and decomposing and worms were all over the bruised part when the body was found." [37]

Chapter 8 | Hope Denied – 1907

Garrett began 1907 with a chance to recover from his financial crisis. He was still in possession of his ranches, because the Bank of Commerce had to wait one year to take ownership. Garrett was disputing the bank's ownership, even though the bank had bought the ranches in the sheriff's sale, by asserting that the Home Ranch was his homestead, and the Rock House Ranch was owned by Poe Garrett.

There are no records in the Bank of Commerce case file that show the bank took any further legal action, such as evicting Garrett. From this lack of legal action, and later events, it can be assumed that Garrett and Poe's ownership was (belatedly) accepted by the bank.

Both ranches and Garrett's remaining livestock were mortgaged to Cox.

Appeals For Help

On January 3, 1907, Garrett wrote to Albert Fall:

"I tried to see you before you left for Cananea, but you were so busy I failed to do so."

"A son of Demetrio Chavez, Manuel, I believe, is offering 200 head of stock cattle for sale at what I consider a fair price. Poe wants to buy them to put on the [Rock House Ranch]. If you can help me to do so, it will be a great favor to us both."

"In case you do not think well of this, I want to take the sheep proposition up with you again, eliminating your proposition that I do the herding."

"Now I will see if you will answer a letter from me or not." [1]

Obviously, Garrett's relationship with Fall was strained. On January 9, Fall replied, writing in part:

"I note what you say with reference to the stock cattle belonging to Chavez, and would be very glad to help you in the purchase of same if it were possible for me to do so. I am overdrawn at the Bank and am living on expectations myself. I have no money coming in, more than sufficient to buy groceries... and have been compelled to borrow money from the Bank...."

Fall added a P. S.

"Where is that fifty dollar check which you were going to return???" [2]

On February 7, Garrett wrote to Emerson Hough, in part:

"You speak of money. Well suppose you are doing well in a financial way, the opposite has been the case with me. Everything seems to go wrong with me."

"I was sold out last fall by the Sheriff. Went on a note with a friend was such judgment obtained execution is here [sic], but we have our ranch and a few stock left and I am going to stay here and build up again."

*"A little money would be worth a great deal to me at present...." * [3]

Following his camping trip with Garrett in late 1905, when the two men had visited Billy the Kid's grave, Hough had published a series of articles (and later a book) recounting Garrett actions during the Lincoln County Wars – including Garrett's account of the killing of Billy. Hough had promised Garrett part of his earnings, but other than an initial $200.00, Hough never paid Garrett anything.[4] The appeal for a "little money" in this letter is a reference to this unfulfilled promise of Hough's.

Hough's response to Garrett's plea was to send him a copy of his book *"The Story of the Outlaw."* In his letter accompanying the book, Hough wrote:

"...this book is just out, and it will be some time before I get anything from it...."

*"...keep your nerve, for money is made quicker now than it ever was, and I have no doubt that it will come your way." * [5]

Wayne Brazel Leases Rock House Ranch

On March 11, 1907, Poe leased the Rock House Ranch to Jesse Wayne Brazel. This lease was more Garrett's decision than Poe's. In his January 3 letter to Fall, Garrett had asked for help buying cattle to put on the Rock House Ranch, *"which will be a great favor to us both."* Authors who have written biographies of Garrett have assumed that the Rock House Ranch was the property of Garrett, and consequently have been unable to explain why this lease was signed by Poe Garrett rather than by Pat Garrett.

The lease, which was probably written by Poe, read:

"I, Poe Garrett party of the first part agree to lease to Wayne Brazel the party of the second part my ranch property which I party of the first part do lawfully claim as being my own indingal [individual] ranch property. The party of the second part does hereby agree to brand for the party of the first part ten head of heffert [Hereford] calves and one mare colt each and ever [sic] year in the month of July for the period of five years.

*This stalk [stock] branded each yr is to be considered full payment for each year and the party of the second part Wayne Brazel does agree to keep annul essessment [annual assessment] work upon said property as required by law and the party of the second part does agree at the end of five years to give peasable [peaceable] possession of said property to Poe Garrett party of the first part. This property is known as the Rocos [Rock] House and sinking springs Ranch and is situated in the north end of the Black mountains mining District of the county of Dona Ana and territory of New Mexico. The party of the second part is to put necessary improvements on the ranch of his expense." * [6]

The annual payment for the lease was ten calves and one mare, which implied that Brazel was going to run cattle and horses on the ranch.

Three months later, Brazel borrowed $574.80 from Cox to buy goats,[7] which he put on the Rock House Ranch, thereby violating the implication of his lease with Poe, which was that Brazel would run cattle and horses on the land (the payment would come from the increase of the livestock). Goats were much harder on the land than cows and horses.

Curry Appointed Governor of New Mexico

On February 18, 1907, President Roosevelt forced the resignation of New Mexico Governor Herbert J. Hagerman so he could appoint George Curry governor. Governor Hagerman was accused of financial mismanagement.[8]

Curry, who was serving as the Governor of the Philippine Island of Samar, had initially declined the position, but at President Roosevelt's insistence, accepted the appointment.[9]

On June 21, 1907, before Curry had returned to the United States, Garrett wrote his friend W. H. H. Llewellyn:

> *"Knowing that you will have an opportunity to see Gov. Curry before I do, when he arrives in New Mexico, I wish you as our mutual friend to talk over with him and see if you can arrange that he settle the judgment that is against he and myself that is held by the [Albuquerque] Bank of Commerce...."*

> *"You may say to him that this judgment has been ruinous to me besides a great deal of annoyance and I wish he would satisfy the Bank and get me a final release; furthermore, tell him that I have been damaged in actual money three thousand dollars ($3,000) and that I think he should arrange to pay me at least two thousand dollars ($2,000) at an early date."*

> *"Tell him by so doing I will be satisfied and greatly relieved in a financial way."* [10]

There is no record of Llewellyn's reply to Garrett. Garrett did, however, get a chance to speak to Curry on July 23, during which he discussed the issue. The next day, Garrett wrote his wife:

> *"I am going to Santa Fe to the governor's inauguration and want you to send me by bearer my dress suit and prince Albert Coat. I saw Gov Curry yesterday and he is alright. He will do anything he can for me. He wants me to go to Washington with him. He will go to Washington just after he is sworn in. I am going to try hard to do something and feel very much encouragement."* [11]

To celebrate his appointment as governor, a group of Curry's long-time friends decided to hire a special train to go to Santa Fe for his inauguration. The train, which left El Paso at 6:20 in the evening, August 6, consisted of five coaches. Two of the coaches were reserved for invited guests of the inauguration. Garrett was one of these guests.[12]

The train was scheduled to pick up Curry at the train station at Torrance (116 miles south of Santa Fe) the next day. The automobile taking Curry to Torrance broke down, delaying the rendezvous for several hours.[13] While waiting for Curry, a photograph was taken of thirteen of the guests. Included in the photo are Garrett, Fall, and Holt (Garrett's attorney during the ranch seizures.) Garrett is wearing his Prince Albert coat (see photo on page 120).

On his arrival at the Santa Fe train station, Curry was greeted by a huge, enthusiastic crowd. The magnitude of the public's expectation for Curry's job performance was reflected by one newspaper headline, which called him the *"Saviour"* of New Mexico.[14]

Garrett, too, had his expectations of Curry as his savior, as noted in the press:

"Garrett is a close personal friend of governor George Curry and his friends expect that he will be given some appointment...." [15]

Then, in an act of seeming self-destruction, Garrett publicly announced he did not want a Curry appointment:

"Pat Garrett... denies that he is an applicant for any position in New Mexico under Gov. George Curry, and says further that he does not want a territorial job, even if one is tendered him." [16]

Given what Garrett had written to his wife, this statement – issued to the press – is difficult to explain. Why the dramatic change in attitude – which was the equivalent of financial suicide? Did Garrett and Curry have a friendship-destroying argument over the 1890 loan?

Fourth months later Cox renewed his mortgage on Garrett's livestock.[17]

Group photo taken at Torrance, New Mexico, August 6, 1907, while the men were enroute to Santa Fe to attend George Curry's inauguration.

Standing, left to right: W. A. Hawkins, W. C. McDonald, Pat F. Garrett, A. H. Hudspeth, unidentified, C. V. Safford, and Charles Hunt.

Seated, left to right: William Riley, Herbert B. Holt, Feliz Martinez, Albert B. Fall, H. O. Bursum, and Mark B. Thompson.

Garrett is wearing the Prince Albert jacket he asked Apolinaria to send him.
Courtesy Kathy Easterling.

Chapter 9 | Killing Garrett – 1908

In early January, 1908, Garrett tried to get Wayne Brazel's goats thrown off the Rock House Ranch using an old New Mexico statute that made it a crime to herd livestock within a mile and a half of a ranch house or settlement. He filed a complaint with Justice of the Peace C. N. Anthony in Organ alleging that Brazel had violated this statute with his goats. Brazel was arrested, but quickly released.[1] After a tense hearing before the JP in which *"arms were openly carried,"* Garrett withdrew his complaint.[2]

Asked by a friend later about the difficulty with Brazel, Garrett said:

> *"...he had leased pasturage to Brazle [sic], and that contrary to the lease, Brazle had used the property for goats...."*

> *"Garrett declared that he was looking for nobody, and that he did not want any trouble. He said there was no truth in the statement that he was 'gunning' for Brazle, and that he expected no trouble with him."* [3]

Brazel countered *"that nothing was said regarding the [kind] of stock"* to be placed on the ranch.[4] (Brazel was not denying the implication of the wording of the lease.)

On January 7, 1908, at Brazel's request, Albert Fall wrote a letter to Governor Curry recommending that Brazel be hired as a mounted policeman (the New Mexico equivalent of a Texas Ranger):

> *"Wayne Brazel, of Dona Ana County, Organ Post Office, has written me asking my endorsement for appointment as member of the mounted police force. I have known Wayne for years and I believe that he would make a good officer. He is steady, quiet and I think competent."* [5]

This application for a paying job suggests that Brazel was unhappy with what he was earning in the goat-raising business, or tired of the conflict with Garrett, or perhaps both.

Building in Organ where Justice of the Peace C. N. Anthony heard Garrett's complaint against Brazel for herding goats too close to his ranch residence. Photo circa 1908. Courtesy Archives and Special Collections, NMSU.

From right to left: William A. Cravens, Jesse Wayne Brazel, and Jim Lee. Wayne had shaved his head as a joke. Photo circa 1907. Courtesy Nita Stewart Haley Memorial Library and J. Evetts Haley History Center.

The Ranches Deal

Some time in early February, James "Deacon Jim" B. Miller and Carl Isaac Adamson travelled to Las Cruces from El Paso. The purpose of their trip, as reported in the *El Paso Herald*, was to buy John Leatherman's ranch, located four miles east of Garrett's Rock House Ranch.[6] The two men said they were planning to buy Mexican cattle to sell in the United States. They said they were looking for a convenient ranch on which to graze the cattle until late fall.[7]

Miller was an ex-lawman and ex-Texas Ranger with a well-known reputation as a professional killer. He had been tried for murder twice and acquitted. He was the prime suspect in at least half a dozen unsolved killings and attempted killings. His nickname, "Deacon Jim," came from his habit of faithfully attending church.[8]

Adamson was related to Miller by marriage. Adamson's wife Amanda Elizabeth Clements was a cousin of Miller's wife Sarah Frances Clements. Adamson married Amanda in 1905 in Roswell, where they had resided ever since.

Both Miller and Adamson were livestock dealers and had been partners in at least one previous deal. In June, 1905, they purchased 147 head of cattle from D. C. Pratt in Stephens, Texas. Pratt filed charges against Miller and Adamson, claiming that the cattle were re-sold before he had been properly paid. Miller and Adamson were arrested on the complaint, but not charged when the dispute was settled out of court.[9]

Miller's main business was sheep-raising, but he also bought and sold cattle, horses, and goats. In October, 1905, the *Roswell Daily Record* reported that Miller was moving his sheep holdings to Roswell.[10] As Miller lived in Fort Worth, Texas, at the time, it is very likely that Adamson was working for or with Miller in Roswell.[11]

Miller and Adamson were unable to buy Leatherman's ranch, according to a newspaper report, but while in Las Cruces, they learned that Garrett was interested in selling his ranches. To explore that option, on February 6, Miller and Adamson visited Garrett at his Home Ranch. Adamson later testified that this visit to the Home Ranch was his first meeting with Garrett.[12] Miller knew Garrett from numerous previous meetings.[13]

Following their visit with Garrett, Miller and Adamson decided to buy Garrett's two ranches, but there was a huge obstacle blocking the sale – the men did not want the goats that Brazel was grazing on the Rock House Ranch.

On or about February 22, Garrett took Brazel to met Miller and Adamson at their hotel in El Paso, where they reached a deal.[14] Adamson signed a contract with Brazel in which he agreed to buy 1,200 goats for $3.50 a head. At the time the contract was signed, Adamson (and presumably Brazel) believed the number of goats on the ranch to be the 1,200 figure specified in the contract.[15]

Once the goats were off the land, Garrett would be free to sell his ranches to Miller and Adamson. Miller and Adamson agreed to pay $3,000 for the two ranches. As part of the deal:

> *"Garrett was to go to Mexico for the cattle, drive them to the [ranches], and take care of them until November 1st for a dollar a head."* [16]

James B. Miller who arrived in Las Cruces by train on the morning of February 29, the day Garrett was killed. He checked into the Park Hotel. He was waiting for Garrett and Carl Adamson to sign the ranches deal when he learned that Garrett was dead. He left Las Cruces March 4. 1906 photo. Courtesy William Neveu.

Carl Isaac Adamson. Adamson and James B. Miller met with Garrett at Garrett's Home Ranch on February 6, 1908, where they made a deal with Garrett to buy his two ranches, if the goats that Wayne Brazel had on the Rock House Ranch were removed. Undated photo. Courtesy Leon Metz Papers, C. L. Sonnichsen Special Collections, UTEP.

A somewhat garbled version of this deal was announced to the public in the Las Cruces newspaper:

> *"Carl Adamson and J. B. Miller of El Paso have leased the Garrett ranches in the Gold Camp, purchased the goats there, and after they move the goats will put on [the] range a fine lot of cattle."* [17]

With the details of the goat/land transaction settled, Adamson traveled to Las Cruces from El Paso on February 28. He rented a two-horse top-buggy at the livery stable and rode out to Garrett's Home Ranch, a route he was familiar with from his first visit. He arrived at about 5 p.m.[18]

At Garrett's invitation, Adamson spent the night. Also at the ranch that night – according to Adamson – was Garrett, his wife, three children, and three employees: Frank Adams, Tom Emery, and an unidentified Hispanic ranch hand. Some time that night, perhaps while preparing supper, Garrett's daughter Pauline *"met with a rather serious accident."* She was scalded badly by hot water.[19]

To be certain that Brazel was in Las Cruces the next morning, Garrett sent him a note. The note was taken by Garrett's ranch hand to the Cox ranch, where Brazel was working. Unable to locate Brazel, the ranch hand gave it to Olive Boyd, who carried it out to the blacksmith shed where Brazel was helping to shoe horses.[20] Olive was Wayne's future wife – and according to her father, already his fiancé (see page 181 for details).

February 29, 1908 – The Shooting

The next morning, February 29, Saturday, leap day, at about 8:30, Garrett and Adamson got into the buggy to travel to Las Cruces to meet Miller and Brazel to *"fix up the papers."* Adamson was driving, seated on the *"whip end seat of the buggy"* (right).[21]

Miller was waiting in Las Cruces. He had arrived by train and was registered at the Park Hotel, which – conveniently – was located across the street from the county courthouse, where any papers signed by the parties could be filed with the county clerk.[22]

Jarvis Garrett, drawing on family history (he was not yet three in 1908), recounted:

> *"At the moment of departure, Garrett asked that he be handed his shotgun, saying he would get some birds on the way back."* [23]

The gun Garrett asked for was an unusual 12-guage, folding shotgun, manufactured by the Burgess Gun Company of Buffalo, New York. The gun was sold with a specially designed scabbard that could be worn around the waist or under a coat. With a quick motion, the gun owner could grab the stock butt, just as one would a pistol grip, and flip the barrel up so that it locked in place, ready to fire.[24] The gun did not require assembly before it could be used, as some sources have alleged.[25]

> *"No sooner had they left than Mrs. Garrett noticed that her husband had forgotten to take his overcoat. She gave it to her daughter, Pauline, who mounted her horse and galloped in pursuit. She caught up with the two men at the entrance gate to the ranch."* [26]

In 1968, 60 years after the event, Willis Walter said in an interview that Adamson and Garrett stopped their buggy that morning to water their horses at his place located just south of the town of Organ.[27] That this actually happened is doubtful. It is not men-

The . Burgess . "Folding . Gun"

1895   1895

Especially Adapted for United States Marshals, Banks, Prisons, Etc.

ALSO, A GOOD FIELD GUN.

The barrel and stock parts fold together to shorten the gun to the length of the barrel, and can be conveniently carried in a holster with belt or in a valise, or kept in a place where a long gun could not be concealed, or made available.

It will take the place of a revolver and do much better and more certain work. Holds six 12-guage cartridges and can be drawn from holster and shot six times in three seconds.

At 40 yards, loaded with buck shot, it gives a spread of about three feet with strong penetration, and is a very destructive weapon up to 100 yards. When choked bored, it may fully take the place of longer and heavier guns for field shooting.

It is the simplest, quickest and handsomest saddle gun ever brought before the public.

FOR SALE BY

TURNER HARDWARE COMP'Y
MUSKOGEE.

Advertisement for the Burgess "folding" shotgun carried by Garrett on his fatal trip to Las Cruces, February 29, 1908. *Muskogee Phoenix,* May 25, 1895.

tioned by Adamson when he recounted the events of the day under oath, nor was it necessary to water the horses for the trip to Las Cruces.[28] This story parallels a story told by Louis B. Bentley that Adamson and Garrett stopped at his store in Organ on the way to Las Cruces that morning – and that Garrett *"looked angry:"*

"Long afterward, he [Bentley] used to tell how Pat's jaw shook as the talked." [29]

Bentley's story is not supported by Adamson's testimony and is believed by most researchers to be made up.

The description of the events that follow are derived from Carl Adamson's sworn testimony in Brazel's preliminary examination to determine whether there was sufficient evidence to hold Brazel for murdering Garrett.[30]

About a mile past Organ on the way to Las Cruces, Adamson and Garrett saw Brazel ahead of them riding his horse. Brazel had a Winchester rifle in a saddle holster on his horse. Although neither Garrett nor Adamson knew it, Brazel was also carrying a .45 revolver in the *"waistband of his breeches."* [31] Asked what Brazel was doing when he first saw him, Adamson replied:

"I think when we first seen him he was talking to some fellow in the road and then before we got to him, he [the fellow] started on ahead this way and we passed him."

Adamson could not identify the man to whom Brazel was speaking. A number of writers have suggested the man was Archie Prentice "Print" Rhode.[32] (See page 195.)

When Adamson and Garrett caught up with Brazel, Brazel asked Adamson what time he should meet him in Las Cruces. Adamson replied:

"...I supposed that we would get there about the same time."

Following this brief conversation, Adamson and Garrett passed Brazel. However:

"...when I struck a sandy place in the road I would drive slow and he [Brazel] would catch up with us."

The two parties continued in this manner, with Brazel catching up to the buggy and then dropping behind, for *"over five or six miles – something like that."*

At a point about five miles from Las Cruces, at a moment when Brazel had caught up with the buggy, the men began talking about the deal they planned to sign:

"The conversation came up about a deal I had made with the defendant for 1200 goats and Mr. Brazel told me that there were something over 1800."

Asked how that question came up, Adamson said:

"I don't remember exactly but I think it was Mr. Garrett asked Brazel how it come that he signed a contract with me for 1200 goats when he had 1800 goats and Mr. Brazel answered that he didn't know that he had more than 1200 goats until he counted them."

In response to the larger number of goats, Adamson said:

"...I didn't know whether I wanted the 1800 goats or not and that this might break up the deal with me – the fact is I didn't want the 1200 but I bought them in order to get possession of the ranch that Mr. Garrett had leased to Mr. Brazel."

Asked what was Brazel's reply, Adamson said:

"Well, Brazel says, 'If I don't sell the whole bunch I won't sell none' or he says, 'I will either not sell the 1200 or I will keep the 600 and keep possession of the ranch' or something like that."

Both Garrett and Brazel were getting angry:

"Garrett asked him [Brazel] how he came to sign the contract for 1,200 goats when he had 1,800...?"

Brazel answered that he did not know he had that many goats.

"He and Mr. Garrett went on talking that way and Mr. Garrett said, 'Well, I don't care whether you give up possession of the ranch or not.' He says, 'I can get you off there anyway.' I think Brazel said, 'I don't know whether you can or not.'"

"About then I stopped the buggy to get out to urinate and when I got out of the buggy Mr. Garrett reached over and took the lines and while I was standing there, why I heard Mr. Garrett said, 'Well damn you, if I can't get you off that way, I will another and I will do it now' or something like that."

Note that Adamson was asserting that Garrett explicitly threatened Brazel's life: *"I will do it now."*

Here is what happened next – according to Adamson testifying under oath (the questioner is James M. Hervey, Attorney General for the Territory of New Mexico) The time was between 10 and 11 a.m:

"HERVEY: Where were these people with respect to you, on the front or to the side of you or behind you, at the time you heard the remark?"

"ADAMSON: Mr. Garrett was in the buggy and Brazel was on the horse."

"HERVEY: Where were they with respect to you?"
"ADAMSON: They were to my back."

"HERVEY: You say that Garrett was in the buggy when he made this remark?"
"ADAMSON: I think he was."

...

"HERVEY: Did you turn your face to them at any time?"
"ADAMSON: After these words passed I heard a racket, and I just turned my head like that, and when I turned it Garrett was on the ground."

"HERVEY: How close to the buggy?"
"ADAMSON: About two feet."

"HERVEY: To the side or the front or the back?"
"ADAMSON: To the side."

...

"HERVEY: When you saw him was he all out or was he getting out of the buggy?"
"ADAMSON: No, sir, as I remember I think he was on the ground when I seen him."

...

"HERVEY: How soon after you heard this remark was it that you looked around?"
"ADAMSON: It was just three or four seconds, a very short time...."

"HERVEY: What else happened?"
"ADAMSON: I heard a shot fired."

"HERVEY: Was the shot fired before or after you turned around?"
"ADAMSON: Just about when I turned around."

"HERVEY: Who shot?"
"ADAMSON: I should judge Brazel."

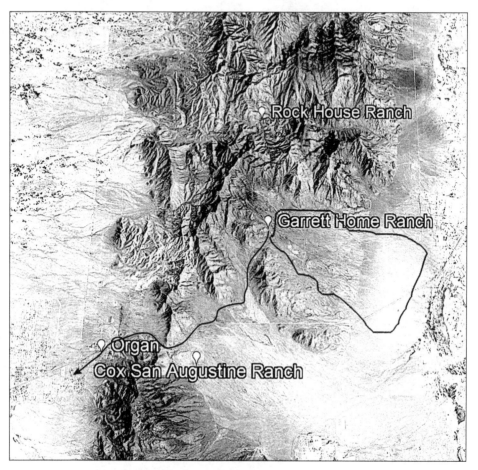

Satellite image showing the location of Garrett's two ranches, town of Organ, and W. W. Cox's San Augustine Ranch. The area enclosed by the black line is the Gold Camp district (see page 154). The line with the arrowhead indicates the route that Garrett and Carl Adamson travelled on February 29, 1908, to the spot where Garrett was killed. This is the normal route that Garrett took to get to Las Cruces from his Home Ranch. The distance between the Rock House Ranch and Garrett's Home Ranch is about 30 miles. The mountain range to the north of Organ is the San Andres Mountains. The range to the south is the Organ Mountains.

"HERVEY: What makes you think so?"

"ADAMSON: Well I didn't see him but I judge he was the one that done the shooting."

...

"HERVEY: What was the defendant [Brazel] doing, what was his attitude?"

"ADAMSON: When I first seen the defendant he was sitting on the horse with a six shooter in his hand."

"HERVEY: Any other shot?"
"ADAMSON: Yes, another."

"HERVEY: How soon after the first one?"
"ADAMSON: Well, as quick as a man can cock a pistol."

"HERVEY: Who shot it?"
"ADAMSON: Brazel."

"HERVEY: Did you see him?"
"ADAMSON: Yes sir."

"HERVEY: In what direction was that shot fired?"
"ADAMSON: In the direction of Garrett."

"HERVEY: When you first turned around at this first shot what did Garrett do?

"ADAMSON: After the first shot Garrett kind of staggered, and staggered back and fell."

"HERVEY: What was the attitude of Garrett, his position with respect to the defendant [Brazel]?"
"ADAMSON: When I looked he was facing him."

"HERVEY: Were they facing each other?"
"ADAMSON: Well, I rather think Brazel was kind of sideways."

"HERVEY: Had Garrett commenced to stagger as you looked around?"
"ADAMSON: Yes sir."

"HERVEY: So you didn't see him standing upright at all?"
"ADAMSON: No sir, I think when I seen Garrett the first shot had been fired and he was staggering."

...

"HERVEY: What did you do after this second shot was fired?"
"ADAMSON: One of my horses started to run and I grabbed the lines and wrapped them as quickly as I could around the hub of the wheel and went back to where the defendant and Mr. Garrett was."

"HERVEY: Where was Garrett?"
"ADAMSON: Lying on the ground."

"HERVEY: Was he dead?"

"ADAMSON: Well, he never spoke a word. When I got to him, he was just stretching out, kind of this way, and grunted a little, that is all."

"HERVEY: Did he die?"
"ADAMSON: Yes sir."

...

"HERVEY: What did you do then?"
"ADAMSON: I got in the buggy and came into Cruces."

"HERVEY: Anyone with you?"
"ADAMSON: Mr. Brazel came in with me."

"HERVEY: Did you make any examination of the body?"
"ADAMSON: No sir. I was badly frightened myself and did not know what to do."

"HERVEY: Did either of you disturb the body in any way or touch it?"
"ADAMSON: No sir, all I did was to take the lap robe out of the buggy and cover him up, but I don't remember touching the body. I came back about 12 to 1."

"HERVEY: How long did you and the defendant stay after the shooting?"
"ADAMSON: Not more than three or four minutes, a very short time."

Adamson provided the following additional details when cross-examined by the attorney representing Brazel, Herbert B. Holt. (Yes, this is the same Holt who had represented Garrett in his legal defense in the matter of the foreclosure of his ranches and livestock by the Albuquerque Bank of Commerce):

"HOLT: Was Mr. Garrett armed?"
"ADAMSON: Yes sir, he had a shot gun."

"HOLT: Was it loaded?"
"ADAMSON: I didn't know that it was but I have since heard that it was. That they took out the shells out there where the body was found."

"HOLT: Was the body in the same position when you went out with the coroner's jury as it was when you left it?"
"ADAMSON: I think it was."

"HOLT: What kind of shotgun was it that Mr. Garrett had?"
"ADAMSON: I don't know what kind it was. I had never seen anything like it – don't think there is another one like it. It breaks right up and you can put it in a small case."

"HOLT: Where was the shot gun?"
"ADAMSON: When I got down the shot gun was between Mr. Garrett and myself."

"HOLT: Was it pointing up or down?"
"ADAMSON: The muzzle was pointing down."

"HOLT: Did you hear the defendant [Brazel] say anything about that moment?"

"ADAMSON: He says, 'This is hell' or something that way. I think maybe he asked me 'What must I do or something?'"

"HOLT: Did the defendant surrender to you?"
:ADAMSON: Yes sir."

"HOLT: Did you ask him to?"
"ADAMSON: I didn't ask him to surrender to me but I told him he had better surrender and he said 'All right.'"

"HOLT: Did he give you his arms?"
"ADAMSON: He gave me his revolver."

"HOLT: Did you give it to the sheriff in the same condition?"
"ADAMSON: Yes, I just took the pistol and put it in the bottom of the buggy."

"HOLT: Did you accompany the defendant to jail?"
"ADAMSON: Yes sir." (33)

After hearing Adamson's courtroom testimony, many observers said his testimony left them with unanswered questions. (This issue will be addressed in the next chapter.)

Coroner's Jury

Brazel, with Adamson trailing in the buggy, rode into Las Cruces and voluntarily surrendered to Dona Ana County Sheriff Felipe Lucero. Twenty years later, Sheriff Lucero recalled the moment as follows:

"I was getting ready to go to lunch...when the door to the sheriff's office opened and in walked Wayne Brazil, looking hurried and upset. He had his gun in his hand, and as he came up to my desk he laid it down in front of me."

"'Lock me up, I've just killed Pat Garrett!' he said. I laughed at him, saying, 'What you trying to do, Wayne, josh me?' But he insisted he'd just shot and killed Pat Garrett with his 45 out on the Organ road. I gave him a second look and saw he wasn't joking. I put his gun into the safe and locked him up in a cell."

"'The man who was with Pat when I killed him,' Wayne told me, 'is outside the jail sitting in Pat's buggy. He's a man named Adamson, and he saw the whole thing and knows I shot in self-defense.'" [34]

Sheriff Lucero quickly organized a coroner's jury consisting of Justice of the Peace Manuel Lopez, and Las Cruces citizens D. F. Baker (jury foreman), Hugh Clary, Vincent B. May, Cesario S. Pedragon, J. F. Sattley, and Fay Sperry. These men knew Garrett well and could readily identify him. The coroner's jury, accompanied by Sheriff Lucero, Dr. William C. Field, and Adamson, rode out to the scene of the killing.

Sheriff Lucero described the death scene as follows:

"I found Pat in the spot Wayne had described, laying flat on his back in the sand, one leg drawn up, his gun lying near him. We could plainly see the wheel

Coroner's jury report on the death of Patrick Floyd Garrett, February 29, 1908. This report was found in April, 2017, in the Dona Ana County Courthouse, in a box of unexamined legal records, after being lost for over six decades. Courtesy Dona Ana County Clerks Office.

tracks of the buggy and the impression of the horses' hooves in the sand, the depressions they'd made when they'd plunged at the sound of the shots. I trailed the tracks back for about two miles and saw where the horse Wayne had been riding joined the buggy at the old chalk hill."

"It was plain to see the team and the horse had been walked side by side, the men apparently talking together as they rode." [35]

The coroner's jury produced its official report on returning to Las Cruces. The report read:

"We the undersigned Justice of the Peace and Grand Jury have attended the investigation of the body of Pat Garrett who was reported dead within limits of Precinct No. 20 of County of Dona Ana, territory of New Mexico on about 5 miles north east of the town of Las Cruces and find the deceased came to his death by one Wayne Brazel." [36]

Dr. Field in a 1939 newspaper interview described the death scene as follows:

"There was poor Pat, lying in the sand. I made a careful physical examination of the body. Pat had been shot twice, once in the head, once in the body. He was lying flat on his back, one knee drawn up."

"His clothes were open and disarranged, showing that he had gotten from the buggy to relieve himself at the time he was killed. He'd taken the glove from his left hand, but a heavy driving glove was still on is right hand. I couldn't help but ponder on that point. It would have been difficult handling a gun with that glove on his hand...."

"Pat's gun lay parallel to his body about three feet from him. It was a shotgun, the kind he generally carried, broken, in its scabbard. It lay without any sand kicked up around it."[37]

Sheriff Lucero and Dr. Field's 31-year-old descriptions match the descriptions of the death scene published in the newspapers at the time of the killing:

"The body was lying on its back, the arms outspread. The shotgun, loaded with No.8 shot, was lying three feet away and the trousers of the dead man, it is said, were unbuttoned." [38]

With the investigation at the death scene completed, Garrett's body was removed to Strong's Undertaking Parlor, arriving there at about 3:30 p.m. Reverend H. C. Strong's parlor was not the only undertaking establishment in Las Cruces, but it was the most respected, and the only one using modern embalming techniques. Strong explained his practice to the local newspaper:

"[Strong's Undertaking Parlor uses a new] fumigating apparatus which forces the fumigating gas through the [casket] keyhole and is the only absolutely sure destroyer of the consumptive germ. This is the same apparatus recently installed by the Southern Pacific Railway to fumigate the sleeping cars on their lines." [39]

Dr. William C. Field. Dr Field visited the site of Garrett's killing and performed the autopsy on Garrett's body. *The New Mexico Sentinel,* April 23, 1939.

It was discovered that Strong had no casket long enough to accommodate Garrett's six-feet, five-inch height, so one that would fit was ordered from Nagley & Kaster in El Paso. The casket arrived the next morning by train.[40]

Autopsy

Dr. Field conducted the autopsy. Here are his findings, as he recalled them in a newspaper interview in 1939:

> *"Later at the undertaking parlor I made an autopsy on Pat. He'd been shot twice by soft-nosed bullets from a .45, one shot hitting him in the back of the head and emerging just over the right eye. The second shot was fired when Pat was nearly on the ground, the bullet striking in the region of the stomach and ranging upward."*

> *"I cut this bullet [the second] out behind the shoulder. I was sure he'd been shot in the back of the head because when I examined the hole [the hair was] driven inward into the wound."* [41]

The first bullet, which was at the death scene, was not found.

Dr. Field's description of Garrett's head wound requires that Garrett's head be turned away from the shooter and tilted slightly at the moment the bullet entered the back of the head, which requires a gun held at or above head level, as would be the case if fired by a man on horseback. The description of the second wound suggests that Garrett was in the air falling backwards, more or less parallel to the ground, when hit by the second shot.

Garrett's Last Check

When Garrett's clothes were searched, something surprising was discovered in his pocket – an un-cashed $50 dollar check and accompanying letter from Governor George Curry. Governor Curry had received the following letter from Garrett some days earlier and had responded to Garrett's anguished plea by sending him the desperately needed money:

> *"I am in a hell of a fix. I am flat broke. I have been trying to sell my ranch, but no luck. For God's sake, send me $50.00."* [42]

Asked years later in an interview about this last communication from Garrett, Curry made the following snide comment:

> *"Fortunately, Pat Garrett had not yet had time to cash my check."* [43]

A odious comment by someone who lacked the honor to pay off a loan from which he had received the benefit, allowing the debt to fall solely on Garrett's shoulders, causing Garrett horrendous financial hardship. Curry's $1,000 loan from the Albuquerque Bank of Commerce in 1890, which Garrett had generously co-signed, was the central cause of Garrett's financial downfall. Absent the loan foreclosure, he would not have been forced to sell his ranches.

George Curry, shortly before his death in 1947. Curry took out a loan in 1890 from the Albuquerque Bank of Commerce that Garrett co-signed. Curry never repaid the loan. The bank went after Garrett for repayment, not Curry. The resulting lawsuit was the central cause of Garrett's financial downfall. Courtesy Center for Southwest Research and Special Collections, UNM.

Chapter 10 | Aftermath

The news of Garrett's killing shot across the country. Sunday morning newspaper editions (March 1) from California to New York reported his killing on the front page, in long articles, detailing his resume as the killer of Billy the Kid, lawman, customs collector at El Paso, and rancher in Las Cruces.[1] The *Los Angeles Times* headed its article *"President's Friend, Pat Garrett, Killed,"* noting:

> *"The President never missed an opportunity to visit Pat Garrett when he was in the famous gun man's territory, and when Garrett went to Washington on political or official business, he was always the personal guest of the President."* [2]

Most newspapers lavished praise on Garrett, calling him *"a man of rare bravery and nerve,"* and noting the critical role he played in bringing the law to New Mexico.[3]

Garrett's two oldest daughters, Elizabeth and Annie, were living in El Paso, where they would have read of Garrett's killing in the *El Paso Times* or the *El Paso Herald.* Garrett's wife and kids at the Home Ranch, however, were not notified of Garrett's killing until about 1:30 p.m. Sunday, more than 24 hours after the event.[4] Apolinaria immediately brought her family to Las Cruces, accepting Oscar Lohman's offer to lodge at his house.[5] Frank Adams, Garrett's foreman, was left in charge of the ranches.[6]

Garrett's friend Major W. H. H. Llewellyn sent Governor Curry a two-page letter, detailing what he understood about the killing: that Garrett and Brazel had quarreled on the road to Las Cruces, that Garrett had *"jumped out"* of the buggy and threatened Brazel, and that Brazel in response had shot Garrett twice with his pistol, killing him.

Llewellyn quoted coroner's jury member Vincent May:

> *"...he [May] was of the opinion that Pat did not intend to do any thing except run a blazer, that his gun was only loaded with bird shot and that he [Garrett] had evidently thought Brazil would run away when he made the break he did."* [7]

Apolinaria sent Governor Curry a telegram asking for territorial legal help:

> *"No one here to represent territory in murder of Mr. Garret please send some one answer"* [8]

Vincent May, probably unaware of Apolinaria's telegram, sent Governor Curry a telegram counseling the opposite:

> *"Do not think necessary to send any one to investigate murder."* [9]

Governor Curry replied to Apolinaria's telegram with a telegram of condolences. Numerous other telegrams of commiseration flooded the family, including one from President Roosevelt.[10]

Emerson Hough wrote Apolinaria saying the news of Garrett's death was *"inexpressibly shocking."* He added:

"[Garrett] was a brave and noble man. I am sure as though I had seen the whole deed, that he never was killed in any fair encounter. I know how averse he was to going armed or starting any kind of quarrels." [11]

On Monday, March 2, Brazel was still being held in the Las Cruces jail, but without formal charges. To ensure he was not released, Poe Garrett filed a formal complaint at 11:30 a.m. that morning, charging Brazel with murdering Garrett.[12]

Garrett's funeral was scheduled for March 2, but it was postponed when Apolinaria received a telegram from Garrett's brothers in Louisiana that they wanted to attend the funeral.[13] The body, lying in an open casket, was made available for public visiting in the front room of Strong's parlor. Viewers reported:

"The features are only slightly discolored by the concussion of the fatal shot, the only evidence that the deceased met a violent death being the small bullet hole through the left eye brow, a little to the left of the center, and the swollen and blackened condition of the flesh surrounding the eye. His heavy iron grey hair is combed back from his forehead, showing the clear cut features of the fearless fighter in all of their rugged strength." [14]

Stacked around the casket were *"magnificent floral wreaths."* [15]

Doubts About Adamson's Account

Observers began to question Adamson's account of the shooting. It appeared to leave two questions unanswered. One, it did not explicitly account for Garrett being shot in the back of the head. Two, it did not account for the newspaper report alleging that Garrett may have been urinating when he was killed. A lesser problem was that he still had his heavy leather riding glove on his right (shooting) hand.

"Friends of Garrett... are bringing out strongly the fact that Garrett's trousers were unbuttoned when his dead body was found, in support of the contention that he did not jump out of the buggy to kill Brazil, but that he had stepped out and was standing beside the buggy, his back to Brazel, relieving himself, when he was fired upon without warning."

"The undertaker, in support of this theory, declares that... men who knew Garrett declare he never would have attempted to climb out of his buggy with gun in hand to kill a man and turn his back on him in so doing. ...and why was there any necessity for him to lose time getting out of the buggy when he might have shot his man from where he was?" [16]

Brazel Pleads Not Guilty

At 10:10 a.m., Tuesday, March 3, Brazel was brought into court to enter his plea to the charge of murdering Garrett. Justice of the Peace Manual Lopez was presiding, as Judge Frank Wilson Parker, the district judge, was in Silver City on another case.[17]

Asked how he pled to the charge, Brazel replied, *"What's that?"*

"The court interpreter repeated the question, 'are you guilty or not guilty?' and the slayer answered 'not guilty' very firmly and quickly, but without show of emotion, and then turned again to look out of the window at the budding

shrubbery in the yard... He stood throughout the brief proceeding and was apparently oblivious of anything save the shrubbery outside." [18]

Brazel with his behavior was making it clear to those in the courtroom that he was totally unconcerned about any legal jeopardy he might face as a result of killing of Garrett.

Following a brief consultation between the lawyers and Judge Lopez, further proceedings were postponed until the next morning. [19]

The *El Paso Morning News* noted that Miller was still in Las Cruces. He was asked not to leave by the sheriff, so as to be available as a witness. [20]

Preliminary Examination – Morning Session

On Wednesday morning, March 4, Governor Curry, having changed his mind about staying in Santa Fe, arrived in Las Cruces. He brought with him James M. Hervey, New Mexico Attorney General. Governor Curry also ordered Mounted Policeman John A. Beal to come to Las Cruces. [21]

Governor Curry's first action, after breakfast, was to direct Sheriff Lucero to bring Adamson to his hotel room for a meeting. In the presence of Hervey, Governor Curry had Adamson recount the events leading to Garrett's shooting. [22]

Following his meeting with Adamson, Governor Curry told the press he wanted Hervey to serve as the prosecutor in the case. Hervey issued the following statement:

"I came to see that the territory is properly represented. If Brazel committed a murder, I do not want to see him at liberty on the streets." [23]

Brazel's preliminary examination began at 10:30 a.m., with Hervey representing the territory and Herbert B. Holt and William Sutherland representing Brazel. (Holt had represented Garrett in his legal battle with the Bank of Commerce – now, apparently lacking any sense of client loyalty, he was defending Brazel for killing Garrett.) Adamson was present as a prosecution witness. Asked about this, Adamson said:

"[He] is in hope that he can get away and drive down to El Paso this afternoon in time to catch the train for his home in Roswell. He came over expecting to return home Saturday or Sunday at the latest, but has been obliged to remain here owing to the killing and says his affairs need his attention at home and that he wishes to return as soon as he can." [24]

Hervey requested that the hearing be adjourned until 2 p.m. to give him time to subpoena additional witnesses. Hervey was considering subpoenaing Miller. The defense agreed to the delay:

"Wayne Brazel, the prisoner, had had a shave since he appeared in court yesterday, and he walked with an elastic step, but seemed to be in a sort of trance till after the close of the brief proceedings, when several of his cowboy and cattlemen friends pressed about him to shake his hands."

"He was asked by The [El Paso] Herald man how he was feeling, and he replied: 'I am feeling bully,' and he looked it."

James M. Hervey, New Mexico Attorney General, 1907-1909. Undated photo.
Courtesy Palace of the Governors Photo Archives (NMHM/DCA), 105460.

Attorney Herbert B. Holt. Holt defended Garrett against the Albuquerque Bank of Commerce suit. He later defended Wayne Brazel against the charge of murdering Garrett. Undated photo. Courtesy Archives and Special Collections, NMSU.

"Sheriff Lucero said this morning that Brazel slept well last night and that he ate heartily at supper and at breakfast and did not seem to be worrying in the least about himself or the crime with which he is charged."

"Miss Annie, one of the daughters of the dead man, was in court, accompanied by Mrs. Felipe Lucero. Poe Garrett, son of the deceased, was also present."

"Gov. George Curry, a personal friend of the slain man, occupied a seat in the jury box... during the brief session...."

"Prior to convening of court, the governor viewed the remains of his old friend at the undertaking parlors and called on Mrs. Garrett and her daughters." [25]

During Governor Curry's visit to the family, he promised to do something to help Elizabeth. He made good on this promise three months later by appointing Elizabeth to the faculty of the New Mexico Institute for the Blind.[26]

Preliminary Examination – Afternoon Session

Brazel's preliminary examination continued at 2 p.m., March 4, as was agreed to in the morning session. Adamson was the only witness. Hervey did the questioning for the prosecution and Holt for the defense.

Adamson's account of the killing is related in Chapter 9 (pages 127-133). Adamson was not asked by Hervey to explain how it happened that Garrett's trousers were, supposedly, unbuttoned when he was shot. This alleged detail had been reported in the newspaper, so Hervey certainly would have known it. If the *crime scene evidence had confirmed* it – and Hervey and Adamson had both viewed the dead body – Hervey would have been legally bound to question Adamson about it. (See page 175 for a discussion.)

Adamson claimed that he got out of the buggy to urinate, and was facing away when the first shot was fired. This was convenient, whether made up or not, because it removed him from supporting one side or the other as far as reporting seeing a threatening physical act by Garrett, such as unfolding his shotgun. But, by testifying that Garrett said:

'Well damn you, if I can't get you off that way, I will another and I will do it now' or something like that." [27]

Adamson was providing all the evidence needed under the law in 1908 to enable Brazel to successfully claim self defense, something Adamson may or may not have known. (See page 175 for a discussion).

Adamson's testimony seemed confusing on one point, but was not. He said that when he turned and first saw Garrett, Garrett was already on the ground:

"HERVEY: When you saw him was he all out or was he getting out of the buggy?"
"ADAMSON: No, sir, as I remember, I think he was on the ground when I seen him." [28]

He said later that when he turned and saw Garrett, Garrett was *"staggering."* But when he said Garrett was on the ground, he meant standing, not lying, on the ground.

"HERVEY: When you first turned around at this first shot what did Garrett do?"

"ADAMSON: After the first shot Garrett kind of staggered, and staggered back and fell." [29]

A key piece of evidence was the unidentified *"racket"* that Adamson testified to hearing immediately before the first shot was fired. He asserted this under both Hervey's and Holt's questioning:

"HERVEY: Did you turn your face to them at any time?"

"ADAMSON: After these words passed I heard a racket, and I just turned my head like that, and when I turned it, Garrett was [standing] on the ground."

"HOLT: Then you heard the noise or racket immediately followed by the discharge of the pistol?"

"ADAMSON: All that happened almost all the same time." [30]

It is obvious that both Hervey and Holt recognize the source of the racket. It was the sound the buggy made as Garrett climbed out – a detail that directly contradicted the newspaper accounts that Garrett was urinating when he was shot.

Another critical piece of evidence was that Adamson said that Garrett's shotgun was on the ground between Garrett and the buggy. (The buggy tracks at the scene would have shown if this was true.) The shotgun's location there was consistent with Garrett being shot just after he jumped out of the buggy and spun around so he could grab the shotgun (putting the back of his head in Brazel's gun sight).

Hervey's goal in this hearing was not to convict Brazel of murdering Garrett, but simply to present enough evidence to enable the judge to rule that Brazel be held for trial. That was easily achieved by Hervey's questioning.

Holt, in his questioning of Adamson, laid a firm groundwork for a claim of self-defense by Brazel.

At the conclusion of the preliminary examination, Judge Lopez ruled that Brazel be held for trial. Holt asked for bond. Hervey acceded and recommended a bond of $10,000, which the judge accepted. [31]

W. W. Cox arranged the bond, soliciting $1,400 from seven different sureties (one stood for $1,500):

"He [Cox] had no trouble raising that amount.... he could easily have raised a hundred thousand.... It was the desire of Mr. Cox that the bondsmen should not be selected entirely from among the cattlemen of the section, as he did not want to create the impression that it was a cattleman's fight. For this reason he selected the bondsmen from the merchants, physicians, farmers, and cattlemen of the county." [32]

Brazel was held in the court until his bond was raised. He then rode out of town with Cox for Cox's San Augustine Ranch. [33]

Miller was undoubtedly pleased he had not been called as a witness in the examination. He left Las Cruces that afternoon (March 4) for El Paso. [34]

Visit to Death Site

Following the conclusion of the afternoon session of the preliminary examination on March 4, Hervey had Adamson take him and Dr. Field to the site of the killing. Adamson was asked to explain again what had happened, which he did, *illustrating the events in situ,* and giving an account that *did not differ* from his sworn courtroom testimony.[35] Note, also, according to the newspaper report of this death site visit, Hervey was accompanied *only* by Adamson and Dr. Field. (No Fred Fornoff! See page 197.)

In an interview in 1938 with lawyer and author William A. Keleher, Hervey said that while at the death site he asked Adamson how he would explain that Garrett was shot in the back of the head, and Adamson said he *"could not explain this."* [36]

In 1961, *True West* published the text of a manuscript that Hervey wrote before he died in 1953 giving his memories of and speculations on Garrett's killing. In that account, Hervey wrote that he found a rifle shell at the death site:

> *"While Fred Fornoff and Adamson were talking... I walked back some thirty or forty feet to where Adamson said he had stood and at that place I happened to spy a new Winchester rifle shell on the ground."* [37]

Yet, this possible evidentiary find *is not mentioned* in Hervey's 1938 interview with lawyer Keleher, a very surprising omission, casting *serious doubt* on the statement made in the 1953 article that Hervey wrote fifteen years later.

Nor does the coroner's jury report any such finding. It was the duty of the coroner's jury to thoroughly investigate the *observable* facts of the killing.

Sheriff Lucero reported that on the day of the killing:

> *I trailed the tracks back for about two miles and saw where the horse Wayne had been riding joined the buggy at the old chalk hill."*

No mention there of finding a Winchester rifle shell or tracks suggesting an ambush!

By the time that Hervey was visiting the site on the evening of March 4, it is four days after the killing. The site has undoubtedly been visited – and probably disturbed – by many curious people; even if Hervey had found such a shell, it would have had dubious evidentiary value.

Captain Fornoff supposedly produced a report of the killing for Governor Curry, but that report, if it existed, has been lost.[38] All that is known of the supposed report today is based on a third hand account – what a co-worker of Fornoff's – Fred Lambert – told a friend of Lambert's – Chuck Hornung. According to this third-hand account, Fornoff found a spot near the killing site where there were:

> *"...horse tracks, cigarette remnants, and other signs that indicated, to him [Fornoff], that this site could have served as an ambush nest for an unknown killer."* [39]

For a fuller discussion of the Fornoff Report, and strong evidence that the Fornoff report *never* actually existed, see page 197.

Interviewed at his hotel that night, Hervey said he *"had made no effort at the preliminary to prevent Brazel from getting bond."* He said he *"had not introduced all of the evidence that he had gathered for the prosecution,"* and he expected that *"important facts"* would develop before the case came to trial.[40]

Governor Curry added that he was:

"... of the same opinion as attorney general Hervey, that there are points in the case which have not yet been brought to light...." [41]

Garrett's Funeral

Garrett's funeral service was held March 5, at 3:00 p.m., the day after the preliminary hearing, at Strong's Undertaking Parlor. John L. and Alfred J. Garrett, two of Garrett's brothers, attended, having arrived in Las Cruces the night before:

"[The two brothers] are quiet men and unassuming, these two planters from Louisiana, but they carry with them the quiet dignity and reserved strength that made Pat Garrett the strong New Mexican that he was. They speak quietly, but there is a depth of feeling in their assertion, a note of finality in the completed utterance, that carries conviction." [42]

The pall bearers were Governor Curry, Morgan O. Llewellyn, Harry Lane, Charles A. Kinnes, Numa G. Buchoz, Hugh Clary, and Tom Powers.

Following a non-religious service in the funeral parlor, a long procession of mourners followed Garrett's body to the Odd Fellows Cemetery, where the remains were laid to rest in a grave next to his daughter Ida. At the burial site, Tom Powers read the funeral oration given by Robert G. Ingersoll upon the death of his brother Ebon. (Governor Curry was asked to read the oration, but declined, pleading political repercussions.[43]) Here is part of the address:

"Life is a narrow vale between the cold and barren peaks of two eternities. We strive in vain to look beyond the heights. We cry aloud, and the only answer is the echo of our wailing cry." [44]

Ingersoll, who died in 1899, was well-known during his life as an advocate of atheism. *The El Paso Herald,* in reporting on Garrett's funeral, wrote:

"Garrett was an atheist and a great admirer of Ingersoll and it is said that he had requested some of his closest friends to have Ingersoll's oration read over his grave." [45]

The charge of atheist had been hurled at Garrett at various times during his life by his enemies. For example, in 1898, Oliver Lee had called Garrett an *"infidel"* during their letter war over the Wildy Well shooting (see page 40.)

The atheist allegation was immediately denied:

"The statement in an afternoon paper that Pat Garrett was an atheist is emphatically denied by friends in this city. He was an Elk, and if he had been an atheist he could never have become an Elk without deliberately perjuring himself; and Pat Garrett's friends say that he would not make solemn oath to a lie to gain admission to any lodge." [46]

The cemetery stone placed over Garrett's grave was paid for by the Elks Association. The stone was stolen in the 1930s, and text on the stone has been lost to time.[47]

For more details on the Garrett family plot in the Las Cruces Odd Fellows Cemetery, see Appendix A.

The Garrett family published the following *"Card of Thanks"* in the Las Cruces and El Paso newspapers:

"To the many friends who have so kindly and generously assisted and sympathized with us in this our time of bereavement we wish in some small measure to tender to them our heartfelt gratitude and appreciation."

"Mrs. P. F. Garrett, And Family" [48]

Conspiracy Allegations

The day before the funeral (March 4), Poe Garrett received an anonymous letter mailed from El Paso claiming to be from a friend of the family. It was *"printed with a lead pencil on cheap paper."* The letter stated that:

"Brazel shot Garrett from the back and that another shot him from the front."

"Hanging without trial is what Brazel should get." [49]

The letter praised Garrett as *"one of the best men that ever lived,"* and said that Poe Garrett, too, would be murdered. The letter was signed: *"One Who Knows."*

Asked about the rumors swirling around Garrett's killing, Garrett's brother Alfred said:

"I believe from what I have heard that my brother was killed as the result of a conspiracy. We are law abiding citizens, and we expect the law to take its course."

"If the killing were justifiable, we do not want an innocent man to suffer, but if it should be proven murder, we want his slayer to pay the penalty." [50]

Contributing to the talk of conspiracy was an event that occurred at Garrett's Home Ranch two nights before Garrett was killed:

"Frank Adams, who has worked for several years for Garrett, says that he was awakened by a noise Thursday night and that he saw two figures sneaking up to the [ranch] house. He awakened Garrett, but Garrett said he thought it must be dogs. Next morning Adams investigated and found the tracks of two men and the horses in a ravine below the house, where they had been tethered." [51]

On April 22, 1908, Annie Garrett received an anonymous letter, which, like the anonymous letter to Poe, was hand-printed with a pencil. The writer said Annie should have "PRINCE RHODES" (Print Rhode) arrested, that he had assisted in killing Garrett. The writer said he was afraid to make himself known in the letter, but would when *"THINGS IS RIGHT."* The writer said that Annie should let the public know the killing was a *"PUT UP JOB."* [52] See opposite page for a copy of the letter.

For a discussion of the conspiracy theories that began to cling to Garrett's killing, including the modern versions, see Chapter 13.

LAS. CRUCES N.M

MISS.

ELPASO. TEX.

DEAR. FRIND. WHY. DONT. YOU.
OR. SOM. OF. YOUR. FRIENDS. HAVE.
PRINCE. RODES. ARRESTE. AND PUT
UNDER BOND FOR. HELPING TO KILL
YOUR FATHER THERE IS NO DOUBT
BUT. WHAT HE. WAS WITH BRAZEL
AND. ADAMSON ON. THAT DAY.
HE WAS. SEEN COMING FROM. THAT
PLACE THE SAME DAY HE KNOWS. ALL
AND SO DO I. AND. IF CAN GET HIM
UNDER. BOND I WILL. GET A ROUND
IN. TIME. I AM AFRAID TO LET MY
SELF BE KNOWN. FOR. A WHILE
YO. SURELY. KNOW. THAT WAS WHY
HE WAS. IN THAT COUNTRY
COME. THERE TO HELP DO THE. DEED
OVER

Page one of the anonymous letter sent to Annie Garrett accusing Print Rhode of killing Garrett. Microfilm roll Roll 54, Frame 201-202. Courtesy State Archives of New Mexico.

Page two and envelope of the anonymous letter sent to Annie Garrett accusing Print Rhode of killing Garrett. Mailed April 20, 1908, from Las Cruces. Received in El Paso April 22, 1908. Microfilm roll Roll 54, Frame 201-202. Courtesy State Archives of New Mexico.

Chapter 11 | Wayne Brazel

Jesse Wayne Brazel was one month and 29 days past his 31st birthday on the fateful morning when he shot and killed Garrett. He was born on December 31, 1876, in Greenwood City, Kansas. His father was Jesse Madison Brazel, his mother Olive Alvery.[1]

A year later, baby Wayne and his parents moved to Brown County, Texas. They were accompanied on this move by Jesse Madison Brazel's older brother, William W. Brazel, W. W.'s wife Sarah J. (Conner) Brazel, and their three children: Marrieta, Clarissa, and William W., Jr. Also moving to Texas as adopted members of W. W.'s family were Mary Elizabeth Conner, James P. Conner, and William A. Conner. These last were the adult siblings of W. W. Brazel's wife Sarah.[2]

Prior to the move, W. W. Brazel was familiar with that area of Texas. In 1872, on a trip to Waco, Texas, to purchase cattle, W. W. Brazel spotted a man who he identified as George W. Petty, who was wanted for a murder in Greenwood County. He reported his sighting to Greenwood County authorities, who, six years later, were able to capture and bring Petty to justice.[3]

In August, 1882, the two Brazel families moved to Lincoln County, New Mexico, where Wayne's father and W. W. Brazel took up adjoining homesteads along Eagle Creek.[4] A visitor to W. W. Brazel's ranch a year later wrote the following:

> *"Monday found us headed for Eagle Creek, the home of Capt. W. W. Brazel.... The Capt. located his farm but a little over a year ago, squatting without seed or other requisites save an industrious family, a few head of cattle, and large experience."*

> *"On his plantation we saw cabbages bigger than the head of a Vera Cruz poet... potatoes large as Eastern squashes... [and] squashes over 50 pounds in weight...."* [5]

W. W. Brazel was Captain of Company F of the Sixteenth Regiment of the Kansas State Militia during the American Civil War. He formed the company. He never saw action in any Confederate engagements, but he did participate in actions against Native Americans.[6]

A year after the Brazels' took up their places on Eagle Creek, Garrett bought land on Eagle Creek, and moved his family there.[7] The Brazels and Garretts became well acquainted. In February, 1886, Garrett *"presented Capt. W. W. Brazel with a fine watch and chain,"* in recognition of Brazel's public service.[8]

It is likely that this recognition was for the log-cabin school house that W. W. Brazel erected on his property and gifted to the Eagle Creek community. During the 1891 school year, the teacher at this school was Eugene Manlove Rhodes.[9]

Original W. W. Brazel homestead on Eagle Creek, Lincoln County. Undated photo.
Courtesy Nita Stewart Haley Memorial Library and J. Evetts Haley History Center.

William W. Brazel. Undated photo. Courtesy Nita Stewart Haley Memorial Library
and J. Evetts Haley History Center.

Cabin built by W. W. Brazel and donated to Lincoln County to serve as the Eagle Creek community school house. Eugene Manlove Rhodes taught here in 1891. Undated photo. Nita Stewart Haley Memorial Library and J. Evetts Haley History Center.

Shooting Frank Terrell

On May 24, 1887, Wayne Brazel was the only witness to the shooting of Frank Terrell by William A. Conner. Wayne, in a sworn statement, described the event as follows:

"I am ten years old. I know that it is wrong to tell what is false and that it would be wrong to swear to it."

"About nine o'clock in the morning I was by myself coming down Eagle Creek.... [Will Conner and Frank Terrell] were at a field a little ways above Uncle William Brazel's when I first saw them. Will Conner was on the other side of the creek and going up and Frank Terrell on this side coming down."

"He hollered to Frank to stop and Frank stopped and got off of his horse and walked around the fence. Will Conner got about as close to him as those three trees (about 40 yards) and threw down his gun on him – pointed it towards him. I was not close enough to see if it was cocked, but I saw him throw a cartridge in his gun before he got there. Frank jerked up his pistol and shot. Then Will shot, and I broke and ran as hard as I could. I was on horseback.... I never heard anything said by Conner as he drew down his gun."

"When Conner drew down his gun on Frank, Frank was standing with his pistol in his hand.... When he [Frank] drew down the gun he did it as if he intended to shoot." [10] *[Signed with an X.]*

Even at the age of 10, Wayne understood the legal significance of self-defense.

Jesse Madison, Wayne's father, in a sworn statement, said that he learned of the shooting only when Conner came to his house:

> *"[Will Conner told me that] he and Frank had had a fight and he guessed he had killed him and he wanted me to go and see him before he died, so Frank could tell me how it started."*

> *"Conner told me he met Frank by the fence and Frank got off his horse and took out his six shooter and laid it on the fence. He (Conner) asked Frank if he was going to take back what he said to him the other day and that Frank said he would not take it back and shot as quick as he said it. Then he (Conner) shot back as quick as he could."* [11]

Jesse Madison jumped on his horse and rode out to the shooting site, followed by William Conner. Frank Terrell's wife was already there, and had brought Frank a hat full of water. Frank Terrell was:

> *"...laying on his face and his arm [was] laying over Conner's gun... he asked me to take the gun. I took the gun and Conner got over the fence and came on about ten feet behind me. I asked him [Frank Terrell] if he was hurt much. He said he was hurt bad. I asked him where he was shot and he said in the leg and the bowels."* [12]

Conner asked Terrell to admit that he, Terrell, was to blame:

> *"Frank said it was no time to talk about it, he was dying."* [13]

The newspaper reported that the cause of the fight was a series of names that Terrell had called Conner previously.[14]

The Conner-Terrell shooting was a family affair. William Conner was the brother of W. W. Brazel's wife Sarah, and Frank Terrell was the husband of W. W. Brazel's daughter Marrieta. (Frank and Marrieta had married 13 months earlier.). [15]

Terrell did not die. He was lucky. The second pistol ball that entered his abdomen turned and travelled inside the skin along his side without breaking the lining of the stomach.[16]

Conner was indicted and tried for attempted murder, but acquitted on the basis of self-defense.[17]

Marrieta Brazel Terrell died June 12, 1888, of unknown causes.[18]

Move to Gold Camp

Following his acquittal, William Conner left Lincoln County and moved to Dona Ana County, where he began gold prospecting in an area on the east side of the San Andres Mountains known as Gold Camp.

Gold Camp was not an actual town – it was a district approximately sixteen miles in length, bound on the north by the Black Mountains and on the south by Bald Mountain (see satellite image on page 130). [19]

On arriving at Gold Camp, Conner:

"...pitched his tent amid the rich croppings of the [area]. The croppings were so numerous he was at first confused as to where to commence sinking, and without hardly noticing what he was doing, he began sinking on a cropping where is now the 200 foot shaft and great dumps of ore of the Mormon Mine." [20]

On December 17, 1889, Conner sold this claim to W. W. Brazel for $600.[21] Conner was unaware of the potential of the claim when he sold it. Seized by the same gold fever as Conner, W. W. Brazel moved to the claim and began mining. By 1892, he had dug the deep shaft noted in the quote above. Why he named it the "Mormon Mine" is unknown. It was quickly recognized as the *"richest [mine] in the district."* [22]

The gold rush frenzy led to some strange beliefs, one which was:

"The water here which is believed to hold gold in solution is wonderfully exhilarating and an excellent substitute for the Keeley Gold Cure." [23]

On November 9, 1893, W. W. Brazel died after a short illness:

"Capt. Brazel was buried on the Mormon claim, in the working of which he had spent the evening of his life." [24]

Following W. W. Brazel's death, there was a campaign by the miners of the district to change the name Gold Camp to Brazel in honor of W. W. Brazel. The proposal failed.[25]

Telles Beating

On February 18, 1893, Levino Telles was travelling by wagon to his home on Eagle Creek when he encountered Jesse Madison Brazel, Wayne Brazel, and W. W. Brazel, Jr., all on horseback.[26]

Riding with Levino were Levino's mother and Olive (Alvery) Brazel, Wayne's mother.

Hard feelings existed between the two parties. Shortly before this encounter, for unknown reasons, Olive Brazel had abandoned her family and moved in with Levino Telles.

Here is what happened next, according to Levino's sworn statement:

"Jesse and Willie Brazel [W. W., Jr.] struck me. Each one had a pistol and each one struck me. My mother and the wife of Jesse Brazel were in the wagon with me."

"...they said nothing before they struck me. We had not quarreled before.... My mother prevented them from going on with the fight. They pushed her. I was hit in the face and the head. I fell to the ground; they continued hitting me after I was down. My mother lay on me with her body to protect me, when they commenced hitting me when I was on the ground. I believe my mother saved me from being killed.... I was senseless after they had beat me." [27]

Wayne did not participate in the attack. In his sworn statement, he said that he knew:

"...that Telles carried a pistol. Did not hear Telles say for whom he carried a pistol, don't know what started the fight – Willie Brazel took out a pistol belonging to Jesse Brazel out of bedding in the wagon that Louis Tellas was

Mormon Mine, located on the White Sands Missile Range. Men unidentified.
Undated photo. Courtesy Archives and Special Collections, NMSU.

Hegan house at Mormon Mine. John Hegan on right. Others unidentified. Undated
photo. Wayne Brazel, Print Rhode, and other Cox cowhands were bunking in
this house at the time that Brazel shot Garrett. Courtesy Archives and Special
Collections, NMSU.

driving. Willie Brazel gave me the pistol and I carried it home. This was before the fight. This pistol was not used in the fight."

"Mother tried to keep them from fighting.... I tried to keep Jesse Brazel from fighting." [28] *[Signed Wayne Brazel]*

Jesse Madison and W. W. Jr. were indicted for attempted murder.[29] The trial was scheduled for mid-1893, but was postponed when Jesse Madison filed a sworn statement asserting that he was presently living at Gold Camp and was too sick to attend court.[30] This led to a postponement until April, 1895, when subpoenas for Jesse Madison and W. W. Jr. were issued requiring their appearance in court.[31] There were no further legal actions, the case apparently being dropped when the defendants ignored the summons.

On October 19, 1895, Sarah Brazel died:

"Mrs. W. W. Brazel, who had been living at the Gold Camp, and who for sometime has been suffering with heart disease and dropsy, started to this city in a buggy for medical aid. The poor woman was beyond the aid of mortal when she reached here, having died in the carriage on the way." [32]

Sarah was buried beside her husband at the Mormon Mine.

Life at Gold Camp

Following W. W. Brazel's death, the house he had built at the Mormon Mine was occupied by W. W. Jr., Jesse Madison Brazel, and Wayne Brazel. Jesse Madison took over as foreman of the Mormon Mine.[33]

"Messrs. Brazel and Bonney have some gold properties in Black Mountain and are preparing to make a test run on ore, using the Mormon mill for that purpose." [34]

Jesse Madison, working with W. W. Cox, established a school in Gold Camp. The first year there were 56 pupils.[35] Wayne's future wife would teach in this school.

On June 7, 1897, Garrett arrested W. W. Brazel, Jr., for the murder of Vicente Sanchez. W. W., Jr. was released when it was determined he was not a participant in the murder.

Wayne preferred working as a cowhand, rather than a miner. In 1898, he was the foreman of the Diamond-X Ranch, but quit over the devastating loss of a girlfriend:

"[Wayne] has thrown up his job and is now preparing to start for Spain, to hunt the lost vessel, since he has lost his best girl. Remember, kind friend, there is hope as long as there is life." [36]

After this episode, Wayne returned to working for W. W. Cox, as he had done many times before.[37]

On March 15, 1905, Wayne's father died in a cave-in at the Mormon Mine. He was working in a shaft about two hundred feet deep, the bottom of which was filled with 35 feet of water:

"Mr. Brazel was at work in a cross-cut on the water level, and while removing a boulder, the timbers gave away and he was caught by the waste rock and carried to the bottom of the shaft."

Brazel cemetery, located on the White Sands Missile Range. 2007 photo.

Brazel cemetery grave maker. Date wrong. 2007 photo.

"A force of men was immediately set at work, but as late as yesterday his body had not been reached. Doctor Johnson of Organ was here yesterday and said that at the rate they were taking the water from the shaft, it would probably be ten days before the bottom would be reached." [38]

It took nine days:

"The body of Jesse [Madison] Brazel was recovered from the bottom of the Mormon mine last Friday afternoon and interred the same day. The body was somewhat bruised and if there had been no water in the bottom of the shaft it is possible he might not have been killed." [39]

Jesse Madison was buried on the Mormon Mine claim next to W. W. and Sarah Brazel.

With Jesse Madison gone, the Mormon Mine went up for sale. On July 16, 1896, it was purchased by a group of investors led by John Hegan.[40] Hegan built a fine house on the property, probably the nicest house in Gold Camp. Using water extracted from the mine, he planted an orchard of fruit trees. At various times in the years that followed, the Hegan house served as a saloon, eatery, and hotel.[41]

Following his father's death, Wayne continued to work as a cowhand for Cox. The local newspaper reported his occasional trip into Las Cruces, but otherwise, Wayne stayed out of the news until the newspaper reported that he had leased Garrett's Rock House Ranch.[42]

At the time of the Rock House Ranch lease, Wayne was living with Print Rhode and several other single men at the Hegan House on the Mormon Mine claim. Hegan had moved out of the house in 1905 and sold the property to W. W. Cox, who used it as a bunk house for his cowhands.[43]

Olive Boyd

Sometime in late 1906, 18-year-old Olive Elizabeth Boyd entered Wayne's life. She met Wayne at W. W. Cox's San Augustine Ranch, where she was working as a children's nanny and tutor.[44] She and 30-year-old Wayne quickly fell in love and began planning to marry.[45]

Olive was born December 21, 1888, in Lake Valley, New Mexico. Her father, Milton A. Boyd, was a railroad foreman. In May, 1906, the family moved to Camp City, a tiny unincorporated community built beside a railroad stop south of Alamogordo.[46] Her father became the post master of Camp City, and ran a small general store.[47] Camp City, later known as Shamrock, then Valmont, no longer exists.[48]

After a year at Cox's ranch, Olive was hired to teach in the little school at Gold Camp, where she taught all grades.[49]

Wayne's decision to lease the Rock House Ranch and get into the goat business was motivated by his strong desire to put himself in a financial position that would justify marrying Olive in the minds of her parents.[50]

Jesse Wayne Brazel, circa 1907. Courtesy Nita Stewart Haley Memorial Library and J. Evetts Haley History Center.

Olive Elizabeth Boyd. Photo taken September 12, 1910, at Silver City, New Mexico. Courtesy Nita Stewart Haley Memorial Library and J. Evetts Haley History Center.

In February, 1912, the Powers Moving Picture Company filmed two silent films on W. W. Cox's San Augustine Ranch. The owner of the movie company and director was Nicholas Powers. This photograph shows the persons who played parts in the second film, a romance in which an American lady flees to the Cox ranch to avoid the unwanted attentions of a wealthy Englishman. Gladys Field played the American lady and Leo White played the Englishman. William W. Cox played the ranch owner and his family members and employees played the ranch cowboys (see *"Screen with a Voice, A History of Moving Pictures in Las Cruces, New Mexico,"* by David G. Thomas, p 33.)

1) William W. Cox, 2) Will Isaacks, 3) Emmitt J. Isaacks, 4) Hal R. Cox, 5) Johnson Davis, 6) James Sterling Rhodes, 7) Jesse Isaacks, 8) Jim W. Cox, 9) A. B. Cox, 10) Jack O'Brien, 11) Gladys Field, 12) Thomas McMahon, 13) Leo White, 14) Enrique Robles, 15) Bill Crosby, and 16) Jess Robinson. Courtesy Archives and Special Collections, NMSU.

Chapter 12 | Wayne Brazel's Trial

Brazel Indicted

On April 3, 1908, the Dona Ana Grand Jury began considering whether to indict Brazel for the murder of Garrett. Carl Adamson was subpoenaed and testified in front of the grand jury – as did Dr. Field.[1]

This was Adamson's *second time* to testify under oath about what he had witnessed. Since his testimony in the preliminary examination a month earlier, the press and public had raised questions about Garrett's killing that the preliminary examination did not seem to answer – what were the explanations for the location of the entry wound and the alleged condition of Garrett's trousers?

These questions would certainly have come up during Adamson's testimony before the grand jury. After three days of deliberations, the jury returned a true bill specifying that Brazel:

> "...unlawfully, feloniously, willfully, deliberately, premeditatedly, of his malice aforethought, and from a deliberate and premeditated design [did] unlawfully and maliciously effect the death of.... Patrick F. Garrett, did kill and murder [him]." [2]

Brazel's trial was set for the October, 1908, term of the Dona Ana District Court "*by consent of both the prosecution and the defense.*" [3]

On May 2, the *Alamogordo News* noted that Brazel was "*very sick*" with the measles.[4]

Adamson Arrested

Carl Adamson's knowledge of the legal jeopardy that Brazel faced evidently had no deterrent effect on his own contemplation of a crime.

On June 21, 1908, Carl Adamson and William Sullivan were stopped by immigration agents three miles south of Tularosa, New Mexico. Adamson and Sullivan were driving a horse-drawn covered wagon. Crammed inside the wagon, hidden from view, were 16 Chinese men.[5]

The agents asked Sullivan who the Chinese were. He replied:

> "*These Chinese belong here, all came from San Francisco.*" [6]

The wagon was escorted to Tularosa, where the two men were arrested and jailed.

The crime had been conceived several days earlier in Thomas Powers' Coney Island Saloon, in El Paso, Texas. Adamson, Sullivan, and John N. Webb met with other persons who were never identified and agreed to smuggle illegal Chinese immigrants from El Paso to northern New Mexico.[7]

After this meeting, Webb rented a wagon and team from an El Paso feed yard. The agreed-on price was four dollars a day, and Webb said he needed the wagon for 12 to 15

The covered wagon Carl Adamson used to smuggle 16 Chinese men into New Mexico. Courtesy U.S. vs Carl Adamson, William Sullivan, and John N. Webb, Case 1287, New Mexico State Records Center and Archives.

The house in Las Cruces to which Apolinaria Garrett moved her family in January, 1909, after selling the Garrett Home Ranch to W. W. Cox. She bought the house January 23, 1909, for $550. The house was torn down in 2002. Undated photo.

days. He instructed the owner to equip the wagon with a covering sheet and a large water keg. The wagon owner was told that the purpose of the wagon rental was prospecting.

On June 18, Adamson went to the feed yard and loaded the wagon with provisions. He rode off in the wagon at sunset that night.[8]

The 16 Chinese, led by two Mexicans, waded across the Rio Grande River from Juarez, Mexico, walked about three miles, and rendezvoused with the wagon. The Chinese were loaded into the covered wagon without being permitted to see the drivers, who were Adamson and Sullivan.

The wagon struck north, across the desert, toward Tularosa.

The next day, about one in the afternoon, Adamson knocked on the door of J. F. Reaves, who lived on an isolated ranch straddling the Texas-New Mexico border. Reaves answered the door:

"[Adamson] said he wanted a team to pull his wagon out; he said he didn't have any load much; he referred to his wife and about what a load he had."

"I says were you hunting help? He said, no, not for myself, but he said, you [do not] often see a big stout man with a sickly wife." [9]

Adamson told Reaves his wagon was stuck in the sand a short distance away. He asked to borrow or rent a team of horses for long enough to pull the wagon loose:

"[Adamson] said his wife was sick... and he was travelling for her health."[10]

Reaves and his son hitched up a team and let Adamson take it.

Later, Adamson returned to Reaves' house with the team and his now freed wagon. He parked his wagon some distance from the house, and neither Reaves nor his son was able to see inside the wagon.[11]

Following Adamson and Sullivan's arrest at Tularosa, they were indicted for conspiracy to smuggle illegal immigrants into the United States. Webb was later indicted on the same charge. The 16 Chinese men, who were Hong Kongese, were found to be in the country illegally and were deported to Mexico.

Adamson and Sullivan's trial began December 7, 1908. They were convicted two days later. Both were sentenced to 18 months hard labor in the state penitentiary. Both appealed their cases, posted bond, and were released pending their appeal decisions.[12]

Apolinaria Sells Home Ranch

On December 5, 1908, Apolinaria sold the Garrett Home Ranch to W. W. Cox. The local newspaper noted that Poe was also planning to sell his ranch, the Rock House Ranch.[13] Apolinaria and Poe were not in a position to operate the ranches without Garrett, even if they had wanted to, which they did not.

On January 23, 1909, Apolinaria bought a two room adobe house in Las Cruces for $550. The funds for this purchase came from the sale of the Home Ranch.[14]

Five months before the move to Las Cruces, Pat Garrett, Jr. developed an abscess on his right leg. He was operated on by Dr. Field. The initial prognosis was good. However, the leg became infected and had to be amputated.[15]

Unidentified, Pauline Garrett, and Apolinaria Garrett, circa 1933. Never before published photo. Courtesy IHSF.org.

The 1910 census shows Apolinaria, Elizabeth, Annie, Poe, Pat Jr., Pauline, Oscar, Jarvis, and Apolinaria's mother Feliciana Valdez Guiterrez living in the tiny Las Cruces house shown on page 164.[16]

Killer of Garrett Confesses

"I am the man who killed Pat Garrett."

"The trouble began when I started to pasture some goats on land I had sub-leased from Brazel, the principal lessee. When we met on the road Garrett started to pull a shotgun from under the seat of the buckboard and I pulled a revolver and fired just in time to save my own life."

"I was tried in Las Cruces and acquitted. Then I skipped out of the county because I was told that Pat's relatives and friends would get on my trail." [17]

This false confession was made by W. D. Whitley to the Denver police on April 16, 1909.

James Miller Lynched

James B. Miller's fate was worse than Adamson's. On April 19, 1909, at about 3:00 in the morning, he was hanged from the rafters of a deserted livery stable by a lynch mob at Ada, Oklahoma.[18]

Miller had been hired by Jesse West and Joe C. Allen to kill former deputy U. S. Marshal Allen "Gus" Augustus Bobbitt. West and Bobbitt were in a vicious, long-running feud that began when West's son Martin was shot. Although the man responsible for the shooting was caught and convicted, West believed that Bobbitt was behind the shooting.[19] When West was arrested after Bobbitt was assassinated, he said:

"I would have killed him on sight. I didn't kill him but the only reason – I didn't get the chance." [20]

On February 27, 1909, at about sunset, Bobbitt was driving a wagon carrying a load of cottonseed when he was hit in the left hip and the left leg by two loads of buckshot fired from a shotgun: [21]

"The shooting occurred in a lonely spot in the road along which Bobbitt had to pass on his way home. Another man driving in a wagon only a few yards behind Bobbitt saw the flashes of the gun and a man approach Bobbitt's wagon after he fell out." [22]

The man driving the second wagon was Robert I. Ferguson, a friend and neighbor. [23]

Bobbitt's wife heard the gun reports and rushed to the scene, where Bobbitt lay dying. Bobbitt *"requested his wife to place his head in her lap."* He told her that he believed he had been shot by a paid assassin, and provided a good description of the shooter before he died.[24]

It is a sign of how poorly Miller planned this killing that by the next day authorities suspected him as the assassin. On March 3, Oscar Peeler, a 17-year old nephew of Miller's was arrested at a house in Ardmore, about 60 miles away. Miller had rented the house some weeks earlier, in preparation for the assassination.[25]

ARDMORE, OKLAHOMA MONDAY MORNING APRIL 19 1909

FOUR MEN PAY PRICE OF BOBBITT'S DEATH
MILLER, ALLEN, WEST AND BURRELL ARE
LYNCHED BY MOB AT ADA THIS MORNING

At Three o'Clock Two Hundred Determined Men Overpowered
Jail Guards, Took Doomed Men From Cells and
Strung Them to Rafters in Old Stable. Work
Done Thoroughly and in Order--
Little Resistance is Made.

Headline announcing the lynching of James B. Miller, Joe C. Allen, Jesse West, and
Berry B. Burrell, *The Daily Ardmoreite,* April 19,1909.

Photo taken by Noah B. Stall of the four men who were lynched in Ada, Oklahoma,
for the assassination of Allen Augustus Bobbitt on April 19, 1909. Left to right:
James B. Miller (wearing hat), Joe C. Allen, Berry B. Burrell, and Jesse West.

On March 4, sheriff deputies arrested John Williamson, the son of Miller's sister. The mare that Miller rode to the location where he shot Bobbitt was identified as belonging to Williamson. Williamson's mare perfectly matched the animal that Ferguson saw the assassin riding before the killing: it was branded "J' with a scar on the left thigh.[26]

Williamson admitted that Miller had come to his house accompanied by Oscar Peeler four days before Bobbitt's killing, and asked to borrow the mare. Miller told Williamson he needed the mare for a cattle deal. Williamson did not want to loan the animal, but Miller said he would ensure that he, Williamson, made good money out of the upcoming deal.

Miller returned to Williamson's house the night of the killing, waking Williamson, who was asleep in bed with his wife. Miller said he was returning the borrowed mare. Williamson noticed the animal was hot and sweaty.[27] Williamson later testified:

> "We fed the pony and went back in the house.... [Miller] sat there and said he was sleepy and had a headache. I told him to wait a few minutes and we would have supper. I told him if he drank some coffee, maybe that would help his head. He drank the coffee and ate a few bites and went to bed." [28]

Put to bed in the same room as Williamson and his wife, Miller slept extremely poorly. The next morning, at breakfast, Williamson asked Miller:

> "...if he had made the deal for the cattle. He said no, but he had made a bigger piece of money, or something to that effect. ...he said he would tell me how he made it after a while" [29]

Miller asked Williamson to rent him a horse and ride with him to the town of Sasakwa, where he could catch a train. While riding along, Williamson asked Miller:

> "...how did you make that piece of money? He told me he had killed a man, he told me not to say nothing about it.... if you do, you are in danger, you are liable to get killed" [30]

Asked who he had killed, Miller said "Bobbitt." Asked how he had killed him, Miller said "a shotgun." Asked what became of the shotgun, Miller said "he throwed it to one side in a branch." [31]

Shortly after the lynching, Oscar Peeler confessed to his part in the crime. Miller had sent him and his sister to Ada in December, 1908, to rent a house as a base of operations. Peeler said that a few weeks later Berry B. Burrell, an associate of Miller's, arrived. Burrell's job in the conspiracy was to identify Bobbitt for Miller. Peeler said that he was paid $150 by Jesse West, that West had paid Miller an unknown amount to kill Bobbitt.[32]

Ada's sheriff learned from Peeler that Joe C. Allen had agreed to pay part of Miller's assassination fee. Burrell was arrested on March 19, in Ft. Worth, Texas.[33] Miller was arrested there twelve days later.[34] West and Allen were arrested April 7 in Oklahoma City.[35] All were brought to Ada for trial.

The carefully planned lynching began late in the evening of April 19, 1909, with a visit by two masked men to the Ada Electric and Gas Company. The night engineer, "at the point of revolvers," was forced to cut off the circuit lighting to the streets.[36]

There were four guards in the jail, two awake and two asleep. Six masked men entered the jail and demanded the keys to the cells, while 20 to 30 men waited outside. When it was found that one of the sleeping guards, Bob Nestor, had the keys, he was roughly awakened by three or four men by yanking his bed covers off. Nestor went for a gun he kept under his bed, and was beaten by a revolver.[37]

Joe Carter, another of the jail guards, described what happened next:

"They took Miller from his cell and fastened a rope around his neck and bound his hands at his back with bailing wire."

"Jesse West was the next man taken out, and the mob says, 'Tell us what you know about this.' West says 'I'll tell you nothing.'"

"The rest of the prisoners then began to plead for their lives." [38]

As the four prisoners were being taken from the jail to be hanged, Miller requested that the diamond stud he was wearing in his shirt be given to a jail guard who had treated him well. He asked that the diamond ring on his finger be sent to his wife. After the hanging, the finger had to be cut off to remove the ring.[39]

The ideal place for the hangings had been found. Behind the jail was an old livery stable with exposed rafters. Miller was the first to be hanged. He asked that his hat not be removed from his head. West was next. He had fought his captors continuously and his body was bloody and bruised when cut down. Burrell and Allen were hanged last.[40]

The four men strangled to death.

Oscar Peeler, who was in the jail with the others, was not molested, apparently because of his age and his lesser role in the conspiracy. Although Peeler was charged as an accessory in Bobbitt's murder, the charge against him was eventually dropped.[41]

None of the lynchers were ever identified. The photo on page 168 was taken by Noah B. Stall before authorities cut down the bodies. It was provided anonymously to the Ardmore police several weeks after the hangings:

"The men... are shown suspended from the rafters in the big vacant barn and the picture is a good likeness of each man and each is easily recognized. The ropes show that slip nooses were used and that death must have come from strangulation.... At the end of the barn may be seen a curious crowd, peering through the latticed doors." [42]

Joseph Stahl Makes Charges

Two days after Miller's lynching, *The Houston Chronicle and Herald* published an interview with Joseph H. Stahl on the killing of Pat Garrett. This interview is the father of today's conspiracy theories regarding Garrett's death. It has most of the elements that are repeated endlessly on the internet today.

Stahl, who had just moved to Houston from Las Cruces, told the interviewer:

"I would like to have seen him [Miller] chained to a tree and roasted alive because he hired a man to kill Pat Garrett...."

"Garrett was killed... about 10 miles from Las Cruces, New Mexico. [Garrett] was decoyed out there at the instigation of W. W. Cox and Oliver Lee, two

noted desperadoes.... Miller was a member of the gang and they paid a cowboy named Wren Brazzel [sic] to do the shooting. "

"I [Stahl] found the body lying just as it fell with the blood oozing out of the hole between the eyes where the bullet came through and I swore I would avenge the murder."

" 'Pat Garrett had... several children. One of them was a blind girl named Lizzie. I led that blind girl up to the coffin and saw her hands flicker over the body until they found the face and when she had found the mouth of the dead man she stooped and kissed it and said: "Poor Papa, they assassinated you; they did not give you a chance." ' " [43]

Stahl went on to tell equally ignorant stories about Billy the Kid (Billy was drunk and in bed with his girlfriend when Garrett shot him) and Oliver Lee (*"[Lee] one time stood off an entire regiment of Mexican soldiers"*).

"[Stahl] was crying when he talked to The Chronicle reporter, partly with joy because he had lived to know that Miller had been hanged and partly with chagrin that Miller met so easy a death."

"Mr. Stahl cites Governor George Currie [sic]... as authority for his statements." [44]

Stahl's assertions appear in all subsequent conspiracy theories.

Wayne Brazel's Trial

Originally schedule for October, 1908, Brazel's trail was postponed a second time to May 3, 1909, 14 months after the killing.

For the October trial, the prosecution had subpoenaed Adamson.[45]

New subpoenas were issued for the May 3 trial. For that trial, the prosecution issued a subpoena for five men: Carl Adamson, Dr. W. C. Field, Hugh Clary, Cesario Pedragon, and Fay Sperry. *Carl Adamson's name was crossed out.* The subpoena showed that *only* Dr. Field, Clary, Pedragon, and Sperry were served a summons by Sheriff Felipe Lucero.[46]

A question that has been asked by Garrett researchers is: *"Why did Adamson not testify at Brazel's trial?"* Their answer has been that he was in jail at the time. This was not true. He was out on bond and could have been subpoenaed and forced to testify. The actual answer is – the prosecution simply decided not to subpoena him for the May trial. [47]

District Attorney Mark B. Thompson was asked by the *El Paso Herald* if Adamson's arrest would adversely impact his ability to testify in Brazel's trial. Thompson replied:

"The last legislature abolished all of the common law restrictions on witnesses and in case Adamson should be convicted and sentenced, he could be brought to Las Cruces to testify without any trouble." [48]

Yet, in spite of this statement, Thompson decided not to subpoena Adamson.

Also subpoenaed by the prosecution from the Western Union Telegraph Company were:

Judge Frank Wilson Parker. Judge Parker presided over Oliver Lee and James Gililland's trial for killing Henry Fountain and Wayne Brazel's trial for killing Garrett. Undated photo. Courtesy Archives and Special Collections, NMSU.

> *"...copies of the telegrams received by and to Wayne Brazel, Carl Adamson,*
> *___ Miller, and W. W. Cox during the months of February and March, 1908."* [49]

The purpose of seeking these telegrams was to look for evidence of a conspiracy between these men to kill Garrett, and to see if the telegrams confirmed the story of the ranches deal between Garrett, Miller, and Adamson.

The defense requested that the court subpoena Miller, but dropped the request when his lynching became known.[50] Clearly, the defense was not worried about anything that Miller might testify to under oath.

The trial opened May 4, 1909. The prosecutor was District Attorney Thompson. Brazel was defended by Albert Fall and Herbert Holt. The judge was District Judge Frank Parker. The first action was the selection of the jury. After five challenges by the defense and none by the prosecution, the following jurors were selected:

Tiburcio Rivas	Casimiro Benavides	Bentura Apodaca
Modesto Aguirre	Santiago Garcia	J. Cordova
Maximo S. Franco	Jose L. Lopez	Pedro Altamirano
Felix Pena	Fabian Samaniego	Francisco Roble, Sr. [51]

Maximo S. Franco was elected jury foreman. A translator was appointed as not all jurors spoke English.

The prosecution opened by calling Dr. Field. Dr. Field had visited the site with the coroner's jury and had performed the autopsy. In an interview 31 years later, Dr. Field said:

> *"I [had] made a careful record of everything I'd found and told the district attorney so. But he said, 'I'll ask for what I want on the witness stand.'"*

> *"Well, I never gave that testimony in detail because I wasn't questioned!"* [52]

Dr. Field was not cross-examined.[53]

Sheriff Filipe Lucero was called. After the killing, Brazel had surrendered to Sheriff Lucero. Lucero's testimony was described by a reporter as *"the most interesting."* [54]

Cesario Pedragon and Fay Sperry were called next, and were the last to testify for the prosecution. As members of the coroner's jury, they would have testified as to what they observed at the death scene.[55]

The defense opened its case by calling Brazel to the stand. There is no trial transcript, so it is impossible to know Brazel's actual words. Brazel was pleading self-defense, so his account of the event would have supported that argument. He would have asserted that Garrett made an explicit threat against him, as recounted by Adamson in his preliminary examination testimony:

> *"About then I stopped the buggy to get out to urinate and when I got out of the buggy Mr. Garrett reached over and took the lines and while I was standing there, why I heard Mr. Garrett said, 'Well damn you, if I can't get you off that way, I will another and I will do it now' or something like that."* [56]

Brazel would have testified that he feared for his life at that moment; and he shot Garrett because he believed that was the *only way* he could save his (Brazel's) life.

Las Cruces courthouse where Wayne Brazel's trial for killing Garrett was held. The courthouse was torn down in 1938. Persons unidentified. Undated photo. Courtesy Archives and Special Collections, NMSU.

Years later, Brazel's brother-in-law John Edgar Boyd, Sr., in a letter, wrote that when Brazel talked about the killing, he said:

> *"He knew plenty about Garrett and was 'skeered' [of him]."* [57]

Following Brazel, defense witnesses Mounted Policeman John A. Beal, James A. Baird, and Jeff Ake testified that they had overheard Garrett threaten Brazel in the days before the shooting.[58] Baird was a friend of Brazel's. Ake was a friend of both Brazel and Garrett. Ake said of Garrett:

> *"Pat Garrett and me was always friendly, and several times I was partners with him in a business deal.... Pat was always honest with me, and I had no kick against him."* [59]

Mounted Policeman Beal's testimony provided the determining collaboration of Brazel's defense to the jurors. He had been ordered to Las Cruces by Governor Curry on the day of Garrett's death to investigate the shooting because he had earlier been assigned to investigate the feud between Garrett and Brazel. The *El Paso Herald* noted:

> *"[Beal] was in this section [Las Cruces] in January [before the shooting] and says the dispute between Garrett and Brazel was in progress at that time, and he made a report on it to the governor."* [60]

Beal had the authority of a territorial policeman, and could testify to the events that led to Garrett's suit against Brazel for herding his goats too close to Garrett's ranch house (see page 121), and to other threats that Garrett may have made against Brazel. Unfortunately, the report that Beal submitted to Governor Curry has been lost.

Beal's role and his crucial importance in Brazel's trial have not been noted before.

After the defense closed, District Attorney Thompson waived making an opening argument:

> *"... attorneys Holt and Fall made brief arguments to the jury for the defense, after which the district attorney closed for the prosecution."*

> *"It took about fifteen minutes for the court to deliver the charge. It was brief, to the point and very clear. The case went to the jury at 5:20 p. m."*

> *"Fifteen minutes later the jury returned with a verdict of 'not guilty' on the ground of self-defense."* [61]

Understanding the Trial Result

In the newspapers at the time, no reporter expressed surprise at the result – acquittal on the ground of self-defense.

Why?

The actual instructions that Judge Parker gave to the jury do not exist, but here are typical instructions to the jury at the time regarding self-defense:

> *"If the circumstances of the shooting were such as to cause an ordinarily prudent man to believe that there was imminent danger to his life or imminent danger of great bodily harm... such circumstances furnishes as complete a defense for the defendant as if the danger actually existed."*

John A. Beal and family. Undated photo taken before his service as a New Mexico mounted policeman and his testimony in Wayne Brazel's defense in Brazel's trial for killing Garrett. Courtesy Kenneth L. Beal.

Jesse Wayne Brazel. Taken about the time of Brazel's trial for killing Garrett. Courtesy Nita Stewart Haley Memorial Library and J. Evetts Haley History Center.

"...it is not essential to the right of self defense that the danger should in fact exist...." [62]

Brazel's account easily met this standard!

The *El Paso Morning Times* wrote:

"Owing to the fact that an acquittal was generally conceded there was very little public interest in the case and but few people were attracted to the court room to hear the evidence." [63]

The headline of the *El Paso Morning Times* was:

"PROVED WAS SHOT IN SELF DEFENSE" [64]

In 2007, the author interviewed Robert C. Cox, the grandson of W. W. Cox. Asked about the shooting, Robert said that the family history was that Garrett verbally threatened Brazel just as he (Garrett) jumped out of the buggy. On alighting on the ground, Garrett turned and reached for his shotgun, which was on the floorboard of the buggy, where Garrett had put it on leaving his Home Ranch. At that moment, Brazel shot Garrett. Garrett's head was turned away from Brazel and tipped slightly forward, causing the bullet to enter the back of Garrett's head and exit above the right eyebrow.[65]

This matches the *El Paso Morning Times* summary of Brazel's defense:

"Garrett is alleged to have jumped from the wagon in which he was riding and on reaching the ground to have reached for a shot gun lying in the bottom of the conveyance, whereupon Brazel drew a sixshooter and shot him twice, killing him." [66]

Brazel probably told the jury that he responded to Garrett's threat so quickly that he did not notice that Garrett was turned away from him.

What about the unbuttoned condition of Garrett's trousers? In the legal proceedings, *this question was never addressed.*

Unless we believe there was utter incompetence on the part of the press and the legal authorities, or a huge conspiracy involving all of the press and the legal establishment, there must have been an explanation for the condition of Garrett's trousers that satisfied the jurors. One possibility is that the report of Garrett's trousers being *"unbuttoned"* was a misdescription. Dr. Field, in reporting on his autopsy, said *"his clothes were open and disarranged."* That is more ambiguous. (For more discussion of this issue, see page 199.)

It has been suggested by some writers that Brazel's acquittal is evidence of total incompetence on the part of the prosecution. The prosecution was certainly lax, as was affirmed by Dr. Field:

"Judge Parker said to Field after he got off the witness stand during a recess: Your testimony was good, but what surprised me was that the District Attorney did not keep pulling that hair out to show that he was shot in the back of the head. Field told Judge Parker: Garrett was shot and murdered in cold blood – not a question in the world." [67]

But rather than supporting incompetence, the existing evidence supports the theory that the prosecution was certain that Brazel would get off on self-defense, and saw no point in trying to disprove something they themselves believed, i.e., the shooting met the standard of self-defense. Subpoenaing the telegrams exchanged with Miller and Cox shows the prosecution investigated the claim that Miller had been hired to kill Garrett, and found nothing in the telegrams that supported a murder conspiracy.

What does the author think? I think, like Dr. Field, that Brazel killed Garrett in cold-blood. I think it is likely that Brazel premeditated it, in that he thought to himself – *"if Garrett pushes me too much, I will shoot the goddamn son of a bitch!"* Brazel had extensive familiarity with the law regarding self-defense. He had personally seen it work twice in his life: once in the shooting of Frank Terrell (page 153) and once in the case of his father beating his mother's lover Louis Telles nearly to death (page 155). He was waiting for a provocation from Garrett sufficient to justify shooting him.

In talking to his future father-in-law Milton Boyd about the shooting, Brazel said:

> *"Now, why did the old fool do that?"* [68]

Brazel meant, *"why was Garrett so foolish as to give me the perfect provocation?"*

Response to Joseph Stahl

Two weeks after Brazel was acquitted, Governor Curry issued a letter disputing Stahl's conspiracy accusations:

> *"I know nothing about the killing of Pat Garrett, excepting what I heard at the preliminary examination of Wayne Brazel, and according to the evidence, Brazel was perfectly justified in his action. I directed the prosecuting attorney and the attorney general, Mr. Hervey, to make a thorough investigation and prosecute the case to the full extent of the law."*

> *"The attorney general reported to me that the evidence did not warrant conviction; however, the district attorney thought it best to let the case go before a jury, which was done with the result that Brazel was acquitted. These are matters of record; and Mr. Stahl's reflection on such men as Oliver [Lee] and W. W. Cox should be resented by every good citizen who knows these gentlemen."* [69]

Albert Fall also released a letter to the press regarding Stahl's statements laying out the facts of the case as they were established by the evidence of the trial:

> *"The trial of Wayne Brazel for the murder of Patrick F. Garrett has just concluded in our district court...."*

> *"The Brazel case for killing of Mr. Garrett occupied the court one whole day in the selection of a jury, examining witnesses, etc. The plea of self-defense and the evidence adduced showed a personal conflict between the deceased and the defendant;"*

> *"...that the defendant was coming from his ranch into the town of Las Cruces at the written invitation of Patrick F. Garrett and his associate, one Adamson, for the purpose of making a trade between the defendant, Adamson and one J. B. Miller, for the purchase of defendant's goats and the release by him of a five-year lease upon a certain spring claimed to be owned by Mr. Garrett;"*

"...that J. B. Miller was in the town of Las Cruces in a hotel awaiting the arrival of the deceased Adamson, and the defendant Brazel;"

"...that Brazel had never met Miller until introduced to the latter by the deceased, Garrett;"

"...that Miller in turn had introduced the defendant to Adamson, Garrett's companion;

...that within about five miles of Las Cruces some controversy arose between the defendant and the deceased;"

"...that the deceased seized from his buggy a sawed-off repeating shotgun loaded with buckshot, and that defendant fired and killed him." [70]

Fall's letter was co-signed by 34 prominent Las Cruces citizens. Other than the exaggerated description of the shotgun, *none* of these findings of fact have been disproven by any evidence that would meet law court standards to this day. Note the *confirmation* that Miller was in a hotel in Las Cruces when Garrett was killed.

Print Rhode Jailed for Murder

On July 8, 1910, Print Rhode killed Henry Lee Murphy, his brother-in-law. According to George Reed, the only witness:

"[Murphy] was coming down the road leading a horse. At the same time, Rhode [advanced] to a fence in front of Murphy. When about 120 feet from Murphy, [Reed] saw Rhode pull a gun from his pocket and fire. The bullet missed its mark, and Murphy advanced toward him."

"Rhode then fired a second shot, and it, too, went wild, Murphy during all this time continuing to advance. The last shot proved the fatal one, entering Murphy's right side, above the hip bone, and lodging in the left side. Murphy fell within eight feet of Rhode." [71]

The shooting occurred near Camp Verde, Arizona, where Rhode and Murphy were partners in a farm. The dispute was over how to split the proceeds of the business. [72]

Upon being arrested, Rhode was asked the reason for the shooting. He replied:

"I do not care to say anything whatever." [73]

On a change of venue, Rhode's trial took place May 16, 1911, in Prescott, Arizona. Cynthia Murphy, Murphy's wife, testified that her sister was married to Rhode. She said that her husband was lame and suffered from a crushed chest. She said that eight or ten days before the shooting, Rhode had threatened Murphy, saying:

"I'll get you and the whole ___ family yet." [74]

Cynthia continued:

"I heard three shots and started to run down the road. All the children I think were following me. I found my husband lying in the road on his face. I saw he was not dead and sent the children back to the house for water. I sat down in the road and took his head in my lap. He did not speak and died a few minutes later." [75]

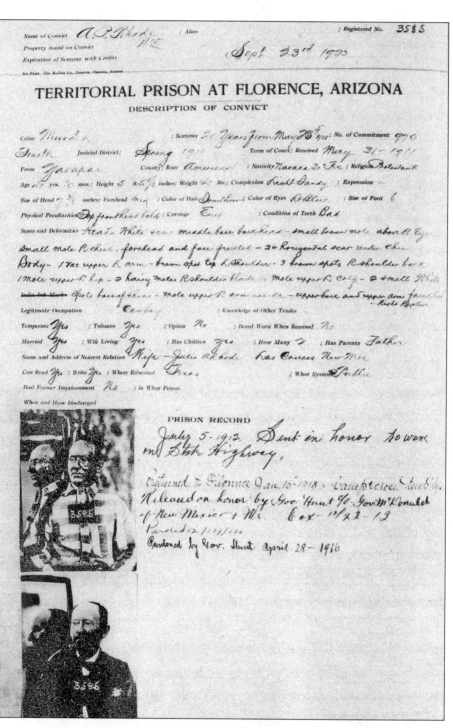

Archie Prentice "Print" Rhode's prison record. Courtesy Pinal County Historical Society Museum.

Rhode took the stand in his own defense. He testified:

> *"...I was hailed by Murphy, who said, 'Get out, I want to talk to you....' He had a rock in his hand and advanced toward me and believing he was going to try to kill me, I pulled my gun and fired it. He still advanced and I fired again. He still came toward me and threw the rock and I shot him and he fell. Murphy had at one time boasted that he had killed a cow with a rock and I feared that my life was in danger."* [76]

After deliberating eight hours, the jury rejected first degree murder and returned a verdict of murder in the second degree.[77]

On May 30, 1911, Rhode was sentenced to 20 years in the state penitentiary. After a little over two years in prison, Rhode was released into the custody of New Mexico Governor William J. Mills and W. W. Cox. Rhode's release was the result of lobbying by New Mexico friends, principally W. W. Cox, who was married to Rhode's sister. Rhode was pardoned by Governor George Hunt of Arizona on April 28, 1916.[78]

Brazel Marries Olive Boyd

On September 5, 1910, Jesse Wayne Brazel married Olive Elizabeth Boyd. The wedding was in the planning stages when Brazel shot Garrett. In a letter about the marriage, Wayne's brother-in-law, John E. Boyd, wrote:

> *"Papa [Milton Boyd] had investigated Wayne immediately after Wayne and Olive made known their homing intentions, before the fatal incident.... We kids liked Wayne for what he was. We learned from elders he attended strictly to business during his trips to Alamogordo."*

> *"...his general conversation with the family in the early evenings and at meal times invariably centered around building up a ranch home where he could do a family proud."* [79]

The wedding was held in the late afternoon at the home of Olive's parents, at Camp City, a tiny settlement south of Alamogordo. The best man was Gene Baird, the son of James A. Baird, who had testified for Brazel at his trial:

> *"Wayne and Olive, with Gene as escort, left in a cloud of dust and a volley of shots."* [80]

Eleven months before his marriage to Olive – and 169 days after his acquittal for killing Garrett – in partnership with W. D. Buck and A. M. Shoemaker, Brazel bought an unpatented 160-acre homestead from James W. Gould, located 12 miles west of Lordsburg (October 20, 1909). The homestead had a primitive adobe house and a good water source known as Harrington's Well.[81]

After a brief honeymoon in Silver City following the wedding, Brazel took his new wife to his homestead – achieving his goal of providing a home for a family. Nine months and two days after the marriage, on June 7, 1911, their son Jesse Vaughn Brazel was born on the homestead.[82]

Life on the homestead was harsh. In November, 1911, Olive, saying she wanted *"a change in environment,"* returned to her father's house for a visit. She became sick with pneumonia and died on November 16, 1911, in the presence of her husband.[83]

Jesse Wayne Brazel and Olive Elizabeth Boyd's marriage photo. September 12, 1910, at Silver City, New Mexico. Courtesy Nita Stewart Haley Memorial Library and J. Evetts Haley History Center.

Olive's death devastated Brazel. Olive's sister, May Boyd, described the impact:

"Wayne left the baby with my father and mother to care for. They were happy to do so. After several months, Wayne told them that he wouldn't be back to see the baby."

"We never heard from him nor saw him again, although my father made quite an intensive search to find out what had happened to him. We do not know where he went or what happened." [84]

Brazel's last words to his father-in-law were:

"If I can only get back into single harness again, I'll be plumb satisfied – but I know myself too doggone, stinkin' well." [85]

Olive was buried in the Monte Vista Cemetery, in Alamogordo.

Brazel's Last Days

Following Olive's funeral, Brazel returned to his homestead – and discovered that the place meant nothing to him anymore. His friend Ed Rhodes said:

"Wayne just seemed to lose interest in everything. All he talked about was getting away from the ranch." [86]

Perhaps to assuage his guilt for abandoning his infant son, Brazel took out a $10,000 life insurance policy with the New York Life and Insurance Company. His son was the beneficiary. Brazel paid the first year's premium, but never paid the second, due a year later.[87]

Brazel completed the proving-up process on his homestead and filed for the patent. As soon as the patent was approved, he sold the homestead to Joseph G. Olney, and took a job with a cattle operation in Arizona.[88]

On the same day that Brazel sold his homestead, February 27, 1913, W. W. Cox filed suit against Brazel for the repayment of two loans, totaling $1,506.16.[89]

- The first loan was for $574.80 and was executed June 29, 1907, three and a half months after Brazel leased the Rock House Ranch from Poe Garrett. The interest rate was 10% per year. Brazel used this loan to buy the goats he put on the leased land.
- The second loan was for $300 and was executed May 18, 1909, two weeks after Brazel's trial and acquittal for murder. This loan also carried an interest rate of 10% per year. Brazel used this loan to pay off the legal costs of the murder trial.

On April 21, 1913, 53 days after his homestead sale, Brazel paid Cox $1506.16 to satisfy his outstanding loans. This amounted to $874.80 for repayment of the principal and $631.36 for repayment of the accumulated interest.[90]

A year later, on April 24, 1914, Brazel, Gould, and Olney were arrested for perjury. Brazel was charged with falsely certifying that he had met the patent requirements on his homestead. Gould and Olney were arrested for witnessing a fraudulent homestead patent application.[91] The *Albuquerque Journal* reported the arrest as follows (!):

OLIVE E. BOYD

Wife of

J. W. BRAZEL;

DEC. 21, 1888;

NOV. 16, 1911.

"Asleep in Jesus."

Olive Elizabeth Boyd's gravestone, Monte Vista Cemetery, Alamogordo. 2018 photo. Olive died of pneumonia during a visit to her parents. Wayne left his 6-month-old son with his parents-in-law and never saw his son or his parents-in-law again after Olive's funeral.

"Wayne Brazel, who was known as the best friend [!?] of the late Pat Garrett, and who leaped into fame at the time Garrett was killed, has been arrested in Dona Ana county on the charge of perjury in a homestead entry." [92]

Only July 10, 1914, Brazel registered to vote at Ash Fork, Yavapai County, Arizona. He gave his height as five feet, seven inches, and his weight as 180 pounds.[93]

Brazel's homestead perjury case was originally scheduled for trial in May, 1914, but was postponed until November, 1914. On November 11, 1914, with Wayne Brazel present, the Assistant District Attorney for New Mexico asked that the case be dismissed due to lack of evidence.[94]

That is the last known documentary evidence of Jesse Wayne Brazel's existence.

In 1936, Brazel's son, Jesse Vaughn Brazel, hired attorney H. L. McCune to find his father. If his father could not be found, then McCune was to attempt to collect on the life insurance policy Brazel had taken out in 1912.

McCune reported the results of his investigation to Jesse Vaughn in a letter dated April 28, 1936. McCune wrote that the last verifiable evidence he could find of Brazel being alive was an acquaintance who remembered seeing him in the spring of 1913, in Ash Fork, Arizona. McCune reported that some of his informants suggested that Brazel had gone to Mexico or South America and never returned – a theory that Brazel's father-in-law had also heard.[95]

McCune said the insurance policy could not be collected because Brazel had never made the second payment, and it could not be proven that he was dead (nor could it be proven that he was alive).[96]

Over the years, various people have told stories of Brazel being seen alive after his 1914 disappearance, with no actual evidence provided, other than their words. Without evidence, such tales are just that – *tales.* It would have been extremely difficult for Brazel to have lived out his life in this country without leaving some corroborating evidence. Brazel either left the country as his brother and father-in-law believed, or died an unrecorded death soon after his November 14, 1914, courtroom appearance.

That Brazel paid his debt to W. W. Cox for his loans, registered to vote, and met all his legal obligations in the homestead lawsuit, indicates that he was living a normal life, contradicting the assertion by some authors that he had developed a paranoid desire to disappear from history, and to spend the rest of his life hiding his existence.

(Shortly before he disappeared, Brazel traded the pistol that he used to kill Garrett to his friend Charlie Burch. See Appendix C.)

Elzy Brown and wife, Jesse Wayne Brazel, Buster Brown and wife. Phoenix, Arizona, 1914. Last known photo of Brazel. Courtesy Leon Metz Papers, C. L. Sonnichsen Special Collections, UTEP

Chapter 13 | Debunking the Conspiracy Theories

In 1970, Colin Rickards published *"How Pat Garrett Died."* A second edition of the book was published in 1986 as *"Sheriff Pat Garrett's Last Days."* [1]

Rickards puts forth a grand conspiracy to kill Garrett involving W. W. Cox, Albert Fall, Oliver Lee, Jim Gililland, Print Rhode, James B. Miller, Carl Adamson, and Emmanuel "Mannie" Clements. He states these men, and *"possibly more,"* met at the St. Regis hotel in El Paso, Texas, in the fall of 1907 to force Garrett *"out of the country,"* or if that failed, to assassinate him. [2]

The reason the men were acting against Garrett was so that Cox could obtain his Home Ranch. Rickards writes:

> *"Garrett had got a bit of water in the heart of the Cox range and moved in a bunch of stock horses. This I think was the impelling motive."* [3]

The first step of the alleged plot was to precipitate Garrett's financial problems by getting the Albuquerque Bank of Commerce to foreclose on the loan Garrett had co-signed with George Curry in 1890. According to Rickards, encouraging foreclosure were a number of financial ploys by Cox using the mortgage that he held on Garrett's ranches. [4] Actually, the foreclosure was in 1906, a year *before* the plotters allegedly first met.

Miller was hired to murder Garrett when he refused to leave *"the country"* – as the alleged plotters anticipated. Miller would be paid $1,500 to $10,000 – probably $5,000. According to Rickards:

> *"One of [Miller's] stipulations was that W. W. Cox must find somebody who would take the blame for the murder and keep his mouth shut."*

> *"...it was agreed that the murder fee would be handed to Mannie Clements, who would collect it from Albert Fall's office if and when it became necessary to kill Garrett."* [5]

Cox took on the job of finding a willing stooge. He picked as his sacrificial lamb his old family friend and loyal employee Jesse Wayne Brazel. [6] Brazel *"idolized"* Cox and thus was the *"perfect tool."* [7]

When the financial machinations failed, the assassination was on:

> *"The plan was a complex and careful one, calling for the involvement of at least eight people...."* [8]

To initiate the plot, Brazel leased the Rock House Ranch from Garrett. [9] Next, Brazel brought goats onto the land, not the cattle and horses Garrett expected. [10] In January, 1908, Brazel drove his herd of goats close to Garrett's Home Ranch, to enrage Garrett. [11] This action led to Garrett's attempt to sue Brazel in the Justice of the Peace court in Organ (see page 121):

St. Regis Hotel in El Paso, Texas, where the plot to murder Garrett supposedly was conceived in the Fall of 1907. The attendees and alleged conspirators were William W. Cox, Albert B. Fall, Oliver Milton Lee, Jim Gililland, Print Rhode, James B. Miller, Carl Adamson, Emmanuel "Mannie" Clements, and others. The plan was to pay Miller $5,000 to kill Garrett if he could not be *"forced out of the country"* by financial ploys. The goal of the plot was to obtain Garrett's Home Ranch. Overlooked by the plotters was the fact that Garrett's ranch had been evaluated the year before by two independent appraisers as being worth only $475. Undated photo. Courtesy El Paso Public Library, Border Heritage Center.

"The plotters left Garrett to fume and fuss for a while and then sent Carl Adamson to see him." [12]

Adamson introduced Miller to Garrett, who offered to buy Garrett's ranches if all of the goats were removed. Rickards writes:

"Miller said he was willing to pay $3.50 a head for the twelve hundred goats which Brazel said he had." [13]

This is a factual error that does nothing for Rickards' credibility – it was Adamson, *not* Miller, who was offering to buy the goats.

The deal the plotters were offering Garrett was irresistible:

"Garrett was exultant. He had never hoped for such a solution." [14]

With all the elements in place, it was just a question of luring Garrett to an isolated location where he could be murdered by Miller, without Miller being seen or caught.

Adamson travelled to Las Cruces, having exchanged earlier (according to Rickards) a series of plot-revealing telegrams with the other conspirators, Miller, Cox, and Print Rhode.[15] This allegation was disproved when District Attorney Thompson subpoenaed and examined those telegrams in preparation for Brazel's murder trial (see page 173).

On February 28, Adamson rode to Garrett's Home Ranch, where he spent the night. As they had planned, Garrett and Adamson left the next morning for Las Cruces to sign the papers:

"Carl Adamson knew the spot which had been chosen for the killing and as the neared it he began to fidget. He told Garrett he wanted to get out of the buckboard to relieve himself." [16]

Garrett, according to Rickards, also got out to relieve himself:

"Up the road a piece, hidden in the scrub, Jim Miller got the back of the old gray head in the sights of his rifle and squeezed the trigger." [17]

After Miller shot Garrett the second time, Adamson allegedly took Garrett's shotgun out of the floor of the buggy and *"put it in the sand near its late owner's outstretched hand."* [18] Dr. Field's descriptions of the bullet wounds found in Garrett's body *do not fit* this scenario of Garrett being shot by a rifle from a distance (see page 137). This applies especially to the shot to the back of the head, which was fired at head height.

Miller sneaked off, and Adamson and Brazel rode into Las Cruces, where Brazel confessed to the killing to Sheriff Felipe Lucero.

Rickards' conspiracy theory relies on three essential, but completely unsubstantiated assertions:

- Cox wanted Garrett's Home Ranch so badly that he was willing to hire an assassin to kill Garrett.
- Brazel was a willing stooge, happy to face hanging or life in prison for the person he idolized, W. W. Cox.
- Miller needed elaborate pre-staging with Brazel and Adamson luring Garrett to Las Cruces to be able to assassinate Garrett.

Robert C. Cox, grandson of William W. Cox, points toward the entrance of the dirt cave where his grandfather lived with his wife and first child for two years after coming to Dona Ana County in 1887. Located on White Sands Missile Range in the Gold Camp area. August 14, 2007 photo.

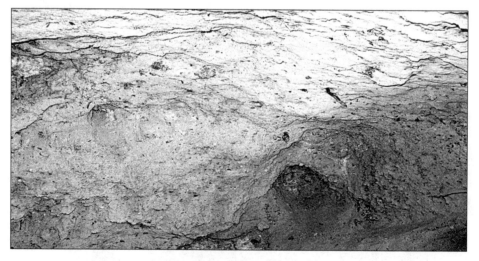

Inside the cave described above. August 14, 2007 photo.

As revealed in previous chapters, Cox had originally sold the Home Ranch to Garrett (see page 31). And further, when the ranch and spring had been appraised during the Albuquerque Bank of Commerce foreclosure, it had been evaluated by two independent appraisers as being worth only $475 (see page 115). Cox was holding the mortgage on the property, so he could have obtained it *legally* by simply foreclosing (see page 113). There was no risk to Cox in doing so, as Garrett had peaceably complied with all of the court-issued legal orders he had received when the Albuquerque Bank of Commerce had foreclosed on his ranches in 1906. To cap it all, Cox, in a totally unnecessary and generous act, paid Apolinaria for the ranch after Garrett's death (see page 165).

Yet, according to Rickards, Cox wanted the ranch he had sold Garrett a few years earlier *so badly* that he was happy to pay Miller $5,000 to kill Garrett, and to take on the very real risk that his ringleader role in the killing would be discovered – something he (Cox) would hang for. It makes *no sense* that Cox was willing to pay Miller $5,000 and Brazel $1,500 (or more) to *potentially* get a ranch worth one-thirteenth that amount.

"Potentially" is the correct word, because Garrett's death did not mean the ranches would automatically go to Cox. The ranches would have been sold by Garrett's heir, Apolinaria, and it is possible that someone would have been willing to pay Apolinaria enough for the property that she could have paid off Cox's mortgage. In that case, Cox would not have gotten the ranches.

Cox, who in Rickards' portrayal was so desperate for Garrett's ranch, was in truth a very successful man with *no motive* to hire Miller to murder Garrett. The local paper, in a biographical profile of Cox, wrote:

> *"Mr. Cox owns five ranches aggregating 12,000 acres.... He is a stockholder and director of the Bowman Bank and Bascom French Company, a stockholder in the American National Bank at El Paso.... He leases a large acreage of range from the government and pays for every acre the usual tax into the territorial fund...."* [19]

No one at the time would have been exaggerating to have described Cox as a financial genius. He had come to Dona Ana County in 1887 with nothing. For the first two years he lived in a dirt cave with his wife and first child that he had dug into the side of an arroyo in the Gold Camp area. He gradually built up his livestock holdings, and was able to buy the San Augustine Ranch in 1893. His remarkable financial acumen was recognized by everyone who knew him – he was president of the Bowman Bank of Las Cruces for twelve years, an officer of the American National Bank of El Paso, and Dona Ana County Treasurer twice.[20]

It was not only Cox who was running the risk of hanging if the plot was discovered. All of the alleged conspirators were taking that risk: Fall, Lee, Gililland, Print Rhode, Adamson, and Clements. It is difficult to believe that a lawyer as wily as Albert Fall would bet his life that *no one* in such a large group of conspirators would ever talk, or ever trade their knowledge of the conspiracy to escape punishment for another offense. Nor is it reasonable to imagine that Lee and Gililland, who had narrowly escaped being convicted of murdering Henry Fountain, and who had seen the imposing power of the legal system up close, would risk hanging again for something offering no personal gain.

ALBERT B. FALL
GENERAL COUNSEL
24 BROAD ST., NEW YORK CITY
GUARANTY TRUST BUILDING, EL PASO, TEX

LEGAL DEPARTMENT
W. C. GREENE
24 BROAD STREET, NEW YORK

CODES:
BEDFORD MC NEILL
LIEBERS
WESTERN UNION

Three Rivers, New Mexico, February 7th, 1908.

Governor George Curry,

Santa Fe, New Mexico.

My Dear Governor:-

Wayne Brazel, of Dona Ana County, Organ Post Office, has written me asking my endorsement for appointment as member of the mounted police force.

I have known Wayne for years and I believe that he would make a good officer. He is steady, quiet and I think competent.

Very sincerely yours;

ABF/r

Letter from Albert Fall to Governor Curry, February 7, 1908, recommending Wayne Brazel for the position of New Mexico mounted policeman. Written 22 days before Brazel shot Garrett. According to the conspiracy theorists, at the time this letter was requested by Brazel, written by Fall, and mailed to Curry, both Brazel and Fall *knew* that Brazel was in a conspiracy to assassinate Garrett. That makes no sense. TANM reel 165, frame 417. Courtesy N. M. State Records Center and Archives.

As for the stooge of the plot: Brazel was supposed to do this for his love of Cox – and for money. One of Rickard's sources says it was at least $1,500.[21]

Rickards was ignorant of the following facts, so he did not have to try to invent an argument to counter them:

- Brazel was in love with a beautiful woman, engaged to be married, and planning to begin a family (see page 181).
- Just 22 days before Garrett's shooting, Brazel had requested and received from Albert Fall, one of the New Mexico's most powerful politicians, a personal recommendation that he be hired as a territorial policeman – a prestigious position equivalent to that of Texas Ranger, which Brazel had an excellent chance of getting (see page 192). (Try to fit this detail into Rickards' conspiracy theory. Brazel *knew* he was going to kill Garrett. Fall *knew* it. In spite of this, Brazel asked for a written letter of recommendation to the position of territorial policeman, and Fall wrote it and *mailed* it to the governor of New Mexico.)
- After Brazel had allegedly sacrificed himself for Cox's benefit, taking the risk of being hanged or sent to the state penitentiary for life, Cox then had the temerity to sue him for the money he had lent him to buy the goats (an essential element of the alleged plot) and for his legal defense (see page 183).

Consider, also, how absurd the elaborate staging of the shooting was – staging that, according to Rickards, Miller *insisted* upon. Garrett was to be brought to Las Cruces by two witnesses at a time and for a reason that had been published in the local newspaper, and was known to hundreds, maybe thousands, of Las Cruces residents (see page 126). And further, Miller made it known that he was travelling to Las Cruces. He purposely connected his name with Garrett by telling the local newspaper that he was in town to make a deal with Garrett.

If Miller had agreed to kill Garrett, he would have followed the pattern he had used in murdering Allen Augustus Bobbitt in Ada, Oklahoma. He would have sent an accomplice to scout Garrett's daily movements. He would then have ambushed Garrett at a time and place where he was confident that he could get away with the killing. How could he trust someone who he had *barely met* (Brazel) to pretend that *he* (Brazel) had killed Garrett and accept sentencing for murder if necessary – and *never* talk?

Miller-Done-It Theories

There are two main variations of the Miller-done-it theme.

The first variation proposes a watered-down version of Rickards' theory. This theory attributes the motivation to kill Garrett to a desire to obtain Garrett's Home Ranch, but is vague on who masterminded the plot. By simply assuming that Garrett's ranch was worth killing for, these accounts avoid having to offer any evidence that Garrett's Home Ranch *really was* worth killing for.

The advocates of this theory concentrate on Miller and his psychopathic character which, in effect, becomes the *justifying motive* for killing Garrett. As a known killer-for-hire – and being involved in the events surrounding Garrett's killing – it is self-evident to these theorists that he was in the area for the sole purpose of killing Garrett.

The proponents of this theory have different suggestions as to how Miller got into position to kill Garrett. One writer said he sneaked over from Roosevelt County, New Mexico, on a horse that he rode to death on the way back.[22] A recent writer said he sneaked up from El Paso along the east side of the Organ Mountains, and sneaked back the same way.[23]

Let us debunk this absurd theory once and for all time. The facts are that Miller rode into Las Cruces by train on February 29, the day the deal papers were to be signed. He took a room at the Park Hotel (see page 126). If Miller killed Garrett, he would have had to sneak out of the Park Hotel that morning, rent a horse at the livery stable, sneak to where Garrett was shot, sneak back to the livery stable, turn in the horse, and sneak back to the Park Hotel – all without anyone seeing him – *the "Magic Horse" theory*. Just imagine the public's reaction if on the very day that Garrett was killed, Miller was discovered to have covertly rented a horse and disappeared for the exactly the hours needed to ride out and kill Garrett.

Miller was still in Las Cruces four days after the killing (March 4), because he had been asked to stay by Attorney General Hervey and be available to testify in Brazel's preliminary examination if called (see page 141). Miller *was* subpoenaed to testify in Brazel's murder trial by the defense. The subpoena was cancelled due to Miller's hanging (see page 173).

What about the murder weapon? Miller would have had to bring it with him on the train, something easily observed. Another element unexplained by the conspiracists.

Park Hotel in Las Cruces where James B. Miller was staying when Garrett and Carl Adamson rode into town on February 29, 1908, to *"fix up the papers"* for the deal to sell Garrett's ranches to Miller and Adamson. Undated photo. Courtesy Archives and Special Collections, NMSU.

The second variation of the Miller-done-it theory is that Miller killed Garrett because he and Adamson wanted to use Garrett's ranches as a secret base for smuggling Chinese into the country.[24] Smuggling illegal Chinese immigrants into the U. S. was a big business at the time. And Adamson obviously was willing to be involved in illegal smuggling.

But the second variation, like the first, requires Brazel to be the stooge – and he must be willing to kill Garrett for two people he has *never* met before – very risky considering that one of these two was a notorious killer.

And further, after all this painstaking planning so that he would not be blamed for the killing, we are to believe that Miller carelessly left *"horse tracks and cigarette remnants"* at the *"ambush nest"* where he was waiting to shoot Garrett (see page 146).

Carl Adamson Done It

Originating with Will Isaacks, this theory claims that unnamed conspirators hired Adamson, instead of Miller, to kill Garrett. The night before the shooting, Brazel traded pistols with Adamson. Then, on the ride to Las Cruces, using the excuse that he needed to relieve himself, Adamson stopped the buggy and climbed out:

> *"When Garrett started to get out of the buggy, Adamson shot him through the head with Wayne's pistol. Then they exchanged weapons again [and Brazel went in and surrendered to Sheriff Lucero.]"* [25]

Brazel was still the paid stooge who confessed to the crime. Sheriff Lucero accepted his confession because the gun that killed Garrett was Brazel's (the point of the trade). W. W. Cox, although unstated, was the financial mastermind behind the conspiracy.

Print Rhode Done It

This explanation was first proposed in the anonymous letter sent to Annie Garrett just after Garrett's killing (see page 148). Over the years it has been repeated by various sources. In this theory, Print Rhode was shadowing Garrett, Adamson, and Brazel on their trip to Las Cruces the day of the killing, staying out of sight, except for the brief instance when Adamson first observed Brazel (see page 128). Then, when Adamson – who was colluding with Print Rhode – stopped the buggy on the excuse of urinating, Rhode sneaked up and shot Garrett.[26]

It is certain that Rhode disliked Garrett. Garrett had arrested him as one of the accomplices of the Bowman Bank Robbery (see page 75). And Rhode was clearly capable of murder (see page 179). His testimony under oath during the Fountain trial showed he had a retaliatory imagination. In that testimony, he claimed that he just barely foiled a plot to blow up Oliver Lee's Dog Canyon Ranch house using dynamite (see page 60).

The statement repeated by numerous writers that Rhode was Brazel's partner, which is said to be his motive for killing Garrett, is dubious. Rhode did *not* sign the Rock House lease with Poe. He did *not* sign the loan paper with Cox for the money Brazel borrowed to buy the goats. He was *not* joined with Brazel in the justice of the peace suit in Organ for running his goats too close to Garrett's Home Ranch. He did *not* negotiate with Miller and Adamson to sell the goats. And on the day of the killing, Brazel did *not* mention Rhode when he talked about how many goats *he* (Brazel) had, and whether *he* (Brazel) would sell them.

> *"Well, Brazel says, 'If I don't sell the whole bunch I won't sell none' or he says, 'I will either not sell the 1200 or I will keep the 600 and keep possession of the ranch' or something like that."* [27]

Rhode was *not* Brazel's partner in any legal sense of the word. He was probably what today would be called a contract employee – he was working for Brazel for a share of what Brazel made.

According to a recent book author, Rhode killed Garrett because of *"bad blood and plain fear."* The reason Brazel became the willing stooge for Rhode was *"because Rhode had a family...."* [28]

No reason is given as to why Rhode chose the day of the business deal with Miller and Adamson as the day to kill Garrett. If the deal had gone through, Brazel would have been paid for his goats, Rhode would have gotten his share of the "partnership" money, and both would no longer have had to deal with Garrett. *Why risk hanging if they were going to get what they wanted legally?*

If Rhode killed Garrett – and *made* Brazel accept the role of stooge – he would have cost Brazel what his heart intensely desired – marrying Olive Boyd.

Captain Fred Fornoff, of the New Mexico Mounted Police. He is the purported author of the "Fornoff Report," which almost certainly *never existed*. The claimed provenance of the report is: Mounted Policeman Fred Lambert saw Captain Fornoff's notes in 1911, told Chuck Hornung what was in those notes 57 years later, and Hornung recounted those details in a presentation in 1996. Undated photo. Courtesy Leon Metz Papers, C. L. Sonnichsen Special Collections, UTEP.

Did the Fornoff Report Exist?

The primary evidence offered to support the different theories that Garrett's killing was a premeditated assassination is the "Fornoff Report." This report, purportedly prepared by Captain Fred Fornoff, a New Mexico Mounted Policeman, is said to summarize Fornoff's investigation into the murder of Garrett. It is asserted that Fornoff learned from sources in El Paso that there was an elaborately planned conspiracy to kill Garrett. It is also asserted that he learned the names of the conspirators and the details of the plot (so much for conspiratorial confidentiality).

But you can not examine the Fornoff Report – *it does not exist.*

What is known about the putative Fornoff Report was put forth by author and researcher Chuck Hornung. Hornung writes:

> *"The Fornoff Report was composed and typed by Page B. Otero from notes supplied to him by Captain Fornoff. Page Otero served as the Mounted Police office clerk from 1908 to 1910."* [29]

This report was supposedly presented to New Mexico Attorney General Hervey, who, it is claimed, took it with him when he left public office on March 12, 1909. The report was purportedly passed on to Hervey's law partner when Hervey died, and was accidentally destroyed with other Hervey papers in 1963.[30]

The story continues: Hornung, who was researching the New Mexico mounted police for a book, was interviewing Fred Lambert, an ex-mounted policeman who had served with Captain Fornoff. On April 13, 1968, Hornung asked Lambert about the murder of Garrett.[31]

Lambert told Hornung that he had viewed Captain Fornoff's file on Garrett's killing in 1911.[32] Lambert then recounted to Hornung the details he remembered from the file: Garrett was killed as a result of a conspiracy; the architect behind the conspiracy was W. W. Cox, aided by Print Rhode and Oliver Lee; after it had been arranged for Brazel to lease the Rock House Ranch and put goats on it, Adamson was paid to contact Garrett and arrange a deal to buy Garrett's ranches.[33]

The ranches deal would *require* a trip to Las Cruces to sign legal papers, putting Garrett in a secluded location along the way where he could be killed by a paid assassin. *Of course, Garrett made that trip regularly, but ignore that.*

Lambert said that Fornoff suspected the shooter was Print Rhode. Lambert said that Fornoff did not believe Miller was the killer. Lambert said that Fornoff did *not think Brazel knew in advance* that Garrett was going to be killed, *but agreed on the spot to be a stooge and to confess to the killing. Explain the reasoning behind that!* Lambert said that Fornoff suspected the second shot that struck Garrett was fired by Adamson. Lambert said that Fornoff believed W. W. Cox financed the whole operation.[34]

This often cited evidence of a conspiracy to kill Garrett is *third* hand. Lambert saw Captain Fornoff's notes in 1911, told Hornung what was in those notes *57 years later*, and Hornung recounted those details in a presentation to the Sixth Annual Western Outlaw Lawman History Association (WOLA) Convention in 1996.[35]

Oliver Milton Lee. It is said that Lee always carried a side-arm, even after his election to the New Mexico Senate. Undated photo. Courtesy Center for Southwest Research and Special Collections, UNM.

Hervey, in his memoir of the Garrett killing composed shortly before he died in 1953, wrote:

"I went to Las Cruces, and while the Governor was attending the funeral, I saw Carl Adamson and asked him to go with me and show me the exact place where Garrett was killed and how it happened. We took Fred Fornoff from Santa Fe along with us. He was a noted peace officer and Captain of the State Mounted Police." [36]

But Hervey was wrong about Fornoff being with him. Rather, it was territorial policeman John A. Beal, as reported in the newspaper at the time:

"<u>Simultaneously</u> with the arrival of Gov. Curry, ranger J. A. Beal also arrived from Deming. He was in this section in January and says the dispute

between Garrett and Brazel was in progress at that time and he <u>made a report</u> on it to the governor. Following the shooting Gov. Curry wired him to come to Las Cruces at once, and his evidence will be used. He will also co-operate with the local authorities if needed in preserving order." [37]

The reporter obviously interviewed Beal for the information in this report, who he reports arrived *"simultaneously"* with Governor Curry, i.e., *on the same train.*

Governor Curry made the same mistake in his autobiography:

"With Hervey and Fred Fornoff, captain of the Territorial mounted police and a highly efficient officer, I went to Las Cruces." [38]

A search of the New Mexico Territorial newspapers for all of 1908 resulted in 104 mentions of Fornoff, *but not one report of him being in Las Cruces during the 1908 year!* Captain Fornoff was big territorial news – his travels and actions were reported frequently in the newspapers. The Garrett killing was huge news. If Captain Fornoff had come to Las Cruces with Governor Curry and Attorney General Hervey, it would have been reported. There was no reason to keep it secret.

Beal would go on to testify for the defense in Brazel's murder trial, supporting Brazel's contention that he had been threatened by Garrett prior to the shooting (see page 175). It probably was Beal's testimony that convinced the jury to acquit Brazel.

Unless contradictory evidence is found, it appears that Governor Curry and Hervey have mis-remembered which mounted policeman investigated the Garrett killing. And if it was Beal and not Captain Fornoff doing the investigating, there would have been *no* Fornoff Report. There actually *was* a *"Beal Report,"* as disclosed by the newspaper reporter.

There is another curious aspect to Hervey's memoirs. Writing in 1953, Hervey recounted how he found a *"new Winchester rifle shell on the ground"* about 30 or 40 feet from where Garrett was killed.[39] This, of course, *does not* prove that Garrett was assassinated by a rifle from a distance, although it has been offered as evidence of such by many writers. But what *is* of evidentiary value is that Hervey *does not mention* this rifle shell in a long interview he gave lawyer and author William A. Keleher in 1938.[40]

In the 1938 interview, Hervey said that in the years since the murder, he has come to believe that Garrett was killed by Miller; that Miller was paid $1,500 to do the job; and the source of the money was W. W. Cox. He said that Brazel agreed to be the stooge. *He said not one word about finding a rifle shell.*[41]

Conclusion

None of these conspiracy theories can be proved because *not one* comes close to the actual evidence or tallies with the account of the eyewitness to the killing. The evidence offered by the conspiracy theorists consists of handpicked details culled from selected oral accounts (related long after the event), implications of actions, hearsay comments, character judgments, and the willful disregard of all contradictory facts.

There *is* a mystery in Garrett's killing. Were Garrett's trousers unbuttoned when he was shot, indicating that he had got out of the buggy to urinate, as alleged *once* in *one* newspaper on the day after the shooting and as remembered by Dr. Field 31 years later?

This detail was *not* mentioned in Adamson's eye-witness testimony – and, indeed, if true – would have *proved* Adamson a liar. Consider how many times Adamson gave his account of the shooting to authorities:

- Immediately after learning of the shooting, Sheriff Lucero appointed a coroner's jury and took the jury, Dr. Field, and Adamson to the scene of the shooting. Adamson gave his account there. Garrett's body *was still* where it had fallen and the scene of the killing was undisturbed, so *any* discrepancy in Adamson's account such as unbuttoned trousers would have been blatantly obvious (see page 133).
- On March 4, Governor Curry had Adamson come to his hotel room and recount the details of the shooting (see page 141).
- Later that same day, Adamson gave his account at Brazel's preliminary examination, under oath (see page 144).
- After the preliminary examination, Attorney General Hervey, Governor Curry, and Dr. Field went with Adamson to the site of the shooting and Adamson once again recounted what he saw in situ (see page 146).
- On April 3, 1908, Adamson returned to Las Cruces and testified to the grand jury investigating Garrett's shooting. This was Adamson's fifth account to officials, and his second under oath (see page 163).

The newspaper accounts of the murder trial's verdict report nothing about Garrett's trousers being unbuttoned, nor do they express any doubt that Brazel was acquitted unjustly. (Shooting a man while he was facing away and urinating would annihilate any attempt to argue self-defense!) There is *no suggestion* that anyone thought Adamson was lying in his testimony. If Adamson was *not* lying, then there were *no* unbuttoned trousers.

When Judge Parker spoke with Dr. Field, following the trial result he said:

> *"Your testimony was good, but what surprised me was that the District Attorney did not keep pulling that hair out to show that he was shot in the back of the head." (See page 177.)*

He did *not* say, *"what surprised me was that the District Attorney did not keep asking about Garrett's <u>unbuttoned trousers</u>."*

This book has produced a huge amount of new information on Garrett's life, the people who intersected with him, his killing, and Brazel's trial. None of this new information supports any of the conspiracy theories. Just the opposite – it debunks these theories.

My belief, as expressed earlier, is that Brazel was intimately familiar with the law regarding self-defense. He was hoping for a provocation from Garrett. When he got it, he killed Garrett, knowing that a conviction of murder was very unlikely. That he was thinking in this way when he killed Garrett is evident from the fact that he claimed self-defense *immediately* upon surrendering to Sheriff Lucero (see page 133):

> *"...[Adamson] saw the whole thing and knows I shot in self-defense.'"*

Brazel fired two shots, the first at Garrett's head, because he wanted to be certain that Garrett was killed. *He had no help from conspirators, and he was not paid for the killing.* Brazel did it because he disliked Garrett intensely by the time of the shooting, and he was afraid *Garrett was <u>also</u> looking for a provocation* – to justify killing *him* (Brazel).

Chapter 14 | Death Site

Where was Garrett killed? In a 1969 newspaper interview, Emmitt J. Isaacks said that he and his brother,

> "...the late Will [Isaacks], heard the shot that killed Pat Garrett.... They were trailing cattle nearby, and by the time they reached the scene, Garrett was lying on the ground, covered over with a carriage blanket." [1]

The Isaacks family had a large 300-acre ranch on the west side of the Organ Mountains, established in 1888.[2]

> "A few years ago, [Emmitt] Isaacks guided some Las Cruces civic leaders to the scene of Garrett's shooting so that it might be identified for posterity. They made a marker out of rocks, topped with a stone bearing a carving of a cross for the site...." [3]

In an introduction to a new 1964 edition of his Father's book, *"The Authentic Life of Billy the Kid,"* Jarvis Garrett wrote:

> "About fifteen years ago, while on a visit to Las Cruces from Venezuela, I chanced to meet Will Isaacs [sic].... The conversation turned to my father's death, and he told me that he was present when Brazel surrendered to Sheriff Lucero, following which he went to the murder scene.... I was very appreciative when he offered to show [me] the exact spot of the murder."

> "We drove about four miles east on the modern highway, stopped the car, and walked along the arroyo bed for another mile in the same direction. After some difficulty, he found the marker, a round stone, which he had placed there in 1908." [4]

Although Emmitt and Will disagree about how they learned where Garrett was killed, the location they marked has been accepted by old-time residents as the spot where Garrett was killed for over 110 years. On November 6, 1965, Dona Ana County Historical Society members Hudson Murrell and John Griggs constructed the monument currently marking the site. [5]

The monument consists of a circle of cement surrounding a blue stone with a cross carved in it. The carved stone was placed at the site by Emmitt and Will Isaacks. The monument is anchored in place by two metal angle-iron stakes driven through the cement into the ground. Roughly scratched in the cement are *"P. Garrett"* and *"Feb 1908."*

Although there can be no absolute certainty that the monument marks the actual spot where Garrett was killed, strong supporting evidence is provided by a 1928 survey map that shows the location of the old road from Organ to Las Cruces that Garrett, Adamson, and Brazel were travelling when Garrett was shot. As you can see from the map, the monument location is next to the road, as described in the courtroom testimony. It is also the approximate distance from Las Cruces described in the coroner's jury report on Garrett's killing.[6]

The location of the site was made public on the internet in 2005 by the Friends of Pat Garrett (friendsofpatgarrett.com), a private organization that had been caring for the site in secret. The decision to make knowledge of the site public was made after the State of New Mexico land on which the monument is located was leased by a real estate developer.

Friends of Pat Garrett is working with the city of Las Cruces to ensure that the site is protected from future real estate development and is preserved for the public benefit. In 2017, a formal request was made to the New Mexico Historic Preservation Division to recognize the monument as a historic site and grant the site the legal protections deriving from that designation. In a stunning decision, the New Mexico Historic Preservation Division refused to designate the site a historic site. Here are the official reasons given by the State and National Register Coordinator:

> "The Historic Preservation Division has reviewed the questionnaire which you submitted on November 13, 2017 on the Pat Garrett Murder Site in Dona Ana County. We have determined that the murder site is not eligible for listing in the National Register of Historic Places. To be eligible for listing in the National Register a property must a) be at least fifty years [old], b) maintain its historic appearance, and 3) be associated with a significant event, significant person, design, or archaeology."

> "Pat Garrett is undoubtedly an important and controversial figure associated with law enforcement in the West, especially in New Mexico and Texas. However, the murder site is not associated with his career in law enforcement. At the time of his murder, Garrett had retired from law enforcement and was struggling economically. His murder, most likely the result of a dispute over livestock or possibly seekers of fame, was not related to law enforcement activities and had no bearing on law enforcement in West."

> "Lastly, a site associated with a person significant to our past is not eligible for listing in the National Register, if there are other appropriate sites or building 'directly associated with his or her productive life.' Lincoln Historic Site, for example is dedicated to interpreting, among other things, the story of Billy the Kid and how he was killed by Pat Garrett. This and other sites are better suited to tell the story of the contributions by Pat Garrett to law enforcement in West." [7]

This is an astonishing – and erroneous – ruling.

The "X" on the 1928 U. S. Survey map reproduced on the opposite page marks the location of the Garrett Monument. This is the location that Emmitt and Will Isaacks identified as the place where Patrick Floyd Garrett was killed. The death site is next to the old road from Organ to Las Cruces (indicated by the arrow). It is also close to the Alameda Arroyo (indicated by the double-headed arrow). The direction that Garrett, Carl Adamson, and Wayne Brazel were travelling is indicated by the dotted line. Las Cruces is off the map to the west (top of page). Organ is off the map to the east (bottom of page). Courtesy Human Systems Research.

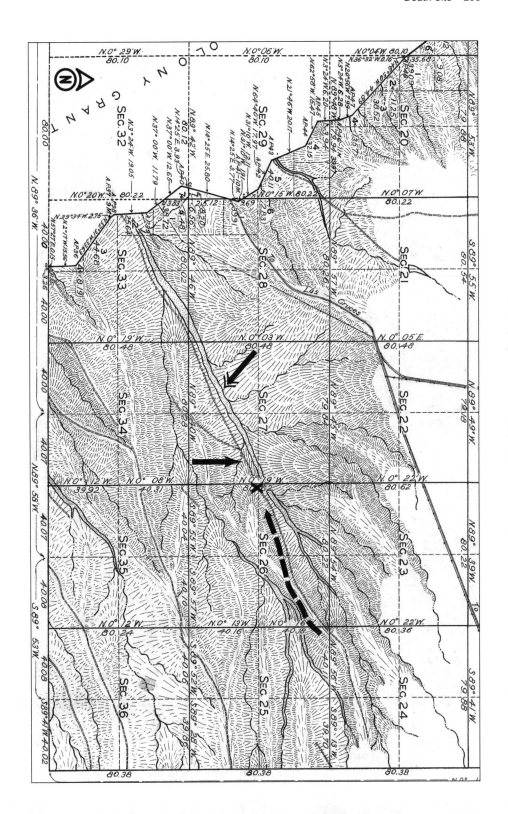

Road that Garrett, Adamson, and Brazel were travelling when Garrett was shot. Looking East. 2007 photo.

Monument at the site where Garrett was killed. The monument was constructed by Dona Ana County Historical Society members Hudson Murrell and John Griggs in 1965. The location was identified by Emmitt and Will Isaacks, who carved the cross in the center stone. 2008 photo.

Appendix A | IOOF Cemetery – Garrett Family Plot

The land for the Las Cruces International Order of Odd Fellows (IOOF) cemetery was purchased by the Las Cruces IOOF lodge on January 29, 1892.[1] Half of the plots were reserved for IOOF members; half were available for purchase by non-members.[2]

The origin of the term "Odd Fellows" is unknown. Its earliest use appears to be in the late 1700s in England for various guilds and orders.[3] The Independent Order of Odd Fellows was founded in Baltimore, Maryland, in 1819. It was named "Independent Order" to distinguish it from other Odd Fellow organizations that existed at the time.[4]

Following the death of Adelaida "Ida" Garrett on October 12, 1896 (born February 20, 1881), Garrett bought a family plot in the southeast corner of the IOOF cemetery. The plot was surrounded by a one-foot-high cement curbing. Ida's burial was commemorated with a stone engraved:

> "Farewell Forever to Ida"
> "Daughter of Mr. and Mrs. P. F. Garrett"
> "Born Feb. 20, 1881"
> "Died Oct. 12, 1896" [5]

Patrick Floyd Jarvis Garrett (born June 5, 1850) was buried in the IOOF family plot on March 5, 1908. His grave was located to the left of Ida's. The cemetery stone placed over Garrett's grave was paid for by the Elks Association.[6]

Feliciana (Valdez) Gutierrez, Apolinaria's Mother, (born 1843) died in 1919. She was buried in the IOOF plot. She had been living with Apolinaria since at least 1910.[7]

Ann "Annie" (Montgomery) Garrett (born October 2, 1889) died August 4, 1922, in Las Cruces and was buried in the IOOF plot August 6, 1922. She was survived by her husband John W. Montgomery and three children.[8]

Patrick Floyd Garrett, Jr., (born February 23, 1896) died May 26, 1927. He was buried in the IOOF plot June 4, 1927. Pat Jr. was working in Mexico when became critically ill, after a two-year period of chronic illness. His company sent him to Mexico City for medical treatment, but he died before a scheduled operation could be performed.[9]

Dudley Poe Garrett (born June 8, 1887) died December 8, 1930, in El Paso. He was taken to the City-County hospital after suffering a stroke, but died shortly after arrival. He was buried in the IOOF plot December 10, 1930. Poe was working as a telephone operator for an El Paso taxi company at the time of his death.[10]

Pat's wife, Apolinaria (Gutierrez) Garrett (born February 9, 1861), died October 21, 1936, in Las Cruces. She was buried in the IOOF plot October 23, 1936. The cause of death was a heart attack. Her parents were Delores Gutierrez and Feliciana Valdez.[11]

In 1938, William A. Keleher travelled to Las Cruces from his home in Albuquerque. He visited the IOOF cemetery and located the Garrett family plot. The only gravestone in the plot at that time was that of Ida Garrett.[12] It is unknown what happened to Garrett's stone. It is also unknown if gravestones were ever placed for the other Garrett family members buried in the plot.

In November, 1952, the remains from the Garrett IOOF family plot were moved to the Las Cruces Masonic Cemetery. In explaining this decision, Jarvis wrote:

"The cemetery was abandoned for many years, and when vandals destroyed Ida's tombstone, my sister Pauline and I decided to arrange for the removal of our beloveds for interment in the Masonic Cemetery across the road." [13]

Oscar Lohman Garrett (born December 30, 1903) died March 21, 1953. He was buried in the Masonic Cemetery family plot.

Pauline Juliet Garrett (born September 11, 1899) died March 7, 1981. She was buried Masonic Cemetery family plot.

Jarvis Powers Garrett (born July 28, 1905) died May 20, 1991. He was buried in the Masonic Cemetery family plot.

Elizabeth Garrett (born October 9, 1885) died October 16, 1939. She was buried in the South Park Cemetery in Roswell, New Mexico.

Abandoned Garrett family plot in the Las Cruces IOOF Cemetery. In November, 1952, the seven burials in the plot were moved to the Las Cruces Masonic Cemetery. 2019 photo.

Appendix B | The Pistol that Killed Billy the Kid

When Garrett was killed, he did not have personal possession of the .44-caliber, single-action Colt pistol that he had carried regularly ever since he had killed Billy the Kid with the gun in 1881. Two years before he was killed by Wayne Brazel, Garrett loaned the pistol to Thomas Powers to display in his gun collection in the Coney Island Saloon.[1]

Powers' gun collection was mounted on the wall behind the main bar of the saloon.

> *"Each [weapon] was tagged with the owner's name and its history. If the tag remained on the weapon it was on loan. If the tag was removed, Powers was the owner."* [2]

Although Powers accepted guns as collateral for small loans, the guns he sought for his valued personal collection had to be owned previously by a *"well-known"* person. He was aware that there were many guns with fake attributions being traded, so he tried whenever possible to get a statement of certification before acquiring a famous gun.

Garrett had two guns that he loaned to Powers for display in the saloon. Both had been taken from Billy Wilson when Garrett captured Wilson, Billy the Kid, and Dave Rudabaugh at Stinking Springs, New Mexico, on December 23, 1880. The two guns were:

> *"...a Winchester 1873 saddle ring carbine, serial #47629, and a Colt Frontier six-shooter, serial #55093."* [3]

The rifle and pistol fired the same ammunition, a .44 Winchester cartridge – a big advantage to a Western lawman, because both weapons could be carried without requiring two kinds of ammunition.

203 days after taking the weapons from Billy Wilson, Garrett used Wilson's Colt pistol to kill Billy the Kid.

In April, 1906, Garrett loaned the guns to Powers to display in his saloon. As a consequence, Garrett did not have the option of carrying the pistol on the day he was killed.

Powers asked for a certification of provenance for the weapons. Garrett provided one that read in part:

> *"This Colt 44 pistol is the one that I used to end the life of William Bonney, also known as 'Billy the Kid.' The gun carries the serial number 55093. I took the gun from one of the 'Kids' gang at the battle of 'Stinking Springs....' My position as Sheriff of Lincoln County allowed me to take and use any equiptment that I so desired...."*

> *"I have been asked to exibit these guns many times, but I was always afraid that they might be lost of stolen. Concent has been given to my friend, Tom Powers, to display them as he so pleases and to retain them until such time as I request their return."* [Spelling as in original]

> *"Signed P. F. Garrett"* [4]

Apolinaria Garrett holding the gun that killed Billy the Kid. The photo was taken October 7, 1934, by *El Paso Herald-Post* editor L. A. Wilke. Apolinaria is standing on the porch of her Las Cruces home. She was too sick to leave her house, so the gun was delivered to her by her attorney U. S. Goen. Pat Garrett loaned the gun in 1906 to Tom Powers for display in the Coney Island Saloon. After Powers died, his estate claimed the gun. Apolinaria sued for the return of the gun, which was awarded to her by the Texas Supreme Court on March 7, 1934. Courtesy Dan Crow, Sally Kading, Bob Gamboa, and Karla Steen.

On Garrett's death, the guns remained on display in the Coney Island Saloon until it closed in 1918.[5]

On October 27, 1926, Powers was interviewed by the *El Paso Herald* about his renowned gun collection. He said there were *"some 60 guns and as many more pistols"* in the collection. Asked about the pistol he got from Garrett, he said:

> *"While Pat Garrett was collector of customs at El Paso following his killing of Billy the Kid, I admired the gun so much that he gave it to me for my collection...."*

> *"After his death I took the gun to his widow, she lives at Las Cruces now, and asked her if she wanted it. She said no that Pat wanted me to have it and she had no use for it. It is my most prized pistol."* [6]

Almost four years later, on October 14, 1930, Powers tried to kill himself:

> *"Powers... shot himself shortly before 10 o'clock yesterday morning at his residence at 1127 Wyoming street. The same pistol used in protecting himself against criminals in the southwest during the 80's and 90's was used to inflict the wound."* [7]

The cause of Powers' suicide attempt was a case of incurable intestinal cancer, causing him excruciating pain.

> *"Police and physicians were called to Powers' residence by Powers a short time before he fired the shot. They found Powers in a rocking chair on the front porch of his home. He was gasping for breath and bleeding profusely. On the floor at his side was his .45 caliber single action pistol."* [8]

Powers had attempted to shoot himself in the heart, but missed the vital organ. He recovered from the gunshot wound, but on January 1, 1931, he died at his home from the cancer.[9]

On January 22, 1933, Apolinaria filed suit against the Powers' estate, claiming that the pistol that killed Billy the Kid belonged to her, that it had only been loaned to Powers. In her suit, she valued the pistol at $500.[10]

The trial began on April 24 1933. Apolinaria, testifying as plaintiff, said that her husband had given her the pistol as a gift in 1904, two years before the loan to Powers. Pauline Garrett, Apolinaria's daughter, testified that Powers had made a promise to her mother to return the pistol after Garrett's death, but never did.[11]

Ed Warren, a long-time Coney Island Saloon employee, testified for the defense. He swore he had seen Powers give Garrett money for the weapon, and that Powers later removed the tag from the weapon, indicating that the gun belonged to Powers.[12]

The court ruled for Apolinaria, awarding her the gun. The Powers' estate appealed to the eighth court of civil appeals.[14] On November 10, 1933, the appeals court affirmed the lower court ruling, that the gun was Apolinaria's.[14]

The Powers' estate appealed to the Texas Supreme Court. On March 7, 1934, the Supreme Court affirmed the awarding of the gun to Apolinaria.[15]

On October 5, 1934, the Colt pistol that killed Billy the Kid was finally returned to Apolinaria:

> *"At a little ceremony in Las Cruces, N. M. Atty. U. S. Goen, who obtained possession of the gun for Mrs. Garrett after a legal battle that went to the supreme court of Texas, will hand her the historic, single-action, .44 calibre revolver."*

> *"Mrs. Garrett is ill but said she would be able to stand on the front porch of her Las Cruces home and receive the gun."* [16]

The photo on page 208 was taken during the award ceremony by L. A. Wilke, editor of the *El Paso Herald-Post*.[17]

Apolinaria, the loyal wife of Pat Garrett, the mother of his eight children, lived two more years. She died October 21, 1936.[18]

In 1978, Jarvis Garrett sold the pistol in a private sale to Calvin Moerbe for an unknown amount.[19] In 1983, Moerbe sold the gun to Jim Earle, who, to the author's knowledge, still owns the gun.[20]

The house in Las Cruces where Apolinaria was living when she was presented with the pistol that killed Billy the Kid. Apolinaria purchased the house in 1929. The house still stands. 2019 photo.

Appendix C | The Pistol that Killed Pat Garrett

In a letter written in 1967, John Edgar Boyd, Sr., Wayne Brazel's father-in-law, described the gun that killed Garrett as a:

> "...pearl-handled, Frontier model Colt .45... [with a] 4-1/2 or 5-inch barrel....

> "The belt clip was on a thin but stiff leather scabbard along with a leather thong which allowed tying securely to either belt of suspender or both at the most comfortable and accessible position around the waist." [1]

When Brazel killed Garrett he was not carrying the gun in a scabbard, but had the pistol stuck in the *"waistband of his breeches."* [2]

In 1972, Jack Carter, who met Wayne Brazel in New Mexico in 1909, wrote in a *Frontier Times* article that Brazel traded the pistol that killed Garrett to a man named Charlie Burch. In exchange, Brazel got Burch's pistol. Carter quotes Brazel as saying to Burch:

> *"Charles, your pistol is smaller than mine. Let's swap."*

Carter wrote that the pistol had a *"file mark on it,"* representing the killing of Garrett. The mark was *"put there by [Sheriff] Felipe Lucero in 1908,"* according to Carter.[3]

Two years earlier, Carter had written Leon C. Metz, who he knew was working on a book about Garrett, that the widow of Charlie Burch possessed the gun that killed Garrett. He said he had made an offer on the gun, but it was refused.[4]

That, to the author's knowledge, is all that is publicly known about the gun that killed Pat Garrett.

Timeline

- June 5, 1850 – Patrick Floyd Jarvis Garrett born in Chambers County, Alabama

- February 9, 1861 – Apolinaria Gutierrez, Garrett's wife, born in Las Vegas, New Mexico.

- December 31, 1876 – Jesse Wayne Brazel born in Greenwood City, Kansas

- November, 1879 – Garrett marries his first wife, Juanita Martinez at Anton Chico. She dies a few days after the marriage. She is buried in the old Fort Sumner cemetery, the same cemetery where Billy the Kid is buried. Many sources falsely state that she was the sister of Garrett's second wife, Apolinaria. Not true. Juanita's parents were Albino and Feliciana Martinez. For more details, see the author's *"Billy The Kid's Grave – A History of the Wild West's Most Famous Death Marker."*

- January 14, 1880 – Garrett marries second wife Apolinaria Gutierrez at Anton Chico. Her parents were Jose Delores Gutierrez and Feliciana Valdez.

- February 20, 1881 – Adelaida "Ida" Garrett born at Lincoln, New Mexico. She was named after one of Garrett's sisters.

- July 14, 1881 – Garrett kills Billy the Kid in Pete Maxwell's bedroom at Fort Sumner, New Mexico. For an account revealing new details about the killing, see the author's *"Billy The Kid's Grave – A History of the Wild West's Most Famous Death Marker."*

- August 1, 1882 – William W. Brazel homesteads a ranch on Eagle Creek

- September 4, 1883 – Garrett buys a ranch on Eagle Creek

- October 9, 1885 – Elizabeth "Lizzie" Garrett born on Eagle Creek

- February 22, 1886 – Garrett presents W. W. Brazel with a watch and chain

- May 24, 1887 – Wayne Brazel is only witness to Conner-Terrell shooting at Eagle Creek. Conner was W. W. Brazel's brother-in-law. Terrell was married to W. W. Brazel's daughter Marrieta.

- June 4, 1887 – Conner acquitted of shooting Terrell on grounds of self-defense

- June 8, 1887 – Dudley Poe Garrett born at Roswell, New Mexico

- December 21, 1888 – Olive E. Boyd, Wayne Brazel's future wife, born in Lake Valley, New Mexico

- October 2, 1889 – Elizabeth Ann "Annie" Garrett born in Roswell

- December 17, 1889 – W. W. Brazel buys Gold Camp mine from brother-in-law William A. Conner

- June 12, 1890 – George Curry, Jno. F. Eubanks, and Garrett sign fateful note for $1000 with the Bank of Commerce in Albuquerque

- 1891 – W. W. Brazel moves to Mormon Mine at Gold Camp from Eagle Creek

- April 13, 1891 – Garrett moves his family to Uvalde, Texas

- April 17, 1891 – Garrett rents his ranch in Lincoln

- May 3, 1891 – Garrett sells his Lincoln ranch for $17,000, $5,000 cash and $12,000 in payments
- October 19, 1891 – Garrett buys a ranch in Uvalde, Texas

- February 12, 1893 – Oliver Lee kills Charles Rhodius
- February 18, 1893 – Jesse Madison Brazel and W. W. Brazel, Jr. assault Levino Telles
- April 13, 1893 – Jesse Madison and W. W. Brazel, Jr. arrested for assaulting Telles
- April 15, 1893 – Jesse Madison and W. W. Brazel, Jr. indicted for assaulting Telles
- November 9, 1893 – W. W. Brazel dies of illness at Gold Camp

- March 10, 1894 – Jesse Madison Brazel sick at Organ
- March 16, 1894 – Wayne Brazel testifies in Levino Telles case

- April 2, 1895 – Subpoena for Jesse Madison Brazel to appear in Lincoln Court
- October 19, 1895 – Mrs. W. W. Brazel dies (Sarah)

- January 12, 1896 – Colonel Albert J. Fountain and Henry leave for Lincoln
- January 30, 1896 – Colonel Fountain leaves Lincoln, spends night at Blazer's Mill
- January 31, 1896 – Colonel Fountain spends night at La Luz
- February 1, 1896 – Colonel Fountain and Henry disappear on road from La Luz to Las Cruces
- February 2, 1896 – Mail carrier Barela notifies Fountain family of suspicious tracks
- February 7, 1896 – Governor Thornton offers a $500 reward to anyone providing information leading to the conviction of the killers of Colonel Fountain and Henry. He also offers immunity to anyone involved who provides such information.
- February 17, 1896 – Governor Thornton increases the reward to $500 per person involved in the killings, and also promises a full pardon to anyone who turns state witness.
- February 21, 1896 – Governor Thornton, Albert Fall, and others meet in El Paso and decide to hire Garrett as a *"private detective,"* and if possible later appoint him sheriff.
- February 21, 1896 – Fitzsimmons-Maher prizefight blocked at El Paso and moved to Langtry, Texas
- February 23, 1896 – Patrick Floyd Garrett, Jr. born in Uvalde, Texas
- February 23, 1896 – Garrett arrives in Las Cruces meets Governor Thornton. He accepts Thornton's job offer to find the Fountain murders.
- February 27, 1896 – Governor Thornton hires Pinkerton Detective John Conklin Fraser to investigate Fountain killing
- March 5, 1896 – Pinkerton operative Fraser arrives in Las Cruces by train
- March 6, 1896 – Garrett in Las Cruces on trail of Fountain killers
- March 8, 1896 – Garrett and operative Fraser meet at Lindell Hotel in El Paso
- March 9, 1896 – Garrett travels to Santa Fe to consult with Governor Thornton
- March 11, 1896 – Garrett returns to Las Cruces from consulting Governor Thornton
- March 18, 1896 – Operative Fraser meets with Oliver Lee in Fall's office
- March 20, 1896 – Numa Reymond declared Dona Ana County sheriff
- March 22, 1896 – Garrett letter to wife about being appointed sheriff
- March 25, 1896 – Garrett acting as sheriff
- March 25, 1896 – Operative Fraser leaves Las Cruces
- March 26, 1896 – Garrett signs contract with Jack Maxwell for $2,000

- April 11, 1896 – Pinkerton Operative William C. Sayers assigned to Fountain case
- April 12, 1896 – Garrett leaves for Uvalde to get family
- April 19, 1896 – Garrett arrives in Las Cruces from Uvalde with his family
- April 22, 1896 – Garrett arrests Luis Herrera
- May 12, 1896 – Operative Sayers discontinues investigating Fountain case
- May 29, 1896 – Dead man found near Wildy Well
- July 3, 1896 – Garrett appointed deputy U. S. Marshall for the Territory of New Mexico
- July 8, 1896 – Ida Garrett visits Van Patten Dripping Springs Resort
- August 8, 1896 – Garrett and Albert Fall travel to Santa Fe and convince Governor Thornton to remove two (Republican) Dona Ana County commissioners so Garrett can be made sheriff
- August 10, 1896 – Garrett appointed sheriff by county commissioners
- October 9, 1896 – Jesus Garcia sentenced to hang for murdering Isabella Montoya.
- October 12, 1896 – Ida Garrett dies of tonsillitis
- October 16, 1896 – Garrett acceptance speech
- October 27, 1896 – Scaffold for Jesus Garcia hanging erected
- November 3, 1896 – Garrett gives campaign speech to Dona Ana County Republican Convention
- November 3, 1896 – Election day for territorial and county offices
- November 6, 1896 – Garrett hangs Jesus Garcia, convicted of first-degree murder.
- November 6, 1896 – Garrett elected Dona Ana County sheriff
- November 6, 1896 – Albert Fall elected to the New Mexico Territorial Council

- January 15, 1897 – Garrett's deputy John McLeod murdered
- February 12, 1897 – Garrett brings carload of horses to Las Cruces
- March 12, 1897 – Garrett and family are now occupying the Christy brick cottage
- March 30, 1897 – Garrett solves Chacon murder
- April 2, 1897 – Garrett in Santa Fe for hanging of Chavez murderers
- April 3, 1897 – Governor Thornton resigns as governor of New Mexico
- April 22, 1897 – Lorion Millier appointed acting governor of New Mexico
- June 2, 1897 – H. D. Bowman of Bowman bank writes Bank of Commerce and says that Garrett *"is not worth anything,"* and is not *"prompt in payment."*
- June 6, 1897 – Miguel A. Otero confirmed by U.S. Senate as governor of New Mexico
- June 7, 1897 – Garrett arrests John Pruit, William W. Brazel, Jr., and Noah Barefoot for the murder of Vicente Sanchez
- June 13, 1897 – Fuentes escapes from Las Cruces jail
- July 30, 1897 – Garrett appointed trustee in the Coghlan property sale
- September 15, 1897 – Cox and Lee buy Coghlan cattle for $22,500.
- September 19, 1897 – Garrett served lawsuit papers by the clerk of the Second Judicial District for 1890 Bank of Commerce loan that he co-signed
- October 16, 1897 – Garrett's attorney files demurrer stating that Garrett has been out of the county for 3 years and should not be liable for the note
- November 23, 1897 – Garrett brings horses from Uvalde
- December 10, 1897 – Garrett purchases Garrett Home Ranch from W. W. Cox

- January 7, 1898 – Lee marries Winnie Pocahontas Rhode, Cox's sister in law.
- January 28, 1898 – Bank of Commerce gets judgment against Garrett for $997.92
- April 3, 1898 – Garrett arrests McNew and Carr for murdering the Fountains
- April 9, 1898 – McNew and Carr preliminary examination begins
- April 16, 1898 – McNew held without bail for trial for murder; Carr dismissed, no charge
- July 10, 1898 – Shootout at Wildy Well
- July 14, 1898 – Kent Kearney dies from gunshot wounds
- August 11, 1898 – Garrett strikes Sam Bean
- August 17, 1898 – *Independent Democrat* article against Garrett
- August 26, 1898 – Garrett announces he will run for a second term as sheriff
- October 6, 1898 – Garrett indicts Carlton Bull, editor of *Independent Democrat,* for libel
- September 7, 1898 – Oliver M. Lee, Jr. born to Oliver Lee
- November 8, 1898 – Garrett re-elected sheriff

- January 30, 1899 – Creation of Otero County from Dona Ana County
- March 13, 1899 – Garrett and Texas Ranger Captain Hughes transport Geronimo Parra by train from Santa Fe to El Paso
- March 13, 1899 – Lee and Gililland surrender to Judge Parker
- March 25, 1899 – Lee and Gililland arraigned for Fountain killings and jailed in Socorro
- March 28, 1899 – George Curry appointed sheriff of Otero County by Governor Otero
- April 26, 1899 – Several of Garrett's children get smallpox
- April 27, 1899 – Lee and Gililland travel to El Paso
- May 24, 1899 – David Wood sells Rock House Ranch to Garrett for $200
- May 25, 1899 – Lee and Gililland trial for killing the Fountains opens at 10 a.m.
- June 2, 1899 – Garrett testifies at Lee and Gililland trial
- June 7, 1899 – Curry testifies at Lee and Gililland trial for defense
- June 9, 1899 – Lee testifies at trial
- June 13, 1899 – Lee and Gililland acquitted after 7 minutes of deliberation (at midnight)
- June 21, 1899 – Geronimo Parra convicted of first degree murder at El Paso
- September 8, 1899 – George Curry resigns as Otero County sheriff
- September 11, 1899 – Pauline Juliet Garrett born in Las Cruces
- October 9, 1899 – Newman shot at Cox ranch by deputy sheriff Jose Espalin
- October 11, 1899 – Garrett libel case against Bull quashed. Fall represented Bull.
- October 15, 1899 – Rincon Post Office robbed

- January 5, 1900 – Geronimo Parra hung in El Paso
- January 12, 1900 – Santa Cruz Garcia captured
- February 12, 1900 – Bowman Bank robbed by two men
- March 19, 1900 – Bowman Bank robbers arrested in San Antonio
- April 25, 1900 – Bowman Bank robbers Wilbur and Wilson convicted
- August 20, 1900 – Garrett takes out life insurance policy
- August 21, 1900 – Claude Barbee kills Deputy Kinney Hamilton

- August 29, 1900 – Garrett reported killed in *El Paso Herald*
- September 24, 1900 – Dona Ana County Republican Convention selects Garrett for US House of Representatives delegate
- October 3, 1900 – Territorial Republican Convention opens in Santa Fe
- October 9, 1900 – Bowman Bank robber Oscar J. Wilbur pardoned by Governor Otero
- December 23, 1900 – Garrett Deputy Carlos Telles kills Juan Telles
- December 31, 1900 – Garrett's last day as sheriff

- January, 1901 – Jose R. Lucero begins term as Dona Ana County sheriff
- February 20, 1901 – Garrett borrows $500 from Catron
- February 21, 1901 – Bank of Commerce asks Bowman to handle debt collection
- February 23, 1901 – Bank of Commerce offers to settle for $1000
- March 1, 1901 – Bank of Commerce writes Bowman asking for him to tell them *"privately what Garrett has. Would it be worth while to run any more garnishments down that way?"*
- March 21, 1901 – Bank of Commerce asks Bowman if he has settled the judgment
- April 2, 1901 – Carlos Telles sentenced to 35 years in penitentiary
- April 9, 1901 – Bank of Commerce asks Bowman if Garrett is trying to get a loan
- May 5, 1901 – Garrett and statehood committee meet with President McKinley in El Paso
- September 6, 1901 – President William McKinley shot by Leon Czolgosz
- September 14, 1901 – President William McKinley dies from wounds
- September 15, 1901 – Theodore "Teddy" Roosevelt, Jr. sworn in as U. S. president
- September 23, 1901 – Fall offers Garrett tax receiver job
- October 1, 1901 – Garrett gets receiver's bond for $5,000
- October 29, 1901 – McKinley's assassin executed
- December 8, 1901 – Garrett in Washington DC to solicit El Paso collector of customs position
- December 11, 1901 – Garrett, Fall, and ex-New Mexico Governor Lew Wallace visit President Roosevelt in White House about his appointment
- December 18, 1901 – Garrett appointed collector of customs

- January 2, 1902 – Garrett sworn in as El Paso collector of customs
- January 22, 1902 – Albert Fall's father made collector at Columbus
- April 8, 1902 – Garrett mortgages his two ranches to Martin Lohman for $3567.50
- April 16, 1902 – Oscar Lohman's daughter burns to death
- July 7, 1902 – Garrett in New York for Corralitos Company customs case
- July 19, 1902 – Garrett visits shooting gallery at Coney Island, New York
- August 4, 1902 – Harry Silberberg, alias James J. Craig, arrives in El Paso
- September 2, 1902 – Board rules against Garrett in Corralitos Company dispute
- September 17, 1902 – Garrett appeals Corralitos Company ruling
- November 13, 1902 – Craig diamonds confiscated by Inspector Dwyer

- January 2, 1903 – Garrett goes to Mexico City to interview Craig
- February 8, 1903 – Garrett writes to President Roosevelt about complaints against him
- February 24, 1903 – I. A. Barnes starts petition to remove Garrett

- March 9, 1903 – Garrett hires George M. Gaither for 30 days as ordered by Agent Evans.
- March 17, 1903 – Garrett ordered to be nicer by Secretary of Treasury Shaw
- April 7, 1903 – Garrett fires Gaither
- April 14, 1903 – Garrett loses Corralitos Company appeal
- April 25, 1903 – Garrett takes Elizabeth Garrett to Austin for eye operation
- May 4, 1903 – Garrett travels to Santa Fe to greet President Roosevelt
- May 5, 1903 – Garrett travels with President Roosevelt to Albuquerque in the President's dining car, sitting at the President's right
- May 8, 1903 – Garrett fights with Gaither
- May 9, 1903 – Garrett fined $5 for fight with Gaither
- May 26, 1903 – Carlos Telles pardoned for killing Juan Telles
- June 17, 1903 – Catron writes Garrett asking that his $500 loan to be repaid
- July 22, 1903 – Garrett's El Paso home is burglarized
- September 1, 1903 – Barnes forced to resign
- September 10, 1903 – Garrett buys $5,000 life insurance policy from New York Life Insurance Company
- December 19, 1903 – Garrett sells his race horse Patchen for $500
- December 30, 1903 – Oscar Lohman Garrett born in El Paso – named after Oscar Lohman

- January 29, 1904 – Garrett appoints Poe clerk in Customs Office
- April 8, 1904 – Renewal of Lohman Mortgage on Garrett ranches for $3567.50
- April 24, 1904 – Bank of Commerce files Certificate of Default for Curry loan
- April 24, 1904 – Garrett travels to Sinaloa, Mexico, to investigate land deal
- June 10, 1904 – Elizabeth Garrett graduates from Blind Institute
- July 18, 1904 – Sheriff Lucero serves court summons on Garrett
- August 19, 1904 – Sinaloa land deal fails
- September 7, 1904 – Bernalillo court issues recovery decree for $1733.13
- September 16, 1904 – Elizabeth Garrett sings at world fair in St Louis, Missouri
- November 8, 1904 – Teddy Roosevelt elected president
- November 22, 1904 – Garrett announces candidacy for re-appointment as Collector

- March 15, 1905 – Jesse Madison Brazel, Wayne Brazel's father, dies in mine cave-in
- April 3, 1905 – Martin Lohman assigns Garrett mortgage to W. W. Cox
- April 7, 1905 – Garrett joins President Roosevelt at Rough Riders reunion, takes Thomas Powers with him
- June 23, 1905 – Adamson and Miller charged with swindling in Stephens, Texas
- July 28, 1905 – Jarvis Powers Garrett born in Las Cruces
- October 14, 1905 – Garrett and Emerson Hough leave El Paso for camping trip
- October 10, 1905 – Craig diamond case settle by court
- October 25, 1905 – Garrett visits Billy the Kid's grave with Hough
- December 5, 1905 – Garrett and Powers leave for Washington D. C.
- December 12, 1905 – Garrett meets with President Roosevelt in Washington D.C.
- December 15, 1905 – Garrett not re-appointed customs collector
- December 20, 1905 – Sharpe confirmed as El Paso Customs Collector by U. S. Senate

- December 31, 1905 – Garrett's last day as collector
- January 1, 1906 – Sharpe takes charge of the El Paso customs office
- January 15, 1906 – Garrett writes Fall that he can't repay $50 loan
- January 16, 1906 – Garrett goes to Mexico to investigate Finstad case
- February 2, 1906 – Garrett meets with President Roosevelt about Finstad case
- March 15, 1906 – Finstad and Coughener sentenced to 12-1/2 years in prison – Garrett attended the trial in Mexico
- May 10, 1906 – Bernalillo Court orders Garrett property confiscated to pay for judgment
- May 25, 1906 – Sheriff Lucero seizes Garrett property (at 6:30 a.m.). Notice of levy given to Apolinaria and Poe Garrett
- May 26, 1906 – Cox renews mortgage on Garrett's ranches and livestock
- June 5, 1906 – Garrett writes Bank of Commerce lawyer Childers with a settlement offer
- June 6, 1906 – Childers writes Garrett saying settlement offer declined. He also states that Garrett's request that the bank go after Curry for the loan is declined by the bank because Curry is in the Philippines and to sue him there *"would be very troublesome and they do not know that he has anything except his salary from the government."*
- June 23, 1906 – Garrett files writ of replevin alleging that certain livestock confiscated by Sheriff Lucero belongs to his wife and must be returned.
- June 23, 1906 – Garrett $580 files bond for replevin – surties are Martin Lohman and Albert J. Fountain, Jr.
- July 6, 1906 – First newspaper notice of sheriff sale of Garrett's property. Date of sale is set as August 4, 1906.
- July 11, 1906 – Garrett lawyer notifies Bank of Commerce that his home ranch is his homestead (residence). Garrett further claims that the Rock House Ranch does not belong to him and did not belong to him at the time of the levy.
- July 28, 1906 – Two appraisers appraise Garrett's Home Ranch and improvements at $225 and his spring at $250. No appraisal of the Rock House Ranch.
- August 4, 1906 – Sheriff Lucero certifies that the seized Garrett property was sold at auction at the courthouse door between 10 am and 3 pm as ordered by the court and that the buyer was the Bank of Commerce. The bank bid and paid $500 for each ranch. No livestock was sold.
- August 17 – Dona Ana County auctions Garrett's livestock for unpaid taxes
- August 17, 1906 – Cox renews mortgage on Garrett's remaining livestock
- August 17, 1906 – Lucero lists prices for all Garrett property, including livestock, bought by Bank of Commerce, plus the costs of men to guard property and round-up stock.
- September, 1906 – Garrett gets property back – Rock House Ranch in Poe's name
- December 29, 1906 – Fall sends Garrett $50 check

- January 3, 1907 – Garrett writes to Fall asking for help buying cattle
- January 9, 1907 – Fall replies to Garrett refusing help on financial grounds
- February 7, 1907 – Garrett writes Hough asking for financial help
- February 12, 1907 – Hough replies to Garret refusing help on financial grounds

- March 11, 1907 – Poe Garrett leases Rock House Ranch to Wayne Brazel for 5 years. Fee is 10 Hereford calves and one mare colt payable every July.
- April 18, 1907 – George Curry appointed governor of New Mexico
- June 21, 1907 – Garrett writes to Llewellyn asking him to ask Curry to pay part of the Bank of Commerce recovery costs
- June 29, 1907 – Cox loans Brazel $574.80 to buy goats for Rock House Ranch
- July 23, 1907 – Garrett meets with Curry and discusses a possible job appointment
- July 24, 1907 – Garrett writes to Apolinaria about his meeting with Curry
- August 6, 1907 – Garrett boards Curry inauguration train from El Paso to Santa Fe
- November 1, 1907 – Cox renews mortgage on Garrett's livestock

- January 1908 – Garrett has Brazel arrested for herding stock within a mile and half of his ranch house. The case is dismissed by the Justice of the Peace in Organ.
- February 2, 1908 – Garrett comes to Las Cruces from El Paso
- February 4, 1908 – Miller and Adamson travel to Las Cruces to buy John Leatherman's ranch
- February 6, 1908 – Adamson and Miller meet Garrett at his Home Ranch and discuss buying his ranches. This is the first time Adamson has met Garrett
- February 7, 1908 – Albert Fall recommends Brazel to Governor Curry for a mounted policeman position
- February 16, 1908 – Garrett comes to Las Cruces from El Paso
- February 17, 1908 – Garrett still in Las Cruces
- February 18, 1908 – Garrett returns to El Paso
- February 22, 1908 – Adamson and Miller meet with Brazel in El Paso to negotiate buying Brazel's goats. Brazel signs a contract to sell 1,200 goats to Adamson at $3.50 a head.
- February 25, 1908 – Brazel comes to Las Cruces from Gold Camp
- February 27, 1908 – Suspicious tracks of two horses found around Garrett's Home Ranch
- February 28, 1908 – Adamson comes to Las Cruces from El Paso by train. He rents a buggy for the trip to Garrett's Home Ranch. He arrives at the ranch at 5 p.m.
- February 28, 1908 – Brazel gets note to meet Garrett and Adamson in Las Cruces the next day to sign the sale papers
- February 29, 1908 – Garrett and Adamson leave Garrett Home Ranch for Las Cruces at 8:30 a.m.
- February 29, 1908 – Miller comes into Las Cruces from El Paso by train, takes a room at the Park Hotel
- February 29, 1908 – Garrett is killed sometime between 10 and 11 a.m.
- February 29, 1908 – Llewellyn writes Governor Curry about Garrett's death
- February 29, 1908 – Garrett's body taken to Strong Undertaking Parlor
- February 29, 1908 – Coroner's jury issues ruling on Garrett's death
- March 1, 1908 – Garrett's family learns of Garrett's death at 1:30 p.m.
- March 1, 1908 – Casket arrives from El Paso – supplied by Nagley & Kaster
- March 1, 1908 – Apolinaria Garrett lodging with Oscar Lohman family in Las Cruces
- March 2, 1908 – Apolinaria Garrett telegrams Governor Curry
- March 2, 1908 – Poe files complaint against Brazel for murder
- March 3, 1908 – Brazel pleads not guilty of murdering Garrett

- March 3, 1908 – Garrett's funeral postponed
- March 3, 1908 – Miller still in Las Cruces at Park Hotel
- March 4, 1908 – Poe gets anonymous letter asserting Garrett was murdered
- March 4, 1908 – Garrett's two brothers arrive from Haynesville, Louisiana
- March 4, 1908 – Governor Curry arrives in Las Cruces from Santa Fe
- March 4, 1908 – Mounted Policeman John A. Beal arrives in Las Cruces
- March 4, 1908 – Governor Curry, Attorney General Hervey, and Sheriff Lucero meet with Adamson in Curry's hotel room
- March 4, 1908 – Preliminary examination to determine whether to charge Brazel with murder
- March 4, 1908 – Brazel released on $10,000 bail raised by Cox
- March 4, 1908 – Adamson and Print Rhode travel to El Paso
- March 4, 1908 – Attorney General Hervey, Dr. Field, and Adamson visit death site (there is *no* evidence that Captain Fornoff was with them, or even in Las Cruces)
- March 5, 1908 – Garrett's funeral held – Governor Curry is one of the pallbearers
- March 5, 1908 – Garrett buried in Odd Fellows Cemetery
- April 3, 1908 – Adamson and Dr. Field testify before grand jury
- April 6, 1908 – Brazel indicted for murdering Garrett in the first degree
- April 22, 1908 – Annie Garrett receives anonymous letter stating Print Rhode helped to kill Garrett
- April 28, 1908 – Brazel trial postponed until October, 1908, session of court
- May 2, 1908 – Brazel gets the measles
- June 16, 1908 – Adamson, William Sullivan, and John N. Webb meet at the Coney Island Saloon and conspire to smuggle Chinese immigrants into New Mexico
- June 21, 1908 – Adamson and Sullivan arrested for smuggling 16 illegal Chinese immigrants into New Mexico
- July 7, 1908 – Renewal of Garrett debt to W. W. Cox
- August 15, 1908 – Renewal of loan on Garrett livestock
- October 23, 1908 – Brazel trial for killing Garrett postponed
- November 27, 1908 – Adamson et al indicted for conspiracy to smuggle Chinese
- December 1, 1908 – Poe and Apolinaria Garrett to sell ranches
- December 5, 1908 – Cox buys Garrett Home Ranch
- December 7-8, 1908 – Adamson tried for conspiracy to smuggle Chinese
- December 9, 1908 – Adamson convicted of conspiracy to smuggle Chinese
- December 14, 1908 – Adamson sentenced to 18 months in the penitentiary
- December 14, 1908 – Adamson files appeal and released on $4,000 bond

- January 23, 1909 – Apolinaria Garrett buys house in Las Cruces for $550
- February 27, 1909 – Allen Augustus Bobbitt assassinated by James B. Miller
- March 12, 1909 – Hervey resigns as NM Attorney General
- April 16, 1909 – W. D. Whitley claims he killed Garrett
- April 19, 1909 – James B. Miller and three others lynched at Ada, Oklahoma
- April 21, 1909 – Stahl makes conspiracy claims
- May 4, 1909 – Brazel acquitted of killing Garrett by reason of self-defense
- May 18, 1909 – Cox loans Brazel $300 to pay off his trial costs
- May 19, 1909 – Governor Curry debunks Stahl's accusations
- May 24, 1909 – Finstad and Coughener released from jail in Mexico

- July 23, 1909 – Fall issues letter debunking Stahl's claims and stating the facts of the Brazel murder case as established by the evidence of the trial
- October 20, 1909 – Brazel and two partners buy Harrington Ranch for $1,000

- January 6, 1910 – New Mexico Supreme Court affirms Adamson conviction
- January 16, 1910 – Adamson appeals to 8th District Circuit Court of Appeals
- March 31, 1910 – Brazel enumerated in 1910 census at Steins Pass, New Mexico
- July 8, 1910 – Print Rhode kills Lee Murphy
- August 21, 1910 – 8th Circuit Court of Appeals affirms Adamson's sentence
- September 5, 1910 – Wayne Brazel marries Olive Boyd

- May 11, 1911 – Print Rhode sentenced to 20 years in the penitentiary
- June 7, 1911 – Wayne Brazel's son Jesse Vaughn Brazel born
- August 21, 1911 – Adamson sentenced to 18 months in the penitentiary for smuggling Chinese.
- November 16, 1911 – Olive Boyd Brazel dies of pneumonia

- 1912 – Brazel takes out $10,000 life insurance policy with his son as beneficiary

- February 20, 1913 – Adamson enters penitentiary to serve 18-month sentence
- February 27, 1913 – Brazel sells his homestead to Joseph G. Olney
- February 27, 1913 – Cox sues Brazel for repayment of two loans ($1506.16)
- April 21, 1913 – Brazel pays $1506.16 to Cox to settle his loan debt
- December 23, 1913 – Print Rhode released to custody of New Mexico governor

- April 24, 1914 – Brazel arrested for perjury on a homestead filing
- May 22, 1914 – Brazel perjury case postponed
- July 10, 1914 – Brazel registers to vote at Ash Fork, Yavapai County, Arizona
- November 11, 1914 – Brazel perjury case dismissed
- November 11, 1914 – Last documented evidence of Brazel being alive

- September 23, 1915 – McNew kills Robert H. Raley

- April 15, 1916 – McNew acquitted of killing Raley
- April 18, 1916 – Print Rhode issued pardon by governor of Arizona

- 1919 – Feliciana (Valdez) Gutierrez, Apolinaria's Mother, dies in Las Cruces

- August 4, 1922 – Ann "Annie" (Montgomery) Garrett dies in Las Cruces

- May 26, 1927 – Patrick Floyd Garrett, Jr., dies in Mexico City, Mexico

- December 8, 1930 – Dudley Poe Garrett dies in El Paso, Texas

- March 7, 1934 – Apolinaria awarded the pistol that killed Billy the Kid by Texas Supreme Court

- April 26, 1936 – New York Life Insurance Company refuses to pay insurance policy on Brazel's life taken out in 1912.
- October 21, 1936 – Apolinaria (Gutierrez) Garrett dies in Las Cruces

- December 25, 1950 – Expedition to locate Fountain bodies fails to find remains

- November, 1952 – Garrett family remains moved from Las Cruces IOOF cemetery to Las Cruces Masonic Cemetery

Notes

1 – A Fresh Start

1. *Daily New Mexican*, Feb. 21, 1896; *Western Liberal (Lordsburg)*, Feb. 2, 18, 1896.

2. *San Antonio Daily Light*, Feb. 8, 1896; *The Eagle (Bryan, TX)*, Feb. 11, 1896; Brownsville Herald, Feb. 22, 1896.

3. *Sierra County Advocate*, Feb. 28. When the news of the meeting was published, Albert Fall told the press that he had not agreed to the hiring Garrett, and was strenuously opposed to it.

4. David G. Thomas, *Billy the Kid's Grave - A History of the Wild West's Most Famous Death Marker* (Doc45 Publications, 2018), p. 13.

5. Patrick F. Garrett, Letter to Apolinaria Garrett, Feb. 25, 1896. Copy provided to author by Sally Kading.

6. *Roswell Record*, Apr. 18, 1891; Jarvis P. Garrett, Foreword to *The Authentic Life of Billy, the Kid, the Noted Desperado of the Southwest, Whose Deeds of Daring Have Made His Name a Terror in New Mexico, Arizona, and Northern Mexico*, by Pat F. Garrett, (Horn & Wallace, 1964), p 22.

7. Garrett, Letter to Ida Garrett, Mar. 2, 1896. Copy in author's possession.

8. Garrett, Letter to Apolinaria, Feb. 25, 1896. Copy in author's possession.

9. *Independent Democrat*, Mar. 25, 1896.

10. Garrett, Letter to Apolinaria, Feb. 25, 1896. Copy in author's possession.

11. John Conklin Fraser, Letter to New Mexico Governor William T. Thornton, Feb. 27, 1896. *Pinkerton Report Regarding Disappearance of Colonel Albert J. Fountain*, Arrell Gibson Collection, MSSU Archives and Special Collections

12. C. L. Sonnichsen, *Tularosa, Last of the Frontier West* (Devin-Adair Co., 1980), p 117.

13. Lincoln County Court Records, William A. Keleher Papers, MSS 742 BC, Center for Southwest Research, UNM. Brand defacing was charged when it could not be proved that an animal was stolen, but it could be proved that its brand had been changed.

14. A. M. Gibson, *The Life and Death of Colonel Albert Jennings Fountain* (Univ. of Oklahoma Press, 1965), p 219.

15. Cree, Letter from Colonel Albert J. Fountain, Oct. 3, 1895. Mary Daniels Taylor Papers, Archives and Special Collections, NMSU.

16. Gibson, *Life and Death*, p 227. This is the same Lincoln County Courthouse that Billy the Kid had escaped from.

17. *El Paso Times*, Apr. 16, 1898.

18. *El Paso Times*, Apr. 16, 1898.

19. *El Paso Herald*, June 2, 1899.

20. *El Paso Times*, Apr. 12, 1898; *San Francisco Chronicle*, May 31, 1899; *El Paso Herald*, June 1, 1899.

21. *El Paso Times*, Apr. 12, 1898.

22. *El Paso Herald*, June 2, 1899; *El Paso Herald*, May 31, 1899.

23. *El Paso Times*, Apr. 12, 1898.

24. *El Paso Herald*, June 1, 1899.

25. *El Paso Herald*, June 1, 1899.

26. *El Paso Herald*, June 1, 1899.

27. *El Paso Herald*, June 2, 1899.

28. *El Paso Herald*, May 31, 1899.

29. *El Paso Herald*, May 31, 1899.

30. *El Paso Herald*, May 31, 1899.

31 *El Paso Herald*, June 5, 1899.

32. *El Paso Herald*, June 6, 1899.

33. *El Paso Herald*, June 5, 1899.

34. *El Paso Herald*, May 31, 1899.

35. *El Paso Herald*, June 2, 1899.

36. *Pinkerton Report*, Mar. 5, 1896.

37. *Pinkerton Report*, Mar. 5, 1896.

38. *Pinkerton Report*, Mar. 23, 1896.

39. *El Paso Times*, Feb. 27, 1896.

40. *Rio Grande Republican*, Mar. 6, 1896.

41. *Pinkerton Report*, Mar. 7, 1898.

42. Thornton, Executive Order, Feb 17, 1896, State Records Center and Archives, Fr. 161.

43 Many sources incorrectly spell the name Gilliland. I have corrected all documents.

44. *Pinkerton Report,* Mar. 12, 1898.

45. *Pinkerton Report,* Mar. 12, 1896.

46. *El Paso Herald,* June 2, 1899.

47. *El Paso Herald,* June 3, 1899. Charles C. Perry was sheriff of Roswell.

48. *Pinkerton Report,* Mar. 18, 1896.

49. *Pinkerton Report,* Mar. 18, 1896.

50. *Pinkerton Report,* Apr. 14, 1896.

51. *Pinkerton Report,* Apr. 14, 1896.

52. *Pinkerton Report,* Apr. 15, 1896.

53. *Pinkerton Report,* Apr. 15, 1896.

54. *Pinkerton Report,* May 11, 1896.

55. *Las Vegas Daily Optic,* May 16, 1896; *Las Vegas Daily Optic,* May 29, 1896.

56. Garrett, Letter to Apolinaria, Feb. 25, 1896. Copy in author's possession.

57. *Rio Grande Republican,* Mar. 20, 1896.

58. *Independent Democrat,* Mar. 25, 1896.

59. Garrett, Letter to Apolinaria, Mar. 22, 1898. Copy in author's possession.

60. *Independent Democrat,* Mar. 25, 1896.

61. *Independent Democrat,* Mar. 25, 1896.

62. *Independent Democrat,* Apr. 1, 1896.

63 *Independent Democrat,* Apr. 1, 1896.

64. *Daily New Mexican,* Apr. 10, 1896.

65. *Southwest Sentinel* (Silver City), May 5, 1896.

66. *Rio Grande Republican,* May 29, 1896.

67. *The Eagle (Silver City),* Apr. 22, 1896.

68. Garrett, Marshall's Appointment, July 3, 1896, U.S. Marshals Service, National Archives and Records Administration.

69. *Rio Grande Republican,* Aug. 14, 1896.

70. *Independent Democrat,* Aug. 12, 1896.

71. *Rio Grande Republican,* Apr. 17, 1896.

72. Keleher, "Pat Garrett Notes," undated, William A. Keleher Papers. Ida was born Feb. 20, 1881. Billy the Kid was killed July 14, 1881.

73. *Roswell Daily Record,* Oct. 17, 1947.

74. *El Paso Evening Post,* Dec. 9, 1930; Dudley Poe Garrett Registration Card, Fold3.com; Garrett Dudley Poe Texas Death Certificate, No. 18901976, Fold3.com.

75. *El Paso Times,* Mar. 4, 1908.

76. *Lincoln County Leader,* Aug. 7, 1922; *El Paso Herald,* Apr. 24, 1886.

77. Garrett, Letter to Ida, Mar. 2, 1896. Copy in author's possession.

78. *El Paso Herald,* Sept. 9, 1908; Fold3.com, Patrick Floyd Garrett Jr., Draft Registration Card, undated.

79. Thomas, *Billy the Kid's Grave,* p 11.

80. Garrett, Letter to Apolinaria, Mar. 1, 1894. Copy in author's possession.

81. Garrett, Letter to Apolinaria, Mar. 22, 1894. Copy in author's possession.

82. Garett, Letter to Apolinaria, Dec. 18, 1901. Copy in author's possession.

83. Garrett, Letter to Apolinaria, Mar. 22, 1896. Copy in author's possession.

84. *Rio Grande Republican,* Apr. 24, 1896.

85. *Rio Grande Republican,* Oct. 16, 1896.

86. *Independent Democrat,* Oct. 14, 1896.

87. Keleher, Pat Garrett Notes, undated, William A. Keleher Papers.

88. *Rio Grande Republican,* Oct. 9, 1896.

89. *Rio Grande Republican,* Aug. 14, 1896.

90. *Las Vegas Daily Optic,* Nov. 11, 1896.

91. *Las Vegas Daily Optic,* Nov. 9, 1896.

92. *Rio Grande Republican,* Nov. 6, 1896.

93. *Rio Grande Republican,* Nov. 6, 1896.

94. *Rio Grande Republican,* Nov. 6, 1896.

95. *Rio Grande Republican,* Oct. Oct 30, 1896.

96. *Rio Grande Republican,* Oct. Oct 30, 1896.

97. *Rio Grande Republican,* Nov. 13, 1896.

98. *Rio Grande Republican,* Nov. 6, 1896.

2. Hard Working Sheriff – 1897-1898

1. *Rio Grande Republican,* Jan. 22, 1897.

2. *El Paso Herald,* Jan. 20, 1897.

3. *Dona Ana County Republican,* Apr. 1, 1897.

4. *El Paso Herald,* Mar. 30, 1897.

5. *El Paso Herald,* June 14, 1897.

6. *Santa Fe Daily New Mexican,* May 31, 1892.

7. *Santa Fe Daily New Mexican,* May 31, 1892; *Santa Fe Daily New Mexican,* May 6, 1895.

8. *Santa Fe Daily New Mexican,* May 31, 1892.

9. *Santa Fe Daily New Mexican,* Apr. 23, 1895.

10. *Santa Fe Daily New Mexican,* May 9, 1895; *Santa Fe Daily New Mexican,* May 13, 1895.

11. *Santa Fe Daily New Mexican,* May 22, 1895.

12. *Santa Fe Daily New Mexican,* Apr. 2, 1897.

13. *San Francisco Call,* Apr. 3, 1897.

14. Miguel Antonio Otero, *My Life on the Frontier, 1882-1897* (Sunstone Press, 2007) p 271; *Santa Fe Daily New Mexican,* Apr. 3, 1897.

15. John Pruit, Case 1543, 1897, Lincoln County, State Records Center and Archives.

16. John Pruit, Case 1543, 1897,

17. John Pruit, Case 1543, 1897,

18. Certificate of Non-Appearance, Case, 4874, 1897, Leon C. Metz Papers, MS 157, C. L. Sonnichsen Special Collections, UTEP.

19. Note for $1,000 by Curry-Eubanks-Garrett, 1890, Leon C. Metz Papers.

20. Leon C. Metz, *Pat Garrett, The Story of a Western Lawman* (Univ. of Oklahoma Press, 1974) p 288.

21. George Curry, *George Curry 1861-1947, An Autobiography* (Univ. of New Mexico Press, 1958) p 58.

22. Curry, *Autobiography,* pp 18-20, 39.

23. Curry, *Autobiography.*

24. *Western Liberal,* Feb. 28, 1896.

25. Demurrer to Complaint, Case 4874, 1897, Leon C. Metz Papers.

26. *Rio Grande Republican,* Feb 12, 1897.

27. *Rio Grande Republican,* July 30, 1897.

28. *Las Cruces Democrat,* Aug. 11, 1897.

29. *Rio Grande Republican,* Aug. 13, 1897.

30 *Independent Democrat,* Sept. 15, 1897.

31. *Rio Grande Republican,* Feb. 9, 1906.

32. *Las Vegas Daily Optic,* Nov. 13, 1897.

33. *Dona Ana County Republican,* Apr. 1, 1897.

34. *Dona Ana County Republican,* Apr. 1, 1897; *Rio Grande Republican,* Apr. 16, 1897.

35. *Las Vegas Daily Optic,* Apr. 10, 1897; *Rio Grande Republican,* Apr. 9, 1897.

36. *Las Vegas Daily Optic,* May 10, 1897.

37. *Rio Grande Republican,* Mar. 12, 1897; *Dona Ana County Republican,* July 22, 1897.

38. *Rio Grande Republican,* Dec. 10, 1897.

39. *Dona Ana County Republican,* Apr. 3, 1898.

40. *Albuquerque Citizen,* Jan. 15, 1898.

41. *Las Vegas Daily Optic,* Mar. 25, 1898; *Albuquerque Citizen,* Mar. 15, 1898.

42. *Albuquerque Citizen,* Mar. 15, 1898.

43. *Albuquerque Citizen,* Mar. 7, 1898.

44. Iris Rose Guertin, *Navidad Country* (2009), p 272.

45. Guertin, *Navidad Country,* p 273.

46. Judgement Against Garrett, Case 487, 1898, Eve Ball Papers, MSS 3096, L. Tom Perry Special Collections, BYU.

47. *El Paso Herald,* Apr. 4, 1898.

48. Garrett Affidavit to Court for Warrant, William A. Keleher Papers.

49. *Western Liberal,* Apr. 8, 1898.

50. *El Paso Herald,* Apr. 8, 1898; *New Mexican Review,* Apr. 7, 1898.

51. *Rio Grande Republican,* Apr. 15, 1898.

52. *New Mexican Review,* Apr. 14, 1898.

53. *Rio Grande Republican,* Apr. 15, 1898.

54. *New Mexican Review,* Apr. 14, 1898.

55. *New Mexican Review,* Apr. 14, 1898.

56. *El Paso Times,* Apr. 16, 1898.

57. *Albuquerque Citizen,* Apr. 18, 1898.

58. *New Mexican Review,* Apr. 21, 1898.

59. *El Paso Herald,* July 13, 1898.

60. *El Paso Herald,* July 13, 1898.

61. *Rio Grande Republican,* July 15, 1898.

62. *Rio Grande Republican,* July 15, 1898.

63. *El Paso Herald,* July 13, 1898.

64. *El Paso Herald,* July 13, 1898.

65. *Rio Grande Republican,* July 15, 1898.

66. *El Paso Times,* Aug. 2, 1898.

67. *El Paso Times,* Aug. 2, 1898.

68. *El Paso Times,* Aug. 2, 1898.

69. *El Paso Times,* Aug. 2, 1898.

70. *El Paso Times,* Aug. 4, 1898.

71. *New Mexican Review,* Aug. 11, 1898.

72. *El Paso Times,* Aug. 11, 1898.

73. *Rio Grande Republican,* Sept. 2, 1898.

74. *Rio Grande Republican,* Aug. 19, 1898.

75. Thomas, *Billy the Kid's Grave,* p 50.

76. Keleher, *The Fabulous Frontier,* p 256.

77. *El Paso Times,* Sept. 10, 1898; *El Paso Herald,* Sept. 12, 1898.

78. *Las Cruces Citizen,* Feb. 10, 1955.

79. *El Paso Times,* Sept. 10, 1898.

80. *Independent Democrat,* Oct. 19, 1898.

81. *Independent Democrat,* Oct. 19, 1898, *El Paso Times,* June 19, 1955.

82. *Las Vegas Daily Optic,* Dec. 9, 1896.

83. *Albuquerque Daily Citizen,* Oct. 11, 1899.

84. *Rio Grande Republican,* Sept. 2, 1898.

85. *El Paso Herald,* Oct. 20, 1898.

86. *El Paso Herald,* Nov. 9, 1898.

87. *Independent Democrat,* Oct. 26, 1898.

88. *Rio Grande Republican,* Nov. 11, 1898.

3. Second Term – 1899-1900

1. *Santa Fe New Mexican,* Jan. 30, 1899.

2. *Santa Fe New Mexican,* Jan. 30, 1899; Cecil Bonney, *Looking Over My Shoulder, Seventy-Five Years in the Pecos Valley* (Hall-Poorbaugh Press, 1971) p 95;. Martha Fall Bethune, *Race With the Wind, The Personal Life of Albert B. Fall* (Complete Priting, 1989), p 50.

3. *Rio Grande Republican,* Nov. 4, 1898.

4. *Las Vegas Daily Optic,* Feb. 3, 1899.

5. *El Paso Herald,* Mar. 1, 1899.

6. *Western Liberal,* Mar. 17, 1899.

7. *El Paso Herald,* Mar. 13, 1899.

8. *Western Liberal,* Mar. 17, 1899.

9. *El Paso Times,* Mar. 14, 1899.

10. *El Paso Herald,* Mar. 13, 1899; *Daily New Mexican,* Mar. 13, 1899.

11. *El Paso Times,* Mar. 14, 1899; Katherine D. Stoes, "Notes on Garrett and Lee, The Surrender," Katherine D. Stoes Papers, Archives and Special Collections, NMSU; William A. Keleher, "Interview with Oliver Lee," Nov. 4, 1937, William A. Keleher Papers.

12. *El Paso Times,* Mar. 14, 1899.

13. *El Paso Times,* Mar. 14, 1899.

14. *El Paso Times,* Mar. 14, 1899.

15. *El Paso Times,* Mar. 14, 1899.

16. *Daily New Mexican,* Mar. 13, 1899; *Santa Fe New Mexican,* Mar. 13, 1899.

17. *El Paso Herald,* Mar. 27, 1899.

18. *Daily New Mexican,* Oct. 26, 1898.

19. *Daily New Mexican,* Mar. 13, 1899.

20. *Daily New Mexican,* Mar. 13, 1899.

21. *El Paso Times,* Mar. 14, 1899.

22. *El Paso Herald,* Dec. 29, 1899.

23. David Wood to Patrick Garrett, Quick Claim Deed, Herman B. Weisner Papers, Archives and Special Collections, NMSU.

24. La Frontera, *Papers in Honor of Patrick H. Becket,* The Archaeological Society of New Mexico, 25, 1999, Albuquerque.

25. Certification of Delivery, Case 532, Lincoln County Records, State Records Center and Archives.

26. Thomas, *Billy the Kid's Grave,* p 13.

27. *Report of the Governor of New Mexico to the Secretary of the Interior,* 1903 (Government Printing Office, 1903).

28. *El Paso Herald,* May 18, 1899.

29. *El Paso Herald,* June 17, 1899.

30. Patsy Crow King, *Sadie Orchard, The Time of Her Life* (PDX Printing, 2008).

31. King, *Sadie Orchard,* p 78.

32. *El Paso Herald,* Sept. 6, 1899; *El Paso Herald,* May 27, 1899.

33. *El Paso Herald,* Apr. 29, 1899.

34. *El Paso Herald,* Apr. 29, 1899.

35. *El Paso Times,* May 16, 1899.

36. *El Paso Times,* May 16, 1899.

37. *El Paso Times,* May 26, 1899.

38. *El Paso Herald,* May 27, 1899.

39. *El Paso Herald,* May 27, 1899; *Daily New Mexican,* May 27, 1899.

40. *El Paso Times,* May 26, 1899.

41. *El Paso Times,* May 26, 1899.

42. *El Paso Herald,* May 29, 1899.

43. *El Paso Herald,* May 27, 1899.

44. *El Paso Herald,* May 29, 1899.

45. *El Paso Herald,* May 29, 1899.

46. *El Paso Herald,* May 30, 1899.

47. *El Paso Herald,* May 30, 1899.

48. *El Paso Times,* May 31, 1899; *El Paso Herald,* June 1, 1899.

49. *El Paso Herald,* May 31, 1899.

50. *El Paso Times,* June 1, 1899; *El Paso Herald,* May 31, 1899; *El Paso Herald,* June 2, 1899.

51. *El Paso Herald,* June 1, 1899.

52. *El Paso Herald,* June 3, 1899.

53. *El Paso Herald,* June 2, 1899.

54. *Albuquerque Citizen,* June 2, 1899.

55. *El Paso Herald,* June 3, 1899.

56. *Albuquerque Citizen,* June 2, 1899.

57. *El Paso Herald,* June 2, 1899.

58. *El Paso Herald,* June 7, 1899.

59. *El Paso Herald,* June 5, 1899.

60. *El Paso Herald,* June 5, 1899.

61. *Albuquerque Daily Citizen,* June 6, 1899.

62. *El Paso Herald,* June 6, 1899.

63. *Albuquerque Daily Citizen,* June 6, 1899.

64. *Albuquerque Daily Citizen,* June 6, 1899.

65. *Albuquerque Daily Citizen,* June 7, 1899.

66. *Los Angeles Times,* June 5, 1899.

67. *Los Angeles Times,* June 5, 1899.

68. *New Mexican Review,* June 15, 1899.

69. *New Mexican Review,* June 15, 1899.

70. *New Mexican Review,* June 15, 1899.

71. *The Call,* June 9, 1899.

72. *Carlsbad Current,* June 10, 1899.

73. *The Call,* June 9, 1899.

74. *Rio Grande Republican,* June 9, 1899.

75. *Carlsbad Current,* June 10, 1899.

76. *Albuquerque Daily Citizen,* June 9, 1899.

77. *El Paso Herald,* June 12, 1899.

78. *El Paso Times,* Feb. 14, 1893.

79. *Albuquerque Daily Citizen,* June 10, 1899, *El Paso Herald,* June 12, 1899.

80. *Albuquerque Daily Citizen,* June 10, 1899.

81. *El Paso Herald,* June 12, 1899.

82. *El Paso Herald,* June 12, 1899.

83. *Albuquerque Daily Citizen,* June 10, 1899.

84. *Albuquerque Daily Citizen,* June 10, 1899.

85. *Los Angeles Times,* June 11, 1899.

86. *El Paso Herald,* June 13, 1899.

87. *El Paso Herald,* June 13, 1899.

88. *El Paso Herald,* June 13, 1899.

89. *El Paso Herald,* June 13, 1899.

90. *El Paso Herald,* June 13, 1899.

91. *El Paso Herald,* June 13, 1899.

92. *El Paso Herald,* June 13, 1899.

93. *El Paso Herald,* June 13, 1899.

94. *Albuquerque Daily Citizen,* June 12, 1899.

95. *El Paso Herald,* June 14, 1899.

96. *El Paso Herald,* June 14, 1899.

97. *El Paso Herald,* June 14, 1899.

98. *El Paso Herald,* June 14, 1899.

99. *El Paso Herald,* June 14, 1899.

100. *El Paso Herald,* June 15, 1899.

101. *El Paso Herald,* June 15, 1899.

102. *El Paso Herald,* June 15, 1899.

103. *El Paso Herald,* June 16, 1899.

104. *El Paso Herald,* June 16, 1899.

105. *El Paso Herald,* June 16, 1899.

106. *Santa Fe New Mexican,* June 13, 1899; *Dona Ana Republican,* June 17, 1899.

107. *Albuquerque Daily Citizen,* June 14, 1899.

108. *El Paso Times,* Sept. 7, 1899.

109. *El Paso Herald,* June 16, 1899.

110. *Santa Fe New Mexican,* June 15, 1899.

111. *El Paso Herald,* June 15, 1899.

112. *El Paso Herald,* Sept. 4, 1899.

113. Stoes, "Who Killed Col. Fountain & Son," Katherine D. Stoes Papers, Archives and Special Collections, NMSU.

114. Peter L. Eidenbach and Sara L. Eidenbach, *Lee Ranch Legacy, Excavations at the Oliver M. Lee Dog Canyon Ranch* (Human Systems Research, Inc., 1986), pp 12, 16.

115. *El Paso Herald,* Apr. 13, 1916.

116. *El Paso Herald,* Apr. 13, 1916.

117. *El Paso Herald,* Apr. 15, 1916.

118. Lucy Raley, Letter to Albert Fountain, Oct. 27, 1915. Arrell Gibson Collection, SC24, Box: 16, MSSU; Gibson, *Life and Death of Colonel Albert Jennings Fountain,* p 286.

119. Gibson, *Life and Death,* p 286.

120. *El Paso Times,* Nov. 28, 1950.

121. *Las Cruces Sun-News,* Feb. 6, 1955.

122. *El Paso Times,* Nov. 28, 1950.

123. *Las Cruces Sun-News,* Apr. 16, 1959.

124. Metz, *Pat Garrett,* pp 229-231.

125. *Las Cruces Sun-News,* Nov. 27, 1950; *El Paso Times,* Nov. 28, 1950.

126. *Las Cruces Sun-News,* Nov. 27, 1950.

127. *Rio Grande Republican,* Sept. 15, 1899; *Las Cruces Democrat,* Sept. 13, 1899.

128. *Oklahoma Capital News,* July 23, 1899.

129. *El Paso Herald,* Oct. 10, 1899.

130. Robert C. Cox, Interview with David G. Thomas, Aug. 14, 2007. Robert C. Cox is the grandson of William W. Cox.

131. *Rio Grande Republican,* Oct. 27, 1899.

132. *El Paso Herald,* Oct. 18, 1899.

133. Bowman Bank Registry, Bowman Bank Collection, State Records Center and Archives, Accession Number 1974-045.

134. *El Paso Times,* Feb., 13, 1900.

135. *Rio Grande Republican,* Mar. 30, 1900.

136. *El Paso Times,* Feb. 13, 1900.

137. *Dona Ana County Republican,* Feb. 17, 1900.

138. *El Paso Times,* Feb. 13, 1900.

139. *Dona Ana County Republican,* Feb. 17, 1900.

140. *Rio Grande Republican,* Feb. 16, 1900; *El Paso Times,* Feb. 15, 1900; *Santa Fe New Mexican,* Feb. 16, 1900.

141. *El Paso Times,* Feb. 14, 1900.

142. *El Paso Herald,* Apr. 23, 1900.

143. *El Paso Herald,* Apr. 23, 1900.

144. *El Paso Times,* Feb. 14, 1900.

145. *El Paso Herald,* Mar. 27, 1900.

146. *San Antonio Express,* Mar. 20, 1900.

147. *San Antonio Express,* Mar. 20, 1900.

148. *San Antonio Express,* Mar. 20, 1900.

149. *El Paso Times,* Mar. 24, 1900.

150. *El Paso Herald,* Apr. 11, 1900.

151. *El Paso Herald,* Apr. 20, 1900.

152. *El Paso Herald,* Apr. 21, 1900.

153. *El Paso Herald,* Apr. 21, 1900.

154. *El Paso Herald,* Apr. 23, 1900.

155. *El Paso Herald,* Apr. 23, 1900.

156. *El Paso Herald,* Apr. 24, 1900.

157. *El Paso Herald,* Apr. 25, 1900.

158. Harold L. Edwards, "Pat Garrett and the Las Cruces Bank Robbery," *True West,* Feb., 1998, p 13.

159. *Rio Grande Republican,* Apr. 27, 1900.

160. *Albuquerque Citizen,* Sept. 21, 1900.

161. *Santa Fe New Mexican,* Sept. 25, 1900.

162. *Las Vegas Daily Optic,* Sept. 29, 1900.

163. *Santa Fe New Mexican,* Oct. 4, 1900.

164. *Santa Fe New Mexican,* Oct. 4, 1900.

165. *The Lone Star,* Dec. 7, 1881.

166. *Rio Grande Republican,* Sept. 2, 1882.

167. *Rio Grande Republican,* Sept. 23, 1882.

168. *Rio Grande Republican,* Sept. 23, 1882.

169. *Rio Grande Republican,* Sept. 30, 1882.

170. *The New Southwest,* Nov. 4, 1882.

171. *Lincoln County Leader,* Nov. 4, 1882.

172. *Silver City Enterprise,* Nov. 30, 1882.

173. *Carlsbad Current,* Nov. 3, 1900.

174 *Albuquerque Citizen,* Nov. 7, 1900.

175.Jack DeMattos, *Garrett and Roosevelt* (Creative Publishing Company, 1988), p 61.

176. *Santa Fe New Mexican,* Nov. 7, 2015.

177. *Santa Fe New Mexican,* Nov. 7, 2015.

178. *El Paso Herald,* Aug. 30, 1900.

179. *Santa Fe New Mexican,* Feb. 8, 1904; *Socorro Chieftain,* Nov. 19, 1904.

180. *El Paso Herald,* Dec. 24, 1900.

181. *Albuquerque Weekly Citizen,* Mar. 30, 1901.

182. Karen Holliday Tanner and John D. Tanner, Jr., *New Mexico Territorial Penitentiary (1884-1912) Directory of Inmates* (Runnin' Iron Press 2006).

4. Return to Private Life – 1901

1. W. S. Strickler, Letter to Henry D. Bowman, Feb. 23, 1901, Bowman Bank Collection, State Records Center and Archives, Accession Number 1974-045.

2. Bank of Commerce, Letter to Bowman, Mar. 11, 1901, Bowman Bank Collection.

3. Bank of Commerce, Letter to Henry D. Bowman, Mar. 22, 1901; Bank of Commerce letter to Bowman, Mar. 29, 1901; Bank of Commerce, letter to Bowman, Apr. 9, 1901, Bowman Bank Collection.

4. *El Paso Daily Herald,* May 7, 1901.

5. *Evening Star (DC),* Apr. 29, 1901.

6. *El Paso Daily Herald,* May 7, 1901.

7. *El Paso Daily Herald,* May 7, 1901.

8. Miguel Antonio Otero, *My Nine Years As Governor of the Territory of New Mexico, 1897-1906* (Univ of New Mexico Press, 1940), pp 142-144.

9. Otero, *My Nine Years,* p 136.

10. Otero, *My Nine Years,* pp 155-158.

11. *El Paso Daily Herald,* May 7, 1901.

12. *El Paso Herald,* June 3, 1901.

13. *New York Times,* Sept. 7, 1901.

14. *New York Times,* Sept. 8, 1901.

15. *Buffalo Times,* Septermber 7, 1901.

16. *The Sun (NY),* Sept. 7, 1901.

17. *New York Times,* Sept. 8, 1901.

18. *New York Times,* Sept. 7, 1901.

19. *The Sun (NY),* Sept. 7, 1901.

20. *The Sun (NY),* Sept. 7, 1901.

21. *The Sun (NY),* Sept. 8, 1901.

22. *Buffalo Times,* Sept. 7, 1901.

23. *New York Times,* Sept. 13, 1901.

24. *Buffalo Times,* Sept. 23, 1901.

25. *Buffalo Times,* Sept. 26, 1901.

26. *Buffalo Times,* Oct. 29, 1901.

27. *El Paso Herald,* Aug. 5, 1901.

28. Fall, Letter to Garrett, Sept. 23, 1901, MS 282, Item 17, Archives and Special Collections, NMSU.

29. Lawrence R. Soljeitberger, Letter to Henry D. Bowman, Oct. 1, 1901, Bowman Bank Business Papers.

30. *El Paso Herald,* Oct. 7, 1902.

31. *El Paso Times,* Nov. 10, 1901.

32. *Washington Times,* Dec. 9, 1901.

33. *Evening Star (DC),* Dec. 11, 1901; *San Francisco Call,* Dec. 13, 1901.

34 Rodey, Letter to President Roosevelt, Dec. 13, 1901, Leon C. Metz Papers.

35. *El Paso Herald,* Dec. 14, 1901.

36. *El Paso Herald,* Dec. 14, 1901.

37. *Congressional Record, Volume 35* (Washington, Government Printing Office, 1902). p 315

38. *El Paso Herald,* Dec. 19, 1901.

39. *Congressional Record, Volume 35,* p 389.

40. *El Paso Herald,* Dec. 26, 1901.

41. *El Paso Herald,* Dec. 26, 1901.

42. Catron, Letter to Pat Garrett, June 17, 1903, Leon C. Metz Papers.

5. Collector of Customs – 1902-1903

1. *Dallas Morning News,* Jan. 3, 1902.

2. *Dallas Morning News,* Jan. 22, 1902.

3. *El Paso Herald,* Dec. 22, 1902.

4. *El Paso Herald,* Jan. 6, 1902.

5. *El Paso Herald,* Jan. 21, 1902.

6. *El Paso Herald,* Jan. 21, 1902.

7. *El Paso Times,* Apr. 17, 1902.

8. *El Paso Times,* Apr. 17, 1902.

9. Garrett to Lohman, Mortgage, Apr. 8, 1902, Eve Ball Papers.

10. *El Paso Herald,* Apr. 17, 1902.

11. *Holbrook Angus (AZ),* Dec. 1, 1900.

12. *El Paso Times,* Apr. 23, 1902.

13. *El Paso Herald,* Apr. 28, 1902.

14. *El Paso Herald,* May 26, 1902.

15. *El Paso Herald,* May 28, 1902.

16. *El Paso Herald,* May 23, 1902.

17. *Dallas Morning News,* July 8, 1902; *El Paso Herald,* July 10, 1902.

18. *Las Cruces Citizen,* July 19, 1902.

19. *El Paso Herald,* Aug. 4, 1902.

20. *El Paso Herald,* Sept. 2, 1902.

21. *El Paso Herald,* Sept. 20, 1902.

22. *El Paso Herald,* Apr. 14, 1903.

23. *El Paso Times,* Aug. 12, 1902.

24. *El Paso Herald,* Aug. 18, 1902.

25. *El Paso Herald,* Oct. 12, 1905.

26 *El Paso Herald,* Dec. 11, 1902.

27. *El Paso Herald.* Dec. 8, 1902.

28. *El Paso Times,* Jan. 9, 1903.

29. *El Paso Herald,* Oct. 12, 1905.

30. *Minneapolis Journal,* Dec. 24, 1903.

31. *El Paso Herald,* Oct. 12, 1905.

32. *Tonopah Bonanza (Butler, NV),* Nov. 24, 1906.

33. *St Paul Globe,* Feb. 27, 1905.

34. *New York Herald,* Aug. 24, 1921.

35. Garrett, Letter to President Roosevelt, Feb. 8, 1903, quoted in Jarvis P. Garrett, Foreword to *Authentic Life of Billy the Kid,* pp 38-40.

36. Garrett, Letter to President Roosevelt, Feb. 8, 1903, quoted in Jarvis P. Garrett, Foreword to *Authentic Life of Billy the Kid,* pp 38-40.

37. *El Paso Herald,* Jan. 2, 1902.

38. *El Paso Herald,* Feb. 24, 1903.

39. *El Paso Herald,* Mar. 6, 1903.

40. *El Paso Herald,* Apr. 16, 1903.

41. *El Paso Herald,* Apr. 22, 1903.

42. *St Louis Post-Dispatch* (MI), Apr. 1, 1903.

43. *El Paso Herald,* May 5, 1903.

44. *El Paso Herald,* May 6, 1903.

45. *El Paso Herald,* May 6, 1903.

46. *El Paso Herald,* May 8, 1903.

47. *El Paso Herald,* July 8, 1903.

48. Garrett, Letter to Leslie M. Shaw, Apr. 7, 1903, quoted in *Garrett and Roosevelt,* Jack DeMattos, p 69.

49. Maury Kemp, Letter to I. A. Barnes, May 27, 1903, Leon C. Metz Papers.

50. Joseph F. Evans, Letter to I. A. Barnes, May 27, 1903, Leon C. Metz Papers.

51. George M. Gaither, Letter to I. A. Barnes, May 22, 1903, Leon C. Metz Papers.

52. Garrett, Letter to I. A. Barnes, May 22, 1903, Leon C. Metz Papers.

53. *El Paso Herald,* July 13, 1903.

54. *Las Vegas Daily Optic,* July 15, 1903.

55. *El Paso Herald,* July 15, 1903.

56. *El Paso Times,* Sept. 3, 1903.

57. *El Paso Herald,* Apr. 13, 1905.

58. *El Paso Herald,* Dec. 29, 1903.

59. *El Paso Herald,* Dec. 29, 1903.

60. *El Paso Herald,* Jan. 24, 1904.

61. *El Paso Herald,* Oct. 31, 1903.

62. Garrett, Letter to Thomas B. Catron, June 17, 1903, copy in author's possession.

63. Thomas B. Catron, Letter to Garrett, Sept. 24, 1903, copy in author's possession.

64. *El Paso Herald,* July 22, 1903.

65. Garrett Life Insurance Policy, Sept. 10, 1903, copy in author's possession.

66. *Albuquerque Weekly Citizen,* Dec. 19, 1903.

67. *El Paso Herald,* Dec. 30, 1903; *El Paso Times,* Dec. 21, 1903.

6. Collector of Customs – 1904-1905

1. Renewal of Garrett Mortgage, Apr. 8, 1904, Eve Ball Papers.

2. Case against Garrett filed, Apr. 26, 1904, Eve Ball Papers.

3. Summons Served on Garrett, July 18, 1904, Eve Ball Papers.

4. Recovery Order Against Garrett, Sept. 7, 1904, Eve Ball Papers.

5. *El Paso Herald,* Apr. 26, 1904.

6. *El Paso Times,* Jan. 27, 1904.

7. *El Paso Herald,* May 20, 1904.

8. *El Paso Herald,* Aug. 19, 1904.

9. *El Paso Herald,* June 13, 1904; Goldie Rouse Buckner, *Elizabeth Garrett Lived With a Song in Her Heart,* undated, IHSF.org, p 4.

10. *El Paso Herald,* June 13, 1904.

11. *El Paso Times,* Sept. 16, 1904.

12. Buckner, "Elizabeth Garrett Lived with a Song in Her Heart," undated, IHSF.org, p 7; Las Cruces Sun News, Aug. 3, 1915.

13. Georgia B. Redfield, "Life of Elizabeth Garrett," Feb. 9, 1937, IHSF.org, p 1.

14. Buckner, "Elizabeth Garrett," pp 8-9.

15. *El Paso Herald-Post,* June 29, 1937.

16. Buckner, "Elizabeth Garrett," p 16.

17. Buckner, "Elizabeth Garrett," p 3.

18. *Roswell Daily Record,* Oct. 17, 1947.

19. *El Paso Herald,* Nov. 21, 1904.

20. *El Paso Herald,* Nov. 22, 1904.

21. *El Paso Herald,* Nov. 22, 1904.

22. *The Washington Post,* Apr. 7, 1905.

23. *El Paso Times,* Apr. 10, 1905.

24. *Buffalo Courier,* Apr. 8, 1905.

25. *El Paso Times,* Apr. 10, 1905.

26. *Austin American-Statesman,* Apr. 6, 1892.

27. *El Paso Times,* Apr. 10, 1905.

28. Jarvis Garrett Draft Card, Fold3.com.

29. *El Paso Herald,* Oct. 2, 1905.

30. *El Paso Herald,* Oct. 14, 1905.

31. *Albuquerque Journal,* Nov. 2, 1905.

32. *El Paso Herald,* Dec. 9, 1905.

33. Thomas, *Billy the Kids Grave,* p 47.

34. *El Paso Times,* May 2, 1905; *El Paso Herald,* Mar. 27, 1905.

35. *El Paso Times,* Dec. 5, 1905.

36. *El Paso Herald,* Dec. 13, 1905.

37. *El Paso Herald,* Dec. 13, 1905.

38. *El Paso Herald,* Dec. 13, 1905.

39. *New York Times,* Dec. 14, 1905.

40. *El Paso Herald,* Dec. 20, 1905.

41. *El Paso Herald,* Dec. 13, 1905.

42. *El Paso Times,* Dec. 23, 1905.

43. Emerson Hough, Letter to President Roosevelt, Dec. 19, 1905, quoted in DeMattos, *Garrett and Roosevelt,* pp 114-115.

44. Hough, Letter to President Roosevelt, Dec. 19, 1905, quoted in DeMattos, *Garrett and Roosevelt,* p 116.

45. *Evening Star* (DC), Dec. 16, 1905.

46. *Washington Times,* Dec. 16, 1905.

47. *Dallas Morning News,* Dec. 24, 1905.

48. *El Paso Herald,* Dec. 22, 1905; *El Paso Herald,* Dec. 27, 1905.

7. Financial Woes Deepen – 1906

1. Garrett, Letter to Albert B. Fall, Jan. 15, 1906, Albert B. Fall Family Papers, MS 8, Archives and Special Collections, NMSU.

2. *El Paso Herald,* Dec. 23, 1905.

3. *El Paso Herald,* Dec. 23, 1905.

4. *Los Angeles Times,* Dec. 26, 1905.

5. *El Paso Herald,* Dec. 23, 1905.

6. *Los Angeles Times,* Dec. 26, 1905.

7. *El Paso Herald,* Dec. 26, 1905.

8. *El Paso Herald,* Dec. 27, 1905.

9. *El Paso Times,* Jan. 29, 1906.

10. *El Paso Times,* Jan. 18, 1906.

11. Garrett, Letter to President Roosevelt, Jan. 21, 1906, Pat F. Garrett Family Papers, MS 282, Archives and Special Collections, NMSU; El Paso Times, Jan. 29, 1906.

12. *El Paso Herald,* Feb. 5, 1906; *El Paso Herald,* Feb. 2, 1906.

13. *Austin-American Statesman,* Jan. 30, 1906.

14. *El Paso Herald,* Dec. 31, 1907; El Paso Herald, June 18, 1906; El Paso Times, Mar. 15, 1906.

15. *El Paso Times,* Mar. 28, 1906.

16. *New York Times,* May 25, 1909.

17. Certification of Seizure of Garrett Property, May 25, 1906, Eve Ball Papers.

18. Amended Certificate of Seizure, May 28, 1906, Eve Ball Papers.

19. Sheriff Certifies Garrett Seizure, May 26, 1906, List of Garrett Property Seized, July 13, 1906, Eve Ball Papers.

20. Prices Bid on Garrett Property, Aug. 17, 1906, Eve Ball Papers.

21. Lohman Assigns Mortgage to Cox, Apr. 3, 1905, Cox Renews Mortgage on Garrett place, May 26, 1906, Eve Ball Papers.

22. W. B. Childers, Letter to Garrett, June 6, 1906, Pat F. Garrett Family Papers, Archives and Special Collections, NMSU.

23. *Santa Fe New Mexican,* Aug. 28, 1899; *Western Liberal,* May 17, 1901; Curry, *Autobiography,* p 173.

24. Action to Recover Wife's Property, June 23, 1906, Eve Ball Papers.

25. Garrett Bond for Replevin, June 23, 1906, Eve Ball Papers.

26. John Houston Merrill, ed., *The American and English Encyclopedia of Law, Vol. XX* (Edward Thompson Company, 1892), pp 619, 1071, 1075, 1078.

27. Court Orders Return of Property by Replevin, June 23, 1906, Eve Ball Papers.

28. *Rio Grande Republican,* July 6, 1906; Rio Grande Republican, July 20, 1906.

29. Garrett Designation of Homestead, July 11, 1906, Eve Ball Papers.

30. Appraisal of Garrett Property, July 28, 1906, Eve Ball Papers.

31. Certification of Sheriffs Sale, Aug. 4, 1906, Eve Ball Papers.

32. Certification of Sheriffs Sale, Aug. 4, 1906, Eve Ball Papers.

33. Prices Bid on Garrett Property, Aug. 17, 1906, Eve Ball Papers.

34. Bill of Sale - Garrett to Cox, Bill of Sale, Aug. 17, 1907, Eve Ball Papers.

35. Prices Bid on Garrett Property, Aug. 17, 1906, Eve Ball Papers.

36. *Rio Grande Republican,* Sept. 14, 1906.

37. *Rio Grande Republican,* Sept. 21, 1906.

8. Hope Denied – 1907

1. Garrett, Letter to Albert B. Fall Letter, Jan. 3, 1907, Albert B. Fall Family Papers, Archives and Special Collections, NMSU.

2. Albert B. Fall, Letter to Garrett Letter , Jan. 9, 1907, Albert B. Fall Family Papers, Archives and Special Collections, NMSU.

3. Garrett, Letter to Emerson Hough, Feb. 7, 1907, quoted in DeMattos, *Garrett and Roosevelt,* p 138.

4. DeMattos, *Garrett and Roosevelt,* p 137.

5. Emerson Hough, Letter to Garrett, Feb. 12, 1907, quoted in DeMattos, *Garrett and Roosevelt,* pp 139-140.

6. Poe Garrett Lease of Ranch to Brazel, Mar. 12, 1907, Eve Ball Papers.

7. Cox Sues Brazel for Loan, Feb. 27, 1913, Eve Ball Papers.

8. *Albuquerque Citizen,* Apr. 18, 1907.

9. Curry, *Autobiography,* pp 186-187.

10. Garrett, Letter to W. H. H. Llewellyn, June 21, 1907, Pat F. Garrett Family Papers, Archives and Special Collections, NMSU.

11. Garrett, Letter to Apolinaria Garrett, July 24, 1907, copy in author's possession.

12. *Santa Fe New Mexican,* Aug. 7, 1907.

13. *Santa Fe New Mexican,* Aug. 7, 1907.

14. *El Paso Herald,* Aug. 8, 1907.

15. *Albuquerque Journal,* Aug. 3, 1907.

16. *El Paso Herald,* Aug. 3, 1907.

17. Renewal of Garrett Mortgage Cox, Nov. 1, 1907, Eve Ball Papers.

9. Killing Garrett – 1908

1. *El Paso Herald,* Mar. 2, 1908; Some oral sources put this event in Dec., but the newspaper dates it in Jan.

2. Sterling Rhodes interview, Herman B. Weisner Papers; *San Antonio Light,* Mar. 5, 1908; *El Paso Herald,* Mar. 2, 1908; Herman B. Weisner, "Garrett's Death," *True West,* Nov.-Dec., 1979, p 9

3. *El Paso Sunday Times,* Mar. 1, 1908.

4. *El Paso Herald,* Mar. 2, 1908.

5. Albert B. Fall, Letter to George Curry, Territorial Archives of New Mexico, microfilm roll 165, frame 417, State Records Center and Archives.

6. *El Paso Herald,* Mar. 2, 1908.

7. *El Paso Herald,* Mar. 2, 1908.

8. Leon Claire Metz, *John Wesley Hardin: Dark Angel of Texas* (Univ of Oklahoma Press, 1998), p 218; Bill C. James, *Jim Miller, The Untold Story of a Texas Badman,* (Henington Publishing, 1983), pp 61-64; *El Paso Herald,* Apr. 19, 1909.

9. *Galveston Daily News,* June 23, 1905; The Houston Post, June 25, 1905.

10. *Roswell Daily Record,* Oct. 1, 1903; *Roswell Daily Record,* Oct. 10, 1905.

11. James, *Jim Miller,* p77.

12. *Rio Grande Republican,* Mar. 7, 1908.

13. *El Paso Herald,* Mar. 2, 1908.

14. *Rio Grande Republican,* Mar. 7, 1908; *El Paso Herald,* Mar. 2, 1908.

15. *Rio Grande Republican,* Mar. 7, 1908.

16. *El Paso Herald,* Mar. 2, 1908.

17. *Rio Grande Republican,* Feb. 29, 1908; Many sources say that the ranches were only being bought by Miller, but Adamson makes it clear in his testimony that he would be joint owner of the ranches.

18. *Rio Grande Republican,* Mar. 7, 1908.

19. *Rio Grande Republican,* Mar. 7, 1908; The three Garrett children at the ranch were Pauline, Oscar, and Jarvis.

20. Bert Judia, Interview by Eve Ball, Dec. 30, 1956, Leon C. Metz Papers; Bert Judia, "The Real Pat Garrett, as told to Eve Ball," Frontier Times, Feb.-Mar., 1964; *New Mexico Sentinel,* Apr. 23, 1939.

21. *Rio Grande Republican,* Mar. 7, 1908.

22. Cesario S. Pedragon, Interview by Keleher, May 23, 1938, William A. Keleher Papers; *Rio Grande Republican,* July 23, 1909.

23. Jarvis P. Garrett, Foreword to *Authentic Life of Billy,* p 43.

24. Mark Wright, "The Garrett/Ross Folding Burgess 12 Gauge," The Gun Report, Nov., 1988, pp 14,17.

25. Jarvis P. Garrett, Foreword to *Authentic Life of Billy,* p 43; Judia, Interview by Eve Ball, Dec. 30, 1956.

26. Jarvis P. Garrett, Foreword to *Authentic Life of Billy,* p 43.

27. Willis Walter, Interview by Leon C. Metz, Combined Interviews, No. 17, Jan. 30, 1968, DigitalCommons.utep.edu/interviews/17/.

28. *Rio Grande Republican,* Mar. 7, 1908.

29. C. L. Sonnichsen, *Tularosa, Last of the Frontier West* (The Devin-Adair Company, 1972), p 238.

30. *Rio Grande Republican,* Mar. 7, 1908, Description of events based on Adamson's sworn testimony in the preliminary examination.

31. *The New Mexico Sentinel,* Apr. 23, 1939.

32. Mark Lee Gardner, *To Hell on a Fast Horse* (William Morrow, 2010), p 237.

33. *Rio Grande Republican,* Mar. 7, 1908.

34. *New Mexico Sentinel,* Apr. 23, 1939.

35. *New Mexico Sentinel,* Apr. 23, 1939.

36. Coroner's Report for Pat Garrett, Feb. 29, 1908, Dona Ana County Clerk's Office; This report was found in Apr., 2017, in the Dona Ana County Courthouse, in a box of unexamined legal records, after being lost for six decades.

37. *New Mexico Sentinel,* Apr. 23, 1939.

38. *El Paso Sunday Times,* Mar. 1, 1908.

39. *Las Cruces Citizen,* June 20, 1906.

40. *El Paso Herald,* Mar. 2, 1908.

41. *New Mexico Sentinel,* Apr. 23, 1939.

42. George Curry, Interview by Keleher, July 1, 1937, William A. Keleher Papers.

43. Curry, Interview by Keleher, July 1, 1937, William A. Keleher Papers.

10. Aftermath

1. *New York Times,* Mar. 1, 1908; *Los Angeles Herald,* Mar. 1, 1908.

2. *Los Angeles Times,* Mar. 1, 1908.

3. *El Paso Herald,* Mar. 2, 1908.

4. *El Paso Morning Times,* Mar. 2, 1908.

5. *Albuquerque Citizen,* Mar. 4, 1908.

6. *El Paso Herald,* Mar. 3, 1908.

7. George Curry, Letter from W. H. H. Llewellyn, Apr. 29, 1908, Governor George Curry Papers, 1959-092, State Records Center and Archives.

8. Curry, Telegram Apolinaria Garrett, Mar. 2, 1908, Governor George Curry Papers.

9. Curry, Telegram Vincent May, Mar. 2, 1908, Governor George Curry Papers.

10. *Albuquerque Citizen,* Mar. 4, 1908.

11 Emerson Hough, Letter to Apolinaria Garrett, Mar. 4, 1908, Pat F. Garrett Family Papers.

12. *El Paso Herald,* Mar. 3, 1908.

13. *El Paso Herald,* Mar. 3, 1908.

14. *El Paso Herald,* Mar. 3, 1908.

15. *El Paso Herald,* Mar. 2, 1908.

16. *El Paso Herald,* Mar. 2, 1908.

17. *El Paso Herald,* Mar. 4, 1908.

18. *El Paso Herald,* Mar. 3, 1908.

19. *El Paso Herald,* Mar. 3, 1908.

20. *El Paso Morning Times,* Mar. 3, 1908; *Albuquerque Citizen,* Mar. 4, 1908.

21. Curry, *Autobiography,* p 216; *El Paso Herald,* Mar. 3, 1908; *El Paso Herald,* Mar. 4, 1908.

22. *El Paso Herald,* Mar. 4, 1908.

23. *El Paso Herald,* Mar. 4, 1908.

24. *El Paso Herald,* Mar. 4, 1908.

25. *El Paso Herald,* Mar. 4, 1908.

26. *El Paso Times,* June 12, 1908.

27. *Rio Grande Republican,* Mar. 7, 1908.

28. *Rio Grande Republican,* Mar. 7, 1908.

29. *Rio Grande Republican,* Mar. 7, 1908.

30. *Rio Grande Republican,* Mar. 7, 1908.

31. *Rio Grande Republican,* Mar. 7, 1908.

32. *El Paso Herald,* Mar. 5, 1908; Brazel Bond Sureties, Apr. 13, 1908, Case 4112, Dona Ana District Court Records, NMSU.

33. *El Paso Herald,* Mar. 5, 1908.

34. *El Paso Herald,* Mar. 5, 1908.

35. James Madison Hervy, "The Assassination of Pat Garrett," *True West,* Mar.-Apr., 1961, p 17.

36. James M. Hervey, Interview by Keleher, Feb. 5, 1938, William A. Keleher Papers.

37. Hervy, "Assassination of Pat Garrett," *True West,* Mar.-Apr., 1961, p 40.

38. Chuck Hornung, "The Fornoff Report," *True West*, Mar., 1998, p 12.

39. Hornung, "The Fornoff Report," *True West,* Mar., 1998, p 16.

40. *El Paso Herald,* Mar. 5, 1908.

41. *El Paso Herald,* Mar. 5, 1908.

42. *El Paso Times,* Mar. 5, 1908.

43. Mary'n Rosson, "The Gun That Killed Billy the Kid," *Old West,* Winter, 1977, p 7

44. *El Paso Herald,* Mar. 5, 1908.

45. *El Paso Herald,* Mar. 6, 1908.

46. *El Paso Times,* Mar. 7, 1908.

47. *Las Cruces Sun News,* Aug. 29, 1957.

48. *El Paso Herald,* Mar. 14, 1908.

49. *El Paso Herald,* Mar. 5, 1908.

50. *El Paso Times,* Mar. 5, 1908.

51. *El Paso Herald,* Mar. 2, 1908.

52 Anonymous, Letter to Annie Garrett, Apr. 20, 1908, Territorial Archives of New Mexico, microfilm roll 54, frames 201 to 202, State Records Center and Archives.

11. Wayne Brazel

1. Robert N. Mullin, *The Strange Story of Wayne Brazel* (Palo Duro Press, 1970), p 2.

2. Mullin, *Strange Story,* p 2.

3. *Emporia Weekly News* (Emporia KS), May 31, 1878.

4. Mullin, *Strange Story,* p 3.

5. *Lincoln County Leader,* Oct. 20, 1883.

6. Muster Roll of Captain W. W. Brazel, Company F, Dec. 6, 1864, Adjutant General's Office of the State of Kansas Records, RG 034, p 1.

7. Jose Chavez y Baca and Adam Padillo to Pat Garrett, Sept. 4, 1883, Book E, p 27, Lincoln County Deed Records.

8. *Santa Fe New Mexican,* Feb. 23, 1886.

9. W. H. Hutchinson, *A Bar Cross Man* (Univ of Oklahoma Press, 1956), p 45.

10. Wayne Brazel, Testimony, New Mexico vs Conner, May 24, 1887, Mullin Collection, J. Evetts Haley History Center.

11. Jesse Madison Brazel, Testimony, Lincoln County vs Conner, May 24, 1887, Mullin Collection.

12. Jesse Madison Brazel, Testimony, Lincoln County vs Conner, May 24, 1887, Mullin Collection.

13. Jesse Madison Brazel, Testimony, Lincoln County vs Conner, May 24, 1887, Mullin Collection.

14. *Rio Grande Republican,* June 4, 1887.

15. *Lincoln County Leader,* June 16, 1888.

16. *Lincoln County Leader,* May 28, 1887.

17. *Lincoln County Leader,* June 4, 1887.

18. *Lincoln County Leader,* June 16, 1888.

19. *Rio Grande Republican,* Sept. 28, 1904.

20. *Deming Headlight,* Mar. 17, 1894.

21. William A. Conner to William W. Brazel, Deed, Dec. 17, 1889, Dona Ana County Records.

22. *Independent Democrat,* June 29, 1892; *Deming Headlight,* Mar. 17, 1894; *Las Cruces Democrat,* Mar. 8, 1893.

23. *Rio Grande Republican,* Dec. 30, 1893.

24. *Las Cruces Democrat,* Nov. 15, 1893.

25. *Las Cruces Democrat,* Jan. 3, 1894; *Rio Grande Republican,* Dec. 30, 1893.

26. New Mexico vs. Jesse Brazel and Willie Brazel, Apr. 13, 1893, Case 1342, New Mexico State Records Center and Archives.

27. Louis Telles, Testimony, Apr. 16, 1893, Case 1342, State Records Center and Archives.

28. Wayne Brazel, Testimony Apr. 16, 1893, Case 1342, State Records Center and Archives.

29. Jesse Brazel and Willie Brazel, Indictment, Apr. 15, 1893, Case 1342, State Records Center and Archives.

30. *Rio Grande Republican,* Mar. 10, 1894.

31. New Mexico vs Jesse Brazel and Willie Brazel, Apr. 2, 1895, Case 1342, State Records Center and Archives.

32. *Rio Grande Republican,* Oct. 25, 1895.

33. *Rio Grande Republican,* June 10, 1898; *Albuquerque Citizen,* Dec. 17, 1902; *Rio Grande Republican,* Feb. 2, 24, 1899; *Rio Grande Republican,* Feb. 18, 1898.

34. *Independent Democrat,* Oct. 2, 1895.

35. *Rio Grande Republican,* June 9, 1894.

36. *Rio Grande Republican,* Mar. 4, 1898.

37. Mullin, *Strange Story,* p 9.

38. *Las Cruces Citizen,* Mar. 18, 1905.

39. *Rio Grande Republican,* Mar. 25, 1905.

40. *El Paso Times,* July 16, 1896.

41. *Las Vegas Daily Optic,* July 30, 1903; *Las Vegas Daily Optic,* Mar. 15, 1905.

42. *Rio Grande Republican,* Nov. 15, 1901.

43. Mullin, *Strange Story,* footnote, p 13.

44. Mullin, *Strange Story,* Footnote, p 12; John Edgar Boyd, Sr., Letter to Robert N. Mullin, Jan. 10, 1967, Mullin Collection.

45. John Edgar Boyd, Sr., Letter to Robert N. Mullin, Mar. 6, 1967, Mullin Collection.

46. John Edgar Boyd, Sr., Letter to Robert N. Mullin, Sept. 5, 1965, Mullin Collection.

47. John Edgar Boyd, Sr., Letter to Robert N. Mullin, Nov. 27, 1964, Mullin Collection.

48. John Edgar Boyd, Sr., Letter to Robert N. Mullin, Sept. 4, 1967, Mullin Collection.

49. John Edgar Boyd, Sr., Letter to Robert N. Mullin, Sept. 7, 1964; Boyd, Sr., Letter to Mulling, Jan. 25, 1967, Mullin Collection.

50. Mullin, Strange Story, footnote, p 13; John Edgar Boyd, Sr., Letter to Robert N. Mullin, Mar. 6, 1967, Mullin Collection.

12. Wayne Brazel's Trial

1. *El Paso Herald,* Apr. 2, 1908; NM vs Wayne Brazel, Indictment, Apr. 6, 1908, Case 4112, Dona Ana District Court Records, Archives and Special Collections, NMSU.

2. *El Paso Times,* Apr. 19, 1908; New Mexico vs Wayne Brazel, Indictment, Apr. 6, 1908, Case 4112, Dona Ana District Court Records.

3. *El Paso Herald,* Apr. 28, 1908.

4. *Alamogordo News,* May 2, 1908.

5. U.S. vs Carl Adamson, William Sullivan, and John N. Webb, Case 1287, State Records Center and Archives.

6. U.S. vs Carl Adamson, William Sullivan, and John N. Webb, Case 1287, State Records Center and Archives.

7. U.S. vs Carl Adamson, William Sullivan, and John N. Webb, Case 1287, State Records Center and Archives.

8. U.S. vs Carl Adamson, William Sullivan, and John N. Webb, Case 1287, State Records Center and Archives.

9. U.S. vs Carl Adamson, William Sullivan, and John N. Webb, Case 1287, State Records Center and Archives.

10. U.S. vs Carl Adamson, William Sullivan, and John N. Webb, Case 1287, State Records Center and Archives.

11. U.S. vs Carl Adamson, William Sullivan, and John N. Webb, Case 1287, State Records Center and Archives.

12. U.S. vs Carl Adamson, William Sullivan, and John N. Webb, Case 1287, State Records Center and Archives.

13 *El Paso Herald,* Dec. 1, 1908; *Rio Grande Republican,* Dec. 15, 1908.

14. Patricio Ballejos to Epolinaria Garret (sic), Jan. 23, 1909, Deed 3459, Dona Ana Country Records.

15. *El Paso Herald,* Sept. 9, 1908.

16. 1910 U.S. Census, Las Cruces Precinct 20, Apr. 26, 1910, sheet B35.

17. *Lincoln Star* (Lincoln NE), Apr. 13, 1909.

18. *The Evening News* (Ada), Apr. 19, 1909.

19. James, *Jim Miller,* p 47; *The Evening News* (Ada), Apr. 21, 1909.

20. *The Evening News* (Ada), Apr. 21, 1909.

21. *The Evening News* (Ada), Apr. 20, 1909.

22. *Daily Ardmoreite,* Jan. 1, 1909.

23. *The Evening News* (Ada), Mar. 1, 1909.

24. *The Evening News* (Ada), Mar. 1, 1909.

25. *The Evening News* (Ada), Mar. 2, 1909.

26. *The Evening News* (Ada), Mar. 3, 1909.

27. *The Evening News* (Ada), Apr. 21, 1909.

28. *The Evening News* (Ada), Apr. 21, 1909.

29. *The Evening News* (Ada), Apr. 21, 1909.

30. *The Evening News* (Ada), Apr. 21, 1909.

31. *The Evening News* (Ada), Apr. 21, 1909.

32. *The Evening News* (Ada), Apr. 19, 1909.

33. *The Evening News* (Ada), Mar. 20, 1909.

34. *Daily Ardmoreite,* Mar. 31, 1909.

35. *The Evening News* (Ada), Apr. 7, 1909.

36. *The Evening News* (Ada), Apr. 20, 1909.

37. *The Evening News* (Ada), Apr. 20, 1909.

38. *The Evening News* (Ada), Apr. 20, 1909.

39. *The Evening News* (Ada), Apr. 19, 1909.

40. *Daily Ardmoreite,* Apr. 19, 1909.

41. *The Evening News* (Ada), Oct. 13, 1909.

42. *Daily Ardmoreite,* Apr. 25, 1909.

43. *Houston Chronicle and Herald,* Apr. 21, 1909.

44. *Houston Chronicle and Herald,* Apr. 21, 1909.

45. NM vs Wayne Brazel, Subpoena for trial Appearance, Sept. 12, 1908, Case 4112, Dona Ana District Court Records.

46. NM vs Wayne Brazel, Subpoena for trial appearance, Apr. 3, 1908, Case 4112, Dona Ana District Court Records.

47. NM vs Wayne Brazel, Subpoena for trial appearance, Apr. 3, 1908, Case 4112, Dona Ana District Court Records.

48. *El Paso Herald,* June 27, 1908.

49. NM vs Wayne Brazel, Subpoena for telegraph records, Oct. 7, 1908, Case 4112, Dona Ana District Court Records.

50. Sutherland and Holt, Letter to Wm. D. Martin, Third District Clerk, Apr. 13, 1909, Case 4112, State Records Center and Archives.

51. *El Paso Herald,* May 5, 1909.

52. *The New Mexico Sentinel,* Apr. 23, 1939.

53. *The New Mexico Sentinel,* Apr. 23, 1939.

54. *El Paso Herald,* May 5, 1909.

55. *El Paso Herald,* May 5, 1909.

56. *Rio Grande Republican,* Mar. 7, 1908.

57. John Edgar Boyd, Sr., Letter to Robert N. Mullin, Mar. 6, 1967, Mullin Collection.

58. *El Paso Herald,* May 5, 1909.

59. James B. O'Neil, *They Die But Once* (Knight Publications, Inc., 1935) p 194.

60. *El Paso Herald,* Mar. 4, 1908.

61. *El Paso Herald,* May 5, 1909.

62. *El Paso Herald,* Apr. 15, 1916.

63. *El Paso Morning Times,* May 5, 1909.

64. *El Paso Morning Times,* May 5, 1909.

65. Robert C. Cox, Interview by David G. Thomas, Apr., 2007.

66. *El Paso Morning Times,* May 5, 1909.

67 *New Mexico Sentinel,* Apr. 23, 1939.

68. John Edgar Boyd, Sr., Letter to Robert N. Mullin, Mar. 6, 1967, Mullin Collection.

69. *Rio Grande Republican,* July 23, 1909.

70. *Rio Grande Republican,* July 23, 1909.

71. *Weekly Journal-Miner* (Prescott), July 20, 1910.

72. *Weekly Journal-Miner* (Prescott), July 20, 1910.

73. *Weekly Journal-Miner* (Prescott), July 13, 1910.

74. *Weekly Journal-Miner* (Prescott), May 17, 1911.

75. *Weekly Journal-Miner* (Prescott), May 17, 1911.

76. *Weekly Journal-Miner* (Prescott), May 25, 1911.

77. *Weekly Journal-Miner* (Prescott), May 25, 1911.

78. *Weekly Journal-Miner* (Prescott), May 31, 1911; Archie Prentice "Print" Rhode Prison

Record, Pinal County Historical Society Museum.

79. John Edgar Boyd, Sr., letter to Robert N. Mullin, Mar. 6, 1967, Mullin Collection; Santa Fe New Mexican, Sept. 10, 1910.

80. John Edgar Boyd, Sr., Letter to Robert N. Mullin, Apr. 4, 1967, Mullin Collection.

81. Emma J. Scofield, Hidalgo County Clerk, Letter to Robert N. Mullin, May 11, 1964, Mullin Collection.

82. Mrs. M. M. Wood, Letter to Robert N. Mullin, Aug. 16, 1964, Mullin Collection.

83. John Edgar Boyd, Sr., Letter to Robert N. Mullin, Oct. 5, 1937, Mullin Collection.

84. Mrs. M. M. Wood, Letter to Robert N. Mullin, Aug. 16, 1964, Mullin Collection.

85. John Edgar Boyd, Sr., Letter to Robert N. Mullin, Nov. 11, 1964, Mullin Collection.

86. Mullin, *Strange Story,* p 31.

87. H. L. McCune, Letter to Jesse V. Brazel, Apr. 28, 1936, Mullin Collection.

88. *Western Liberal,* Mar. 7, 1913; Betty J. Turner, Grant County Clerk, Letter to Robert N. Mullin, Sept. 14, 1966, Mullin Collection.

89. W. W. Cox vs Wayne Brazel, Complaint, Third District Court, Mar. 27, 1913, Case 3387, Herman B. Weisner Papers.

90. W. W. Cox vs Wayne Brazel, Complaint, Third District Court, Mar. 27, 1913, Case 3387, Herman B. Weisner Papers.

91 *Western Liberal* (Lordsburg), Apr. 24, 1914.

92. *Western Liberal* (Lordsburg), May 1, 1914.

93. Voter registration, Ash Fork Precinct, Yavapai County, Arizona, p 215, July 10, 1914. Ancestry.com.

94. *Santa Fe New Mexican,* Nov. 11, 1914.

95. John Edgar Boyd, Sr., Letter to Robert N. Mullin, Oct. 8, 1967, Mullin Collection.

96. H. L. McCune, Letter to Jesse V. Brazel, Apr. 28, 1936, Mullin Collection.

13. Conspiracy Theories

1. Colin Rickards, *Sheriff Pat Garrett's Last Days* (Sunstone Press, 1986); *How Pat Garrett Died* (Palomino Press, 1970).

2. Rickards, *Garrett's Last Days,* pp 27-28.

3. Rickards, *Garrett's Last Days,* p 26.

4. Rickards, *Garrett's Last Days,* p 29.

5. Rickards, *Garrett's Last Days,* p 28.

6. Rickards, *Garrett's Last Days,* p 28.

7. Rickards, *Garrett's Last Days,* p 47.

8. Rickards, *Garrett's Last Days,* p 29.

9. Rickards, *Garrett's Last Days,* p 29.

10. Rickards, *Garrett's Last Days,* p 47.

11. Rickards, *Garrett's Last Days,* p 47.

12. Rickards, *Garrett's Last Days,* p 48.

13. Rickards, *Garrett's Last Days,* p 48.

14. Rickards, *Garrett's Last Days,* p 48.

15. Rickards, *Garrett's Last Days,* p 50.

16. Rickards, *Garrett's Last Days,* p 51.

17. Rickards, *Garrett's Last Days,* pp 51-52.

18. Rickards, *Garrett's Last Days,* p 52.

19. Rio Grande Republican, Nov. 3, 1911.

20. Katherine D. Stoes, "The Story of San Aug.ine Ranch," *The New Mexico Stockman,* Apr., 1957.

21. Rickards, *Garrett's Last Days,* p 83.

22. Dee Harkey, *Mean as Hell, The Life of a New Mexico Lawman* (Ancient City Press, 1986), p 180.

23. Jerry J. Lobdill, "How Jim Miller Killed Pat Garrett," *Wild West,* Aug., 2018, p 43.

24. Lobdill, "Rethinking the Murder of Pat Garrett," *Wild West History Association Journal,* Aug., 2011, p 34.

25. C. L. Sonnichsen, "Pat Garrett's Last Ride," *True West,* Nov.-Dec., 1958, p 31.

26. Mark Lee Gardner, *To Hell on a Fast Horse – Billy the Kid, Pat Garrett, and the Epic Chase to Justice in the Old West* (Harper Collins Publishers, 2010), p 242.

27. *Rio Grande Republican,* Mar. 7, 1908.

28. Gardner, *To Hell on a Fast Horse,* p 242.

29. Chuck Hornung, "Surprising New Information on Pat Garrett's Death," *The Journal, Western Outlaw-Lawman History Association,* Spring-Summer, 1997.

30. Chuck Hornung, "The Fornoff Report: New Light on the Death of Pat Garrett," *True West,* Mar., 1998, p 12.

31. Hornung, "The Fornoff Report," p 12.

32. Hornung, "The Fornoff Report," p 13.

33. Hornung, "The Fornoff Report," p 14.

34. Hornung, "The Fornoff Report," pp 15-16.

35. Hornung, "The Fornoff Report: New Light on the Murder of Pat Garrett," Typewritten Copy of Oral Presentation to the Sixth Annual WOLA Convention, July 17-20, 1996, Leon C. Metz Papers; Chuck Hornung, "The Fornoff Report: New Light on the Death of Pat Garrett," *True West*, Mar., 1998.

36. James Madison Hervy, "The Assassination of Pat Garrett," *True West*, Mar.-Apr., 1961, p 17.

37. *El Paso Herald*, Mar. 4, 1908.

38. Curry, *Autobiography*, p 216.

39. Hervey, "Assassination of Pat Garrett," pp 39-40.

40. James M. Hervey, Interview by Keleher, Feb. 5, 1938, William A. Keleher Papers.

41. Hervey, Interview by Keleher, Feb. 5, 1938, William A. Keleher Papers.

14. Death Site

1. *El Paso Times*, May 11, 1969.

2. *El Paso Times*, May 11, 1969.

3. *El Paso Times*, May 11, 1969.

4. Jarvis P. Garrett, Foreword to *Authentic Life of Billy*, p 47.

5. George Helfrich, Interview with David G. Thomas, Oct. 20, 2017.

6. Coroner's Report for Pat Garrett, Feb. 29, 1908, Dona Ana County Clerk's Office.

7. Steven Moffson, Letter to Sally Kading, Nov 30, 2017, copy in author's possession.

Appendix A: IOOF Cemetery – Garrett Family Plot

1. *Rio Grande Republican*, Jan. 29, 1892.

2. *Las Cruces Democrat*, Mar. 1, 1893.

3. Henry Leonard Stillson, editor, *Official History of Odd Fellowship*, pp 47-50.

4. Stillson, *Official History*, p 67.

5.Keleher, Pat Garrett Notes, undated, William A. Keleher Papers; *Rio Grande Republican*, Oct. 16, 1896.

6. *Las Cruces Sun-News*, Aug. 29, 1957.

7. 1910 U.S. Census, Las Cruces Precinct 20, Apr. 26, 1910, sheet B35.

8. *El Paso Herald*, Aug. 7, 1922.

9. *El Paso Herald*, May 28, 1927.

10. *El Paso Evening Post*, Dec. 9, 1930.

11. 1936-10-21 Apolinaria Garrett Funeral-Record, Oct. 21, 1936, Collections, NMSU.

12. Keleher, "Pat Garrett Notes," undated, William A. Keleher Papers.

13. Jarvis P. Garrett, Foreword to *Authentic Life of Billy*, p 47.

Appendix B: Pistol that Killed Billy the Kid

1. Mary'n Rosson, "The Gun That Killed Billy the Kid," *Old West*, Winter, 1977, p 39.

2. Rosson, "Gun That Killed Billy," pp 6,7.

3. Rosson, "Gun That Killed Billy," p 8.

4. Rosson, "Gun That Killed Billy," p 8.

5. *El Paso Times*, Nov. 11, 1933.

6. *El Paso Herald*, Oct. 26. 1926.

7. *El Paso Times*, Oct. 14, 1930.

8. *El Paso Times*, Oct. 14, 1930.

9. *El Paso Times*, Jan. 2, 1931.

10. *Dallas Morning News*, Jan. 23, 1933.

11. *El Paso Herald-Post*, Apr. 24, 1933.

12. Rosson, "Gun That Killed Billy," p 36; El Paso Herald-Post, Apr. 24, 1933.

13. *El Paso Times*, Nov. 3, 1933.

14. *El Paso Herald-Post*, Nov. 10, 1933.

15. *El Paso Herald-Post*, Mar. 7, 1934.

16. *El Paso Herald-Post*, Oct. 6, 1934.

17. Mike Cox, grandson of L. A. Wilke, Interview with author, June 20, 2019.

18. 1936-10-21 Apolinaria Garrett Funeral-Record, Oct. 21, 1936, Archives and Special Collections, NMSU

19. *De Baca County News*, Sept. 20, 1979.

20. Web site, www.historynet.com/jim-earles-priceless-historic-gun-collection-includes-items-garrett-ringo-hardin.htm.

Appendix C: Pistol that Killed Pat Garrett

1. John Edgar Boyd, Sr., Letter to Robert N. Mullin, January 10, 1967, Mullin Collection.

2. *The New Mexico Sentinel*, April 23, 1939.

3. Jack Carter, "Facts About Wayne Brazel," *Frontier Times*, Jun., 1972, p 3.

4. Jack Carter, Letter to Leon C. Metz, Jul. 5, 1970, Leon C. Metz Papers.

Index

Doc45 Publications

La Posta – From the Founding of Mesilla, to Corn Exchange Hotel, to Billy the Kid Museum, to Famous Landmark, David G. Thomas, paperback, 118 pages, 59 photos, e-book available.

"For someone who grew up in the area of Mesilla, it's nice to have a well-researched book about the area – and the giant photographs don't hurt either.... And the thing I was most excited to see is a photo of the hotel registry where the name of "William Bonney" is scrawled on the page.... There is some debate as to whether or not Billy the Kid really signed the book, which the author goes into, but what would Billy the Kid history be without a little controversy?" –Billy the Kid Outlaw Gang Newsletter, Winter, 2013.

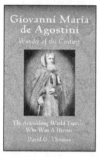

Giovanni Maria de Agostini, Wonder of The Century – The Astonishing World Traveler Who Was A Hermit, David G. Thomas, paperback, 208 pages, 59 photos, 19 maps, e-book available.

"David G. Thomas has finally pulled back the veil of obscurity that long shrouded one of the most enduring mysteries in New Mexico's long history to reveal the true story of the Hermit, Giovanni Maria de Agostini. ...Thomas has once again proven himself a master history detective. Of particular interest is the information about the Hermit's life in Brazil, which closely parallels his remarkable experience in New Mexico, and required extensive research in Portuguese sources. Thomas's efforts make it possible to understand this deeply religious man." – Rick Hendricks, New Mexico State Historian

Screen With A Voice - A History of Moving Pictures in Las Cruces, New Mexico, David G. Thomas, paperback, 194 pages, 102 photos, e-book available.

The first projected moving pictures were shown in Las Cruces 110 years ago. Who exhibited those movies? What movies were shown? Since projected moving pictures were invented in 1896, why did it take ten years for the first movie exhibition to reach Las Cruces? Who opened the first theater in town? Where was it located? These questions began the history of moving pictures in Las Cruces, and they are answered in this book. But so are the events and stories that follow.

There have been 21 movie theaters in Las Cruces – all but three or four are forgotten. They are unremembered no longer. And one, especially, the Airdome Theater which opened in 1914, deserves to be known by all movie historians – it was an automobile drive-in theater, the invention of the concept, two decades before movie history declares the drive-in was invented.

Billy the Kid's Grave – A History of the Wild West's Most Famous Death Marker, David G. Thomas, paperback, 154 pages, 65 photos.

"Quien es?"

The answer to this incautious question – "Who is it?" – was a bullet to the heart.

That bullet – fired by Lincoln County Sheriff Patrick F. Garrett from a .40-44 caliber single action Colt pistol – ended the life of Billy the Kid, real name William Henry McCarty.

But death – ordinarily so final – only fueled the public's fascination with Billy the Kid. What events led to Billy's killing? Was it inevitable? Was a woman involved? If so, who was she? Why has Billy's gravestone become the most famous – and most visited – Western death marker? Is Billy really buried in his grave? Is the grave in the right location?

These questions – and many others – are answered in this book.

CPSIA information can be obtained
at www.ICGtesting.com
Printed in the USA
LVHW082140240220
648106LV00009B/184